SAYINGS OF
GENERALISSIMO
GIULIANI

EDITED BY

Kevin McAuliffe

INTRODUCTION BY

Malachy McCourt

RESEARCH BY

Lawrence L. Ackerman

Welcome Rain Publishers   New York

For Anna, who got angry.

The editor and publisher wish to express their gratitude to David Atlas, Melissa Georges, and Edward Rosenthal of Frankfurt Garbus Klein & Selz for their thoughtful and meticulous work on this manuscript.

Sayings of Generalissimo Giuliani
First Welcome Rain edition 2000.
Printed in the United States of America.

Direct any inquiries to Welcome Rain Publishers LLC, 532 LaGuardia Place, Box 473, New York, NY 10012.

ISBN 1-56649-163-0

First Edition: March 2000
10 9 8 7 6 5 4 3 2 1

Sayings of
Generalissimo Giuliani

At the turn of the last century, United States Senator Corwin opined, "To be successful in politics, never make the populace laugh. Be solemn—solemn as an ass. All great monuments are built over solemn asses." There are exceptions, however, to every rule, and, though unintentionally, Rudolph William Louis Giuliani the Third has many of us howling with laughter, now that many of his profound sayings have been gathered together in this book by Kevin McAuliffe, there will be more laughter still and, in some camps, some weeping.

Herein we meet the Mayor of New York, named after three odd monarchs: Rudolph (a Hapsburg and Holy Roman Emperor), William of Orange, and Louis of France (like Giuliani, married into a House of Hanover, a shaky habitation in the best of times). Rudy is the third in this line, and one wonders about the previous two Rudolphs, but that's another story.

This book is a juicy plum pudding, filled with goodies, and all succulent. McAuliffe takes us back to Rudy's school days, when he was a Democrat who only became a Republican because principle is a terrible impediment to success and ambition.

And from whence did this man spring? Brooklyn, dear reader! Brooklyn, a place that George Washington Plunkitt of Tammany Hall said produces people who are natural-born hayseeds, and who can never become real New Yorkers. Germans, Chinese, Japanese, and Irish can, but not Brooklynites. (I'm a Brooklynite myself.) In that borough of mad Dodger fans, the young Giuliani was sent out into the street, sporting a Yankee uniform, which was as welcome there as a pederast in the St. Patrick's Day Parade. The poor lad was lambasted and attacked, but he was stubborn and wouldn't change allegiance because Yankees are rich, and also some kind of winners. So, Rudy became a lawyer, then a prosecutor, not for the purpose of seeing justice done, but to get the law enforced. "The magic egalitarianism of law," as Anatole France put it, "which forbids rich and poor alike to sleep under bridges, to beg in the streets, and to steal bread," appealed greatly to the Rude man.

Of course, like any strictly toilet-trained person, he will oftentimes do the right thing, not because it's the right thing to do, but because it might reveal his opponents to be wrong and deserving of punishment.

Just as the wave of crime and crack addiction and the AIDS crisis began to recede nationwide, Rudolph G. came to office and promptly grabbed credit for cleaning up the mess, just as Nixon got credit for the moon landing, even though the program had been initiated by John Kennedy. And, the Giuliani administration was going to be a clean one: no nepotism (except for family members), no patronage (except for supporters), and no access for paid lobbyists (except for the law firm of Raymond Harding and Herman Badillo, which, like Little Topsy, just growed and growed and growed). Mr. Harding is the boss of the Liberal party, though he is "liberal" to the degree that Paul O'Dwyer was a conservative.

The Mayor's statement that, "Of course, we are hiring supporters. Who else would we appoint?" is in keeping with the philosophy of the indefatigable G. W. Plunkitt (coiner of the phrase, "Honest Graft"). Plunkitt's credo was that "Every good man looks after his friends. If I have a good thing to hand out in private life, I give it to a friend. Why shouldn't I do the same in public life?" Isn't it nice that the incorruptible Mayor

Giuliani and an old Tammany chieftain adhere to the same principles of patronage?

Our Mayor had decided that no matter what the circumstances, he would never act like Hitler. No, Sir! The Rudolph William Louis the third Bunker was not going to be one of those cowardly underground rabbit warrens for sniveling defeatists! *Au contraire!* This bunker was going to be high up in a skyscraper, in close proximity to a building that's already been bombed because, as everyone knows, terrorists never bomb in the same vicinity twice. From this bunker, our noble First Citizen can peer down on the hostile rabble and, if they become threatening, cauldrons of boiling oil can be spilled over on them (which will also warm them in winter).

What a feast of Rudy words McAuliffe brings to the table, and one wonders whether, if given the opportunity, our noble Mayor would eat his words if served up to him! Most normal people would devour such words posthaste, but then, the subject of this book is hardly normal. He has yet to learn that there is only one thing worse than being wrong, and that is being right. What Jimmy Breslin said about Mayor John Vliet Lindsey is also most applicable to Rudy G., to wit: "He is the man who gave good intentions a bad name."

As Rudy recedes like his hairline from public view, people will wonder about his legacy: for what will we remember this man? Some folk still remember his predecessors—the grim Mayor Hylan and the insouciant Jimmy Walker, the bumbling O'Brien, the silly reformer La Guardia, the whimsical Bill O'Dwyer, the short-lived Impellitteri, the solemn Wagner, the stately Lindsey, the diminutive Beame, the "How Am I Doing?" Koch, and the bewildered Dinkins. Their legacies are still being assessed: some built lasting institutions for the benefit of the cities, and bridges and edifices, while others did little but make pronouncements.

But what about the benevolences of our present man—el Generalíssimo? He hung out with an ex-convict, George Steinbrenner, and tried to use $1 billion of taxpayers' money to build George and his millionaire ballplayers a playground on the West Side. He said that "Bedrooms are for sleeping," despite the fact that many Conservatives are afraid to sleep in their beds because, statistically, 75 percent of people who die do so in bed. Thanks to Rudy, lonely old men no longer have porn parlors to remind them of their late, lamented sex lives. As Chief Magistrate of this City of New York, he has judged us and found us not only wanting, but guilty as well.

When Rudy departs this planet, we may well recall Dorothy Parker's question when informed of the death of Calvin Coolidge: "How do they know?" This mayor drove compassion from the city, so when they autopsy him, they will discover the same man he was in life: No light in the eye, complete absence of heart, no soul to save, and no special spirit to rise in triumph.

Say Good Night, Gracie [Mansion].

Malachy McCourt
January 2000

Editor's Foreword

There are things in this book that are laugh-out-loud funny. But make no mistake: this book is about a tragedy. It is about what we have given up, as a people and as a city, to get what we have today. And it is about what could have been.

Rudolph William Giuliani was swept into government in 1993 by a New York electorate that was fed up with the way things were going, that was in despair the ruling Democratic Party establishment could ever fix what was wrong, and that was ready to take a chance—to take a leap into the unknown with a man many of them had doubts about, but who promised real change, and who seemed strong enough and determined enough to bring it about.

I was there as he came into office, having worked behind the scenes at City Hall as a speechwriter for the previous two Mayors—and, because I had some friends in the incoming Giuliani entourage, having been asked to stay on and organize the transition in my office. The joke I would tell people later was that I worked for Ed Koch for four years, for David Dinkins for four years, and for Rudy Giuliani for six months—which felt like four years. (Actually I worked for Koch for seven years in all, but you get the point.)

For the first three months of 1994, I actually had more up-close-and-personal access, on a day-to-day basis, with the new Mayor than either of the previous two. I got a chance to spend "quality time" with him, one on one, and to observe him closely. Parting company with many of my liberal friends, I found myself in agreement with the philosophical direction in which Giuliani was taking the city. But I also found it very wearying trying to cope with the constant, impulsive energy bursts of a rambunctious amateur who was (like the people around him) prone to issue commands first, and then figure out how—and *whether*—something should be done only later. As best I could, I used my accumulated know-how about government to channel the enthusiasm of these new people in the right direction. But it was a project.

Then, after that three-month period was over, Rudy Giuliani suddenly found his sea legs. And the man who had entered office being impulsive, now that he knew his way around, suddenly became more impulsive and less prone to listen to cautionary advice. More and more, the atmosphere within City Hall—and the attitude of those closest to him— became one of winning through sheer ferocity. I could not help but notice the change: my "face time" with the Mayor was reduced to zero. A major pay raise that had been promised me as an inducement to stay was secretly canceled. A few weeks later, I was told my position was to be eliminated. When I complained that I would miss out on qualifying for the City pension by six months, I was told another job would be found for me, long enough for me to vest. But it took nearly five weeks of being bumped from office to office, in the most demeaning and dismissive manner possible, before—with only 36 hours to go until I was officially terminated—I finally received written confirmation that I could remain on the payroll (in the meantime, my supposedly eliminated job had been offered to someone else). Two weeks after that, on a Friday afternoon, two Personnel Department apparatchiks came around to my office at 4:30 in the afternoon to hand me a one-paragraph letter firing me immediately, shut off my computer, and escort me out of the building. Somehow, in all the confusion, they forgot the gold watch.

I heard various explanations for the sacking, but I knew the ultimate cause was this: I was not an original Giuliani loyalist—and there was no longer room in his Administration for anyone except absolute loyalists. I had already shown the new-comers how everything worked—and drawn up a plan under which the Speechwriting Office could function with far fewer people. So, by their logic, the natural next step was to downsize me, the last holdover. And I had come to be seen as someone who, if I turned against the administration, could be a threat. Which, in a self-fulfilling prophecy, is how they began treating me.

Actually, aside from the pension I will never get (and which, 20 years or so from now, I may really miss), Rudy Giuliani did me a favor when he threw me out on the sidewalk. I went on with my life. And today, as a media and political consultant in the private sector, I am more professionally fulfilled—and better compensated—than I ever was in govern-ment. But I have seen, over and over again, the same behavior patterns I witnessed and experienced—among Giuliani and his minions—being repeated with others. And I have had lots of good company in being driven out: two of the best Police Commissioners that New York has ever had (and someone who would have been an excellent Police Commissioner). Two of the best Schools Chancellors. And, in one convulsive para-noid purge, virtually every veteran press officer who worked for the City of New York.

Yes, New York City is safer today. The economy is stronger. The quality of life is higher. And the government of New York is being run, if not better, at least more decisively. But those things have come at a price. And, more and more, New York-ers are adding up the cost of the collateral damage and wondering if it was necessary. Other cities across America seem to have staged comebacks too, but without the rancor, the raw belligerence and the intimidation factor that have increasingly typified the governing style of Rudy Giuliani.

New York is a city today that is ruled by tyranny, and tem-per tantrums. It is a city in which gratuitous malice has been injected into the political process. It is a city in which people in public life base their decisions, as never before, on the threat of retaliation from a vengeful Mayor.

At one time, as even some of his opponents would concede, Rudy Giuliani was right for what was wrong with New York. But now even supporters of what Giuliani has accomplished find themselves forced to concede that there is also something wrong with him.

He came into office using the term "defining deviancy down" (borrowing the term, actually) to describe conditions in New York. But when he leaves office, his legacy may be—more than anything else—that he defined *dictatorship* down.

It is an age-old problem: people surrender power to a strongman who promises to protect them from great dangers, only to face the question—Now, who is there to protect us from our protector?

That has been Rudy Giuliani's fatal flaw as Mayor. It is his fundamental character defect. It is our problem. And, if he achieves his goal of election to the United States Senate, it may very well become the nation's problem.

Kevin M. McAuliffe
New York City
January 18, 2000

Editor's Note

A few words about the methodology employed in this book.

It was decided early on in this project that—especially because of the chronic propensity of its subject to willfully make assertions plainly at variance with the truth and the known facts (known, at least, by others)—every quotation contained in these pages must come from some documented source in the public record, and must be accompanied by a citation identifying that source. No statement or comment is attributed to anyone in this book that has not already been published—at least once, and in some cases several times—and entered the public domain. I deliberately did not use apocryphal statements, or recollections of other parties in conversations they claim to have had with Rudolph Giuliani, that were available to me. I did not even use statements made for radio or television broadcasts, unless they were also printed in a newspaper or some other print medium, or (in a handful of instances) I was simultaneously taking notes.

Thus, this is not your standard political biography. The core substance of this book is—incontrovertibly and inescapably—Rudy Giuliani in his own words, being himself. Rudy on Rudy. Or, if you will, Rudy does Rudy.

Virtually every quote selected for inclusion herein is from Giuliani directly. In a very few cases, when someone was speaking in his name or on his behalf, and clearly expressing his policies or sentiments, those statements are included—with the name of the person speaking listed in the underlying citation. In cases where a Giuliani statement was complete on the record, it is simply rendered intact, without quotation marks. In instances where the Mayor's statements were reported in partial fragments in the course of a news article, the article (or the relevant sections of it) is reproduced—and the Mayor's comments within the article are in quotes, just as they would have been when originally published.

As for such things as punctuation, I found that different media have different styles and use different syntax. Whenever possible, in reproducing quotes from various publications I generally rendered them in a common style—my own. (Which betrays such things as my long service in City government, with a capital "C" used whenever referring to the legal entity that is empowered to run New York.) But in no case has the substance of an original quotation, as published, been altered.

None of this would have been possible without the superb tracking abilities of Larry Ackerman, whose skills as an Internet detective I would gladly recommend to anyone—and who uncovered things the Mayor had done and said that even I, a well-read and politically aware person, did not realize existed (and, even more fun, were retrievable from cyberspace!). As a veteran of politics, government and the media wars, I had the memory to point him in the right direction. But his dogged persistence did the rest.

Contents

1

Day One:
Rudy's Reign Begins

It should be so, and it will be so.
> Rhetorical refrain from Mayor Rudolph W. Giuliani's
> First Inaugural Address, *New York Times,* January 3, 1994

It should be so, and it will be so.
> Andrew Giuliani, age 7, standing at rostrum throughout
> entire speech and repeating refrain to the audience every
> time his father uses it

The common sense approach of Ed Koch will echo again.
> First Inaugural Address, *New York Times,* January 3, 1994

. . . he's dying for a corruption scandal in my administration so that he doesn't end up with the most corrupt administration in the last half of the 20th Century.
> Comment on former mayor Ed Koch
> *New York Daily News,* December 29, 1998

Mayor Dinkins, I salute your accomplishment for our city. Mayor Dinkins' special dignity and grace will also mark his governance of our city and it's something that we hope to call on in the future.
> First Inaugural Address, *New York Times,* January 3, 1994

If I had his record, I'd be kind of embarrassed to show my face.
> Comment on former mayor Dinkins, *New York Daily News,* February 27, 1998; *New York Post,* April 8, 1999

... Former Mayor Dinkins [and] ... former Mayor Koch both ... perpetuated on the bench a significant number of Democratic machine politicians.

New York Times and *New York Daily News,* Dec. 23, 1995

To Mark Green and Alan Hevesi, I offer my congratulations to you and your wonderful families. I look forward to working with you in government as partners, all three of us committed to working hard, to creating more hope and more optimism, a much better city for all the people of the city.

First Inaugural Address, *New York Times,* January 3, 1994

Idiotic.

Reaction to first policy proposal offered by Public Advocate Mark Green, *New York Times,* March 29, 1994

A typical pandering politician of the latter part of the 20th Century. Mayor Giuliani on Mark Green

New York Times Magazine, August 1, 1999

Comptroller Alan Hevesi has a penchant for putting out reports that tell only half the picture, because if he tells the whole picture he doesn't get any attention.

New York Daily News, February 27, 1998

I don't at this point expect anything better from Alan Hevesi than trying to fudge numbers in order to get himself on television.

New York Daily News, September 7, 1996

Speaker Peter Vallone, I congratulate you on having developed the City Council into such a respected and effective legislative body. And I look forward to our partnership and friendship with you and the other

members of the City Council in working together for our city.

First Inaugural Address, *New York Times,* January 3, 1994

If they override the veto, we would take the viewpoint that their action is null and void. . . . They'd have to go to court.   Statement in midst of budget dispute with City Council. *New York Times,* Nov. 29, 1994

It's too late for negotiations. We will carry out the powers that the City Charter gives the Mayor to hold spending back.   Statement in midst of budget dispute with City Council. *New York Times,* June 15, 1998

It's time to enhance our relationship with the United Nations and to build on it.

First Inaugural Address, January 3, 1994

If they'd like to leave New York over parking tickets, then we can find another use for that area of town. It happens to be just about the most valuable real estate in the world, not just in the United States. . . . Can you imagine what we could do with that?

Comment on the United Nations, *New York Times,* April 11, 1997

Dream with me of a city that can be better than it is now.   First Inaugural Address, *New York Times,* January 3, 1994

2

Rudy the Prosecutor:
Signs of Things to Come

In the 1980s, Rudolph W. Giuliani made his name—and his mark—as a corruption-battling federal prosecutor famous for showing no fear and (some warned) no scruples either.

To make the justice system a reality for the criminal.
U.S. Attorney Rudy Giuliani defining his mission
Time, February 10, 1986

Mr. Giuliani denies that people came to regard him as infallible during his high-profile years as prosecutor. His reputation, he said, is one of solid accomplishment and one that he earned. *New York Times,* July 11, 1989

I think we made cases more successfully during the period of time I was United States Attorney than ever before in the history of the office and that's what did it. I don't think it's a mythlike thing. I think it's a matter of substance. *New York Times,* July 11, 1989

I think that's one of the exhilarations of being a United States Attorney; you feel like you are the good guy.
Interview on *MacNeil-Lehrer News Hour,* PBS,
September 10, 1985

Before I came, young assistants were spending too much time on long, fancy cases and not getting enough trial

experience. They didn't know how to find their way to the goal line quickly. I energized this office. I think maybe for the first six months I may have pushed too much, but I've tried to ease up. If you get too worried about morale, you run the office to please everyone else.
New York Times, June 9, 1985

If I don't tip in favor of law enforcement, who will? The civil libertarians won't. The defense lawyers won't. The liberal editorial writers won't.　　*N. Y. Times,* June 9, 1985

Some characterizations of me as very stiff, very tight, people will be surprised to find out are just wrong. Because I'm a prosecutor, there is a view of me as judgmental, but I'm not—except when it comes to the law.
Village Voice, January 24, 1989

My wife says to me that when I'm on television I never smile, and I tell her that I haven't figured out a way of smiling when I announce the indictment of a drug dealer.　　*Time,* February 10, 1986

My view is: The way you end corruption, you scare the daylights out of people.　　*New York Times,* June 9, 1985

◆ On Organized Crime

Our approach is to wipe out the five families.
Time, February 10, 1986

The Godfather is my favorite movie. I watched the movie back in the 70's and probably it helped me a lot, in a lot of the plans that we put together for how to dismantle the five families in New York. *New York Times,* January 1, 1998

At other times, Giuliani said the autobiography of mob boss Joe Bonnano had given him his game plan to attack the New York crime families.

Using it against the Commission—that was an idea that no one had until I developed it and went down to Washington and started talking about it. And I came to the office with it. *New York Times,* July 11, 1989

When others in the law enforcement community contradicted his version of events . . .

Mr. Giuliani said the others' recollections were simply incorrect. "Absolutely, totally not true. . . . These people are now trying to re-create a good idea."

New York Times, July 11, 1989

◆ On White-Collar Crime

Contrary to his later reputation, Rudy Giuliani did not always treat "crime in the suites" as a major corruption threat.

The previous administration [of Democratic President Jimmy Carter] had one priority, and that was white-collar crime. I think there was almost a McCarthyism to it. It had gotten to the point where these people had become zealots, rather than prosecutors.

1982 statement to legal correspondent Connie Bruck, made as associate attorney general at Department of Justice in Washington, DC. Reprinted in *American Lawyer,* March 1989

It reflected their prejudice against business. A professional prosecutor wouldn't have brought that case.

Explanation of decision, as associate attorney general, to settle (for fines only, no jail time) felony cases pending against four McDonnell-Douglas aerospace executives, *American Lawyer,* March 1989

People have been chasing rainbows, spending two or three years chasing a [white-collar] case they can never make. 1993 statement made to reporter Connie Bruck shortly after taking over as U.S. Attorney in New York. *American Lawyer,* March 1989

But his priorities changed.

. . . We did a survey of the number of insider-trading cases that had been prosecuted by, and were pending in, the U.S. Attorney's office. There'd be prosecution, someone would plead guilty and there was very little attention being given to it. We thought that there should be a little more attention paid to this because it could act as a deterrent to people who were involved in insider trading. *Barron's,* November 26, 1990

A string of high-profile convictions and guilty pleas followed. But in February 1987, something went wrong. Three Wall Street traders were arrested in front of their coworkers and literally taken from their offices in handcuffs. Three months later U.S. Attorney Rudolph Giuliani was forced to ask for dismissal of the case—and to admit that the arrests had been made without any investigation or grand jury indictment, based on information supplied by a lone uncorroborated witness and a complaint that contained factual errors.

The *New York Times* noted that the U.S. Attorney said the Government had been delayed because it had found a more extensive conspiracy and needed further time to investigate and present evidence to a grand jury. *New York Times,* May 14, 1987

Prosecutor Giuliani promised that new and bigger charges would be brought in record-breaking time. *New York Times,* January 4, 1988

But in the end, two years after the arrests, no charges were brought against two of the traders, while the third pleaded guilty merely to one count of mail fraud, a relatively low-level offense.

I should have analyzed those cases personally. . . . I should have gotten more of the acts out before we acted. Eventually, I got involved and realized that we didn't have the kind of case we should have and hadn't investigated the case to the extent that we should have. And it was my mistake. . . .

There was no plan at the time that we authorized going forward with it to handcuff anyone. There wasn't even a discussion of it. There was no plan to seek any kind of publicity except to hand out a press release explaining in moderate language what the complaint said, and answering questions about it. What happened was that when the agents were executing the warrants, one of the individuals refused to come along, and said, Come back after the trading is over.   *Barron's,* November 26, 1990

I had nothing to do with that [the handcuffing]. It was the agent's decision because the stockbrokers refused, thinking the arrest was a joke.

Explanation of the incident given to former mayor
Ed Koch, 1993, quoted by Koch in *New York Daily News*
column, June 12, 1998

In retrospect, was it a mistake? Sure. In retrospect, if we had known the facts we discovered two or three months later, when we realized it was a much bigger case and required more analysis to be done fairly, then we would not have done it. The valid criticism probably

is . . . rather than moving as fast as we did, we should have investigated the case first. [But] they were handled like every other case. What you'll find in these white-collar cases is that in about one-third, people are arrested, and in about two-thirds, they're not. . . . We did not set up new rules for them. As far as we are concerned, we were following the usual procedures. . . . It is not usual—but not unprecedented. Regret? No. As long as you haven't made a decision for a wrong reason, for something unethical, you can't always be regretting.

American Lawyer, March 1989

I should have slowed it down and I should have found out how complex the case was.   *N. Y. Times,* July 11, 1989

A lot of the press coverage assumed that all this was more planned than it actually was. That we wanted to send a message to Wall Street. . . . It may have turned out to be one, but it wasn't planned that way.

Barron's, November 26, 1990

• Giuliani, the Press—and Prosecutorial Ethics

The case of the three handcuffed traders brought to a head rising concern within the New York legal community at what appeared to be a persistent policy of Giuliani and his office try-ing cases in the media through prejudicial pretrial publicity, involving both high-profile news conferences and leaks of sup-posedly confidential information. The concern was shared (and expressed) not only by defense lawyers but by members of the City Bar Association and even the head of the New York State Commission on Judicial Conduct.

Damn them.   *New York Times,* June 9, 1985

I'm a more aggressive prosecutor.

Explanation offered to reporter as to why members of a bar association committee did not like testimony he had just given, in which he called the committee's members "provincial" and said they were "acting like a trade association," *New York Times,* June 9, 1985

Baseless and dishonest.

Reaction to Federal Judge Kevin Duffy's response to demand by Giuliani that Duffy recuse himself from an upcoming prosecution; before agreeing to withdraw, the judge blasted prosecutorial misconduct by Giuliani and his office, citing "intentional leaks" of grand jury proceedings in the case that "can be attributed only to the Government," *New York Times,* January 15, 1988

. . . We didn't find they [leaks] were coming from our office. What people don't realize in an investigation is that there are numerous people co-operating with the Government, or people trying to make deals who are also represented by attorneys, and attorneys very effectively have an interest in trying to spin the case in one direction or another. There was at least one article, I remember, where we were pretty well convinced that it did come from a defense attorney who had a tactical reason for getting it out. But the Assistant U.S. Attorneys handling the case and I were absolutely satisfied we were not giving away any information about the case. After all, every time one of these articles would appear there would be the potential for a motion, or an actual motion, in court. And we would have to defend it, and explain it. Hardly made sense, under the circumstances, for us to leak information.

Barron's, November 26, 1990

I feel a Government office should be open, and I have an obligation to maximize public education.

> Reflecting back on his experience as U.S. Attorney and charges that he manipulated cases through publicity
> *New York Times*, October 19, 1997

It is also very important for the public to see what we do, that we aren't always failing, that we aren't always making mistakes.
> Interview on *MacNeil-Lehrer News Hour*, PBS, September 10, 1985

The only way to deliver a deterrent effectively is to publicize it.
> *Time*, February 10, 1986

You can't delegate talking to someone who only wants to talk to the U.S. Attorney.
> *New York Times*, June 9, 1985

Very little. But if you write something out for me, I could read it.
> Response on being asked by reporter at press conference whether he spoke Spanish, *New York Times*, June 9, 1985

I don't have the foggiest idea why [people objected]. I did it at the request of [Robert] Stutman, head of the DEA [Drug Enforcement Agency]. . . . He asked me to go along so he could draw attention to the crack problem and get more resources to combat it . . . I almost *couldn't* say no. These agents go out, risk their lives, ask me to help them. I think the criticism is *silly*. There could be more legitimate criticism if I refused to do it. People could say, "What is he doing to get resources?"
> Defending decision to dress up as low-level user and make a "street buy" of drugs (accompanied by a similarly garbed U.S. Senator Al D'Amato), while posing for much-derided newspaper photographs showing him and D'Amato in easily recognized disguise. *American Lawyer*, March 1989

People assume I must be doing this because I want to run for public office. It's very hard to convince them that I do it because I feel a Government office should be open, and I have an obligation to maximize public education and public knowledge.   *N. Y. Times,* June 9, 1985

❖ The Myerson Case

After the Wall Street traders came a case that disturbed observers of the U.S. Attorney's office even more. Giuliani brought indictments against Bess Myerson, Miss America of 1945 and Cultural Affairs Commissioner in the administration of Mayor Edward Koch, and Judge Hortense Gabel, charging Gabel showed favoritism to Myerson in a bitter divorce case that involved Myerson in return for Myerson hiring Gabel's daughter Sukhreet for a city job. Not only did Giuliani have Sukhreet, who had long been afflicted with severe mental illness, put on the stand to testify against her own mother; it turned out that Sukhreet had gone through her mother's study searching for papers to use as evidence and brought them back to be reviewed by agents and prosecutors on Giuliani's staff—and had even been used to initiate taped telephone calls to her mother, for the purpose of eliciting incriminating statements. Amid widespread revulsion over his tactics, Giuliani lost the case.

I told her not to, but she [Sukhreet] inadvertently pressed the wrong button and taped her. I explained that to the judge at the arraignment.

> Explanation of the incident given to former mayor, Ed Koch, 1993. Quoted by Koch in *New York Daily News* column, June 12, 1998 (with Koch's addendum, "The arraigning judge later told me such an explanation had never been made"). Requoted in *New York Daily News,* November 29, 1998

We thought about it [having the judge's daughter gather evidence and be a witness against her mother], argued, discussed it—but we decided that was the very essence of the alleged crime. So we had to either use Sukhreet or pass on the prosecution. Judicial corruption is so serious, it didn't seem the kind of case that in fairness I could pass on. And the argument that [Bess Myerson] was prosecuted because she is famous is a bogus argument. . . . We honestly applied the same rules to that case that we did to two or three hundred other cases in this office.   *American Lawyer,* March 1989

Nobody ever came to me and argued that the case should not be indicted. Everyone in the entire chain of command was in favor of prosecution. It's possible that someone, as a passing comment, said it, but I have no recollection of that. . . . A reporter asked me, "Would you have done it again if you knew what you know now?" Well, no [he says with a chuckle]. But the question is, was there anything in the decision-making process we would change, and the answer is no.
                    American Lawyer, March 1989

You don't walk away from difficult cases because the personal complexities of a case are difficult.
                    New York Times, July 11, 1989

This is a case that had to be tried.
                    Washington Post, December 24, 1988

◆ On Haitian Refugees

In the spring of 1982, the notoriously vicious dictatorship of the Duvalier family—which for a quarter century had engaged in systematic terror against the people of Haiti, involving murder, torture, and the use of voodoo to intimidate the nation's largely uneducated population—was tottering. But not before one last killing spree that sent thousands of desperate Haitians fleeing toward the shores of Florida after a dangerous trip through rough Caribbean waters on makeshift rafts. The administration of President Ronald Reagan adopted a policy of discouraging the flood of refugees by using the Coast Guard to intercept the Haitians on the high seas and send them back—and by incarcerating those who made it through.

The prime defender of the policy: Associate U.S. Attorney General Rudolph W. Giuliani.

The third-ranking official of the Justice Department says he is convinced that there is "no political repression" in Haiti.

Associate Attorney General Rudolph W. Giuliani, testifying Thursday at a hearing of a class-action lawsuit seeking the release of 2,100 refugees in Government detention camps, said that repression in Haiti "simply does not exist now" and that refugees had nothing to fear from the Government of Jean-Claude Duvalier.

Mr. Giuliani said he visited Haiti two weeks ago and met with several officials, including President Duvalier. "Political repression is not the major reason for leaving Haiti," Mr. Giuliani said. He said he reached that conclusion after Mr. Duvalier personally assured him that Haitians returning home from the United States were not persecuted. United Press International, April 3, 1982

Amid class-action lawsuits and public quarreling, Mr. Giuliani made a two-day trip to Haiti, then testified about his findings in Federal court. In words that would be unforgettable to a generation of Haitians, he said "political repression, at least in general, does not exist"

in that dictatorship, and that the boat people were in no danger when sent home.

Mr. Giuliani later insisted that his remarks—though repeated many times in his testimony—were quoted out of context. "I know there were people who fled political oppression in Haiti and that they were entitled to asylum," the Mayor said. "But I also knew that the vast majority of people were coming for economic reasons."

The chief purpose of his trip was to guarantee the Haitians' safety upon return. He said. Indeed, during his testimony, he recalled a 75-minute conversation with President-for-Life Jean-Claude Duvalier: Mr. Giuliani demanded and received the brutal dictator's "personal assurance" that the boat people would be safe.

New York Times, October 19, 1997

The imprisonment of the Haitians in Florida was subsequently ruled illegal, and they were ordered released. As for the thousands more who, under the policy advocated by Giuliani, were turned back to face the wrath of the Duvalier regime and its dreaded *tontons macoute* secret police, they could not be reached for comment.

Mr. Giuliani said in the interview he still considered the policy justifiable, considering the problem caused by illegal immigration. *New York Times,* July 11, 1989

◆ Compassion Logged and Noted

Whenever I have heard a sentence being pronounced, I have never felt good about it. It is a horrible thing to think about somebody having to spend much time in prison. And no matter what they did wrong, there is always another part to them. *Barron's,* November 26, 1990

**Few U.S. Attorneys in history can match his record of
4,152 convictions with only 25 reversals.**
> Boast contained in official biography disseminated by
> Mayor Rudy Giuliani's Press Office, 1999

3

1989: Rudy
the First-Time Candidate

The campaign for Mayor of New York in 1989 was not
Rudolph Giuliani's first try for elective office. As a sophomore
at Manhattan College in the early 1960s, he ran for sophomore
class president.

Oh, s - - -, how can I have lost that?
> Reaction by young Rudy Giuliani to his defeat
> at the hands of classmate Jim Farrell, as recalled by
> Giuliani's campaign manager and lifelong best friend,
> Peter Powers, *New York Daily News*, May 13, 1997

**A city out of control . . . a city overwhelmed by crime,
crack and corruption. . . . All the others merely offer
rhetoric. I offer experience and performance. Before
they tell you what they'll do, ask them what they have
done.**
> Announcement of candidacy for mayor
> *New York Times*, May 18, 1989

**For 12 years, one group, one party, has virtually domi-
nated and controlled the jobs, advice, policy and direction of New York City. That isn't good for a democracy.**

It inevitably leads to negligence, to incompetence, to one corruption scandal after another.

> Accepting nomination of Liberal Party for mayor
> United Press International, April 8, 1989

Nobody owns him. Rudy—he'll clean up New York.

> Campaign ad for Giuliani
> Quoted in *Washington Post*, September 11, 1989

In his third term, incumbent mayor Edward Koch was reeling from corruption scandals that had engulfed his administration. Giuliani, who had personally prosecuted and won a conviction against one Koch political ally and whose office had jurisdiction over most of the investigations, entered the race as the prohibitive favorite. But he quickly dropped in the polls, after it was revealed that the law firm he joined upon resigning as U.S. Attorney represented the interests of Panamanian dictator Manuel Noriega, and after a falling-out with Senator Alphonse D'Amato. D'Amato backed a rival in the Republican primary, millionaire Ronald Lauder, who pummeled Giuliani with a barrage of negative television advertising.

Giuliani . . . said Lauder had "made an idiot of himself," that he is a "desperate and dishonest man" unfit to be "dogcatcher." . . .

In their only debate last week, Giuliani gave Lauder a verbal thrashing, declaring at one point: "Suffering to him is the butler taking the night off."

> *Washington Post*, September 11, 1989

Then, having based his strategy on facing off against Koch in November, Giuliani entered the general election campaign against not Koch but the man who unseated him in the Democratic primary, David Dinkins, who sought to become New

York City's first black mayor. There followed a high-minded campaign on the issues, Rudy-style.

Mr. Dinkins has been facing persistent attacks by his Republican-Liberal opponent, Rudolph W. Giuliani, as a "clubhouse politician," a "go-along get-along" patronage appointee, willing to make deals with the "bosses."
New York Times, October 10, 1989

He said Mr. Dinkins was "out of the mainstream" on the crime issue, because "he is almost always on the permissive side."
New York Times, September 20, 1989

Dinkins is the one who has taken the weakest position on criminal justice. . . . He's been in this business for 20 or 30 years. What has he ever said about crime? What has he ever done about crime? How has he fought back? . . . If you took a poll of the organized criminals and drug dealers in this city and said to them, "Which one of the two frightens you as the next mayor of the city, which one of the two says to you this may be a different city when he becomes Mayor?" I guarantee you I win that election. They'd say Giuliani is the guy who scares the living daylights out of them.
New York Times, September 20, 1989

There is definitely a double standard.
Rudy Giuliani on the media's failure, in his view, to give sufficient coverage to Dinkins's failure to pay income taxes over a four-year period in the early 1970s
New York Times, October 2, 1989

Silly . . . a ploy. . . . I really feel sorry for David. He's got a lot of problems. They're mounting. The questions are becoming more serious every day.

> Response to "Dear Mr. Giuliani" public letter from
> Dinkins to him warning him to cease "negative"
> campaign tactics, *New York Times*, October 20, 1989

◆ "A Jesse Jackson Democrat"

In a city where tensions existed between the large black and Jewish communities, Giuliani handled the challenge of criticizing the African American candidate without heightening racial divisions with extraordinary tact.

On the night that I won the Republican primary, I stood there and I laid out a vision of the future for New York. And when David Dinkins stood up, instead of seeing David Dinkins, you saw Jesse Jackson. So I could go around saying, if David wants to engage in this kind of labeling—which I think makes no sense at all—I could say, 'Well, he's a Jesse Jackson Democrat.'" And it's Jesse Jackson who wants to be President of the United States. Ronald Reagan used to be President. That's the past. It's Jesse Jackson who wants to be President. So if they're talking about a beachhead, it seems to me the only one that makes any sense is a Jesse Jackson beachhead in his quest for the Presidency.

> Response to descriptions of him by Dinkins as a "Ronald
> Reagan Republican," *New York Times*, September 26, 1989

Because I've spent a week listening to all of the labeling from the other side, which no one seems to pay any attention to. Explaining why he had now raised the issue *New York Times*, September 26, 1989

Let the people of New York choose their own destiny. Pro-Giuliani ad placed in Yiddish newspapers, showing photos of Dinkins and the Reverend Jackson together September 1989

In response to criticism, including some from Jewish groups, Giuliani insisted that his line of attack was **perfectly fair. . . . It has nothing to do with the color of your skin, your religion or ethnicity. If you subscribe to the philosophy of Jesse Jackson, the people of this city should know about that. David Dinkins himself says that he's proud to be a Jesse Jackson Democrat, so how could it possibly be in bad taste? And was it in bad taste when David Dinkins for four or five months went around the city talking about "Reagan Republican" and "reactionary"? And where the heck was the American Jewish Committee when that was being done? Or where were they when I was being tainted with Nazism, racism and lots of other charges? They were nowhere. I say there's a double standard.**

Jesse Jackson stands for views and policies, that's what it's all about, that some people may think—I do— are antithetical with the good of New York City. Unless you want to say you cannot campaign in this election, I've got to be able to raise issues regarding policies and programs. [Jesse Jackson's] policies and programs [would] bankrupt the city. I think David Dinkins's policies, to the extent there are economic policies, would

mean fiscal disaster for New York City and I think a lot of other people think that. *N. Y. Times,* Sept. 30, 1989

◆ The Jackie Mason Affair

But Giuliani had his own vulnerability on the issue of race relations. It was called Jackie Mason. The Borscht Belt comedian had attached himself to the Giuliani campaign, the candidate was enamored of him, and it seemed they appeared everywhere together—until Mason gave an interview to the *Village Voice* in which he said Jews who supported Dinkins (and other African American causes) were doing so only because they were "sick with complexes. . . . The Jews are constantly giving millions of dollars to the black people. Have you ever heard of a black person giving a quarter to a Jew? I never heard a black person say we have to help the poor Jews."

Amid the outcry and Mason's withdrawal from campaign activity "for my insensitivity," Giuliani refused to condemn Mason's remarks.

He has been very helpful and he's a good friend. He's taken himself out of the campaign so his remarks don't become an issue. The remarks, as reported, do not reflect my views. *New York Times,* September 28, 1989

The article went on to note that

asked if he would have dropped Mr. Mason if he had not stepped aside, Mr. Giuliani said he had no comment. *New York Times,* September 28, 1989

The next day, complaining that he had had to cancel, "at considerable expense," a fund raiser at which Mason was scheduled to perform, Candidate Giuliani said of Mason:

I'm not going to personally attack someone. *New York Times,* September 29, 1989

But it turned out that Mason's comments in the *Village Voice* were not the only thing the comic had said. Within a week the story broke that, two months earlier, Mason—at a lunch with Giuliani and reporters from *Newsweek* magazine—had called Dinkins "a fancy *shvartze* with a mustache." Claiming he had not heard the comment, Giuliani said:

I think the whole thing has been blown out of proportion. . . . As I recall, there were four reporters there. I emphasize that the four reporters did not report it, which means they didn't hear it or they didn't attach any significance to it at the time. . . . I did not pick up on the use of the word. . . . It's not a word I would use.

New York Times, October 2, 1989
(Article reported that "an angry Mr. Giuliani stabbed the air with an index finger" while talking)

Conceding that the word was "offensive," Giuliani reluctantly cut his ties with Mason.

He's taken some unfair hits. He's a comedian.

New York Times, October 2, 1989

But the break turned out to be less than total. When the coast was clear. . .

Two weeks ago, Mayor Giuliani presided at the unveiling of a blue sign reading "Jackie Mason Way" at Eighth Avenue and 45th Streets. The installation was meant to honor the first anniversary of Mr. Mason's latest one-man show, "Politically Incorrect," at the John Golden Theatre. *New York Times*, May 7, 1995

◆ Election Night

On November 7, 1989, David Dinkins was elected Mayor of New York. The vote was much closer than polls had predicted—50 to 48 percent.

I want to congratulate him [David Dinkins] and to wish him and his family the very best for the future.

> Concession speech, which Giuliani "had to shout to quiet the boisterous crowd" that booed every mention of Dinkins's name and demanded a recount, according to the article, *New York Times,* November 8, 1989, "Giuliani, Shouting for Quiet, Fights to Concede Graciously"

David Dinkins will be the first African-American to hold the office of mayor, and that's a historic achievement for which he deserves applause.   "Tepid applause followed"
> *New York Times,* November 8, 1989

You did a miracle. Forty-eight percent of the vote when Republicans are outnumbered 5 to 1!

> (These words, the article reported, "calmed the crowd"), *New York Times,* November 8, 1989

Do they really think I'm mean?

> Quoting reminiscence of that night by Donna Hanover, Giuliani's wife, who described her husband as asking that question of her, "crumpled at the foot of their bed," *New York Times,* October 19, 1997

4

Rudy and the PBA Riot

On September 16, 1992, some 10,000 off-duty police officers gathered for a demonstration in Lower Manhattan organized by their union, the Patrolmen's Benevolent Association. The Dinkins administration and the PBA were already at odds over stalled contract talks, the mayor's apparent opposition to giving

9-millimeter pistols to members of the force, and his support for a pending City Council bill that would create an independent civilian review board to investigate complaints of police misconduct. Added to that list now was a new, more volatile issue. Two months earlier, the mayor had publicly comforted the family of a man with a criminal record who had been shot by an NYPD officer in the drug-infested neighborhood of Washington Heights (where Rudy Giuliani and Al D'Amato had once gone "undercover" to buy drugs), paid for his funeral with city funds, and seemed—at least initially—to be taking the family's side as they charged the officer (falsely, as an exhaustive grand jury probe later documented) with murder.

The demonstration by the cops—sweltering in the heat, most of them irate, many of them drunk and some of them openly drinking alcohol, some carrying signs such as "Fight Crime, Dump Dinkins" or crude racist depictions of the black mayor as a "washroom attendant"—quickly spun out of control. Mobs of erstwhile law enforcement professionals, spouting epithets and obscenities, some of them threatening civilians (including a Caribbean American city councilwoman who reported being racially harassed), stormed the steps of City Hall, literally laid siege to the building, and blocked traffic on the Brooklyn Bridge.

The most prominent public official to appear at the "rally": former candidate for mayor, and former United States Attorney, Rudolph W. Giuliani.

I have the ability to conduct myself in a way I think is dignified.   Interview with columnist Maureen Dowd
New York Times, July 12, 1997

**BULLSHIT!... BULLSHIT!... BULLSHIT!...
BULLSHIT!...**

Chant shouted by Rudolph Giuliani in speech to crowd at PBA demonstration. Reported by several news organiza-

tions, including *New York Times,* September 20, 1992
([Giuliani] "repeatedly screamed a one-word profanity),
September 23, 1992 [Giuliani was heard "repeatedly using
a vulgarity"), and again on March 5, 1998 ("'Bull - - - -!'"
he screamed again and again").

In addition, Giuliani told the crowd that the Mayor of New
York was merely trying to
protect his political ass.   *N. Y. Daily News,* Feb. 27, 1998

**Beer cans and broken beer bottles littered the streets as
Mr. Giuliani led the crowd in chants, using an obscenity
to refer to Dinkins Administration policies. Most officers in the in the crowd agreed with his sentiments,
though they reacted less warmly when Mr. Giuliani said
there was a need to fight corruption and problems
within the police department.**   *N. Y. Times,* Sept. 27, 1992

Asked about the propriety of yelling the word "bullshit" in
such an incendiary situation, Giuliani explained:
**That was the word David Dinkins used talking to police
officers at the 34th Precinct. Guy Molinari [Republican
Staten Island Borough President] quoted him. I was
quoting Molinari.**
　　**At City Hall, there were 2,000 or 3,000 cops chanting
my name. A PBA representative came to me on the
steps and gave me a bullhorn. "Maybe they'll follow
you." So I said into the bullhorn, "Let's go over to Murray Street." A PBA guy grabbed a flag and walked in
front of me. I took someone by the elbow and said, "I
want you please to come over to Murray Street." They
didn't want to. But some did.**
　　**[Criticism of his actions was] just David Dinkins try-
ing to put a spin on this. . . . The effect? Who knows? . . .**

[Dinkins] made the tragic mistake of treating a drug dealer as a hero. . . . I had four uncles who were cops. So maybe I was more emotional than I usually am.

Newsday, September 19, 1992

When Mayor Dinkins denounced the mob's actions as "hooliganism" and denounced Giuliani as "an opportunist" who was "seizing upon a fragile circumstance in our city for his own political gain,"
Mr. Giuliani lashed out at Mr. Dinkins, accusing him of lying about Mr. Giuliani's role in Wednesday's demonstration and of "scapegoating." He added that the Mayor is guilty of hypocrisy for "doing this phony routine about 'I care about your lives' when his own police guards carry automatic weapons."

New York Times, September 20, 1992

This publicity helps him, so he's trying to create an impression that I incited a riot. . . . At some point people are going to say, how can you have a Mayor who has a Police Department where the overwhelming majority of officers think he's putting their lives at risk. . . . He's had two racial riots and he has a Police Department that's out of control.

New York Times, September 20, 1992

Politically inspired. . . . I led at least 2,000 police officers away from City Hall, verbally urging them to come with me. Those actions significantly reduced whatever disturbance may have taken place.

Reaction to call by black police officers' organization
for special prosecutor to investigate his role in the
disturbances, *New York Times,* September 23, 1992

Then a Dinkins deputy mayor added fuel to the fire by comparing Giuliani to Klansman David Duke.

To compare me to David Duke is sick. It indicates that what you're interested in is political division and not political peace. . . . The Mayor is perpetrating a fraud about my activity. When he apologizes for that, when he has the wisdom and the sense to apologize for that, then other people can apologize to him for things. The Mayor plays the race card when he thinks it is to his advantage and he condemns other people when he believes they're doing it and that is very phony. I'll say it once again: Bill Lynch being on WLIB comparing me to David Duke is playing the race card. It is to get a largely African-American audience bitterly angry at me.

New York Times, September 23, 1992

A form of racial politics which is far worse than anything I've seen in this city. . . . Abysmal leadership . . . [Dinkins chided Lynch for his comments but did not require him to resign or apologize.] I think if the shoe were on the other foot, I would certainly be required to go a lot further. *New York Times,* September 28, 1992

Finally Giuliani changed the subject.

We should discuss other things for a while. Maybe we should shut up about this and talk about how we deal with the school system. And if we want to talk about his problem, let's talk about things other than a civilian complaint review board; the substantive things that would be more than just kind of useless symbolism.

WNBC-TV, "News Forum," October 4, 1992

The Patrolmen's Benevolent Association paid a high price for its rally. The disgraceful behavior of so many of its members

· 27 ·

directly paved the way for the independent civilian review board that, ironically, the PBA had assembled its members that day in order to oppose. As for once (and future) mayoral candidate Rudy Giuliani, it was not clear what, if any, lessons in self-awareness he came away with from the episode.

Shouting and screaming is not the way for intelligent people to talk to each other. *N. Y. Times,* March 9, 1995

5

Rudy to the Rescue: The Ambulance Incident

In 1993, kept under tight control by veteran political consultant David Garth, Rudy Giuliani committed no major gaffes in his second race for mayor. Indeed, he emerged looking almost statesmanlike by the end of the campaign, reversing the result of four years before and defeating David Dinkins in another close (51 to 48 percent) contest. But after the election, an incident occurred that had some New Yorkers wondering all over again about the temper of the man they had just elected.

The son of a neighbor in Giuliani's apartment house was struck by a cab and, though not critically hurt, needed to be taken to a hospital. A city ambulance arrived and, according to regulations, prepared to take the boy to the nearest trauma center. The boy's mother wanted him taken to a hospital where his father was a heart surgeon on staff—but which was much farther away. An argument ensued on the sidewalk. Rudy Giuliani, emerging from the building, intervened. The ambulance wound up taking the boy to the father's hospital. Conflicting versions soon emerged as to what happened.

The EMS [Emergency Medical Service] worker was not exercising appropriate judgment here, nor was he acting in the way you or I would like to see people working for the City of New York to act toward its citizens. This was a woman in distress with her child crying next to her. He was making matters worse and arguing with her.... What I said when I ran for Mayor is that New York City is going to get a different kind of Mayor. You're going to get a hands-on Mayor, somebody who acts to help the citizens of this community. *N.Y. Times,* December 16, 1993

The mayor-elect went on to describe to the *Times* how he had found the boy
shivering on the ground *N. Y. Times,* Dec. 16, 1993

and the mother's wish a
perfectly reasonable request. *N. Y. Times,* Dec. 16, 1993

Indeed, he joked about the fracas at a speech that same night.
If I have to leave quickly, it's only because there might be an emergency out there that needs my help.
Remarks at Liberal Party dinner, December 15, 1993
New York Times, December 19, 1993

But a few days later, a different tale emerged.
Immediately he says, "Take him where his mother wants him to go." ... All I could remember was him using expletives and talking about bureaucracy and red tape.
EMS Lieutenant Jimmy Ayuso describing Giuliani's manner during incident, *New York Times,* December 19, 1993
[Article also quoted witness saying the lieutenant "didn't seem to be rude. Mr. Giuliani seemed much more agitated than he did," and reported witnesses' contention that "Mr. Giuliani used a vulgar anatomical reference in talking with the Lieutenant."]

Giuliani blamed it all on the EMS lieutenant's **bureaucratic, rigid attitude.... He got very annoyed, walked away from me, and he had a discussion with someone else. Meanwhile, the boy is kind of lying there. They're doing a few things to him. We finally got the blanket put on him so he would be warm. [The lieutenant] continued to discuss it with someone.... So I went over to him and I did in very strong language tell him what I thought. I didn't use the words he's attributed to me.** *New York Times,* December 19, 1993

I would do it again. It had nothing to do with the fact that it was an EMS employee. I would have done the same thing if it was any other employee.
New York Times, December 19, 1993

And, in what would become a familiar complaint, he blamed the media.

[The article was] very distorted ... numerous people who supported my account [were not interviewed. People who were interviewed] were selectively quoted.
New York Times, December 21, 1993

6

The Generalissimo Takes Charge
- Dr. Rudy's Rx: Cut, Cut, Cut

I ask you to give me a chance to make change happen for us. Don't let those who are so fearful of transformation stop the process before it begins—killing ideas by fear. We don't need to be fearful.

First Inaugural Address, *New York Times,* January 3, 1994

It turned out, however, that in the new mayor's view of things, there was plenty to be fearful about.

Disorder . . . is driving this city down.

1993 stump campaign statement
Requoted in New York Times, February 28, 1994

This state of the city has to end, because if it doesn't end, it will end our city as we have known it.

State of the City address, *New York Times,* February 10, 1994

But Generalissimo Giuliani had a plan.

Despite the tough and difficult steps that I must take to remove our structural budget deficit . . . be sure that I will take them.

First Inaugural Address, *New York Times,* January 3, 1994

Government has a role, but a far less expansive one than has been the norm in New York City.

New York Times, February 28, 1994

We are going to cut the size of government so that we can live within our means.

Televised address to New Yorkers, *N.Y. Times,* Feb. 3, 1994

We have budgeted on the theory that we were unique for the last 10 or 15 years, that we could just increase spending and that we didn't have to take into account the tax burden, the fee burden, the fine burden we were placing on businesses. *New York Times,* February 3, 1994

The fact is if you look broadly in New York City, government has always answered the question of should government do it by answering it yes. What government should have done is occasionally answer it yes and more often answer it no. *New York Times,* February 28, 1994

The City is doing what it traditionally does. The City is attempting to spend more money than we planned to spend and this is why we're making cuts.

New York Times, September 23, 1994

I expect there will be a big reaction against this. [But] there aren't any other options.   *N. Y. Times,* Jan. 29, 1994

It's an offer to sanitation workers and everyone else in this city. "Help us make you more productive. If you do, then this massive change doesn't have to take place. If you don't, then the massive change is inevitable."

Characterizing city's ultimatum to sanitation workers' union that they accept work-rule changes or his administration would begin laying off union members
New York Times, February 3, 1994

Saying the city's fiscal problems required a dose of "reality therapy," Mayor Rudolph W. Giuliani told New Yorkers yesterday evening that he would reduce City spending for the second year in a row and cut public assistance and health care for the city's poorest residents.

New York Times, February 14, 1995

We must confront the reality that we cannot continue spending substantially more money than other American cities. . . . We must confront the reality that the city's fiscal problems will not be solved by Albany or Washington. . . . We really have no other choice.

Televised address to New Yorkers, *N. Y. Times*, Feb. 14, 1995

I see this crisis as a historic opportunity. It is a chance to do what was politically unthinkable just a few years ago.

Televised address to New Yorkers, *N. Y. Times*, Feb. 14, 1995

I don't like the idea of having to remove anyone's job. But it was done in order to stimulate the economy of the city.   *New York Times,* November 14, 1994

You can't have a city where everybody works for the city.
                    New York Times, February 4, 1994

Every time we've proposed those reductions we've been met with a chorus, a cacophony really, of politicians in this city who go around saying the streets will be dirtier, the streets will fall apart. The highways won't work any longer. Crime will go up. There'll be chaos in the city. The human needs of people will not be cared for or taken account of. We hear that over and over again.
    Speech at political fund raiser, *New York Times,* May 10, 1996

I think the most remarkable thing about this report is how little effect that all had on services—not at all the level in which people opposed to those reductions claimed, suggested or argued.
            Statement on release of Mayor's Management Report
                    New York Times, March 3, 1995

[A budget] must be compassionate. [It] must balance the needs of people.
        Statement accompanying release of Mayor's 1996 Financial Plan. Quoted by former mayor Ed Koch in *New York Post* column, March 15, 1996
[The former mayor noted that "within ten days after publishing the financial plan, the mayor announced $700 million in additional cuts. It is inconceivable that he was unaware of the need for these cuts when he announced his fiscal plan."]

Oh, yeah, like, be efficient. Uh. Oh my God, they're going to have to be efficient.

> Mocking critics of his cuts to city public libraries,
> using what a reporter called "a child's whine,"
> WABC Radio show, *Washington Post,* June 30, 1999

With his much-heralded "downsizing" of government, the new mayor effectively destroyed New York City's long commitment to welfare-state liberalism. He also dismissed thousands of government workers from their jobs. But while many of these career professionals were having their livelihoods as public servants ended, other people were finding it quite easy to get positions in government. In fact, on a variety of fronts, the Giuliani administration operated rather differently from the "good government" promises of the Giuliani campaign.

◆ On Lobbying

The U.S. Attorney called for creation of a commission that would bring to public view what he described as "noncriminal, unethical behavior" by New York public officials. . . . The United States Attorney said that "a certain kind of frustration" arose during his office's lingering investigation of corruption in New York City because "much of what you're looking at really isn't criminal" but "raises questions about the way politics is practiced." . . . He suggested that the Top 20 [state legislators who had appeared before state agencies on behalf of clients from their private law firm] be called before the commission to explain the practice, adding that "I think the public would get upset if they saw how much money these people were making."

> *New York Times,* December 9, 1986

The actions of lobbyists such as Sid Davidoff are further evidence as to the failure of New York City's current revolving-door provisions to prevent conflicts of interest.

1993 campaign statement abhorring former top aide to Mayor John Lindsay, who had parlayed government connections and personal friendships to become city's best-known, highest-paid lobbyist during administration of Mayor David Dinkins, *Village Voice,* February 20, 1996

And indeed, under the Giuliani administration, Davidoff's law firm was no longer ranked No. 1 in lobbying fees in New York. But look at whose firm was—that of Liberal Party chairman Ray Harding (who had thrown his party's support behind Giuliani as far back as the 1989 race, and who had two sons working in the new administration) and Herman Badillo (Giuliani's 1993 running mate for city comptroller and, like Harding, a member of the mayor's "kitchen cabinet"), both of whom freely intervened on behalf of their clients with municipal agencies that were fully aware of their clout with the mayor. In the first two years of Giuliani's tenure, in fact, their lobbying client list zoomed from three to sixty, the *New York Times* found. Pure coincidence?

No one has broken any rule, any regulation or any law. Everyone has conducted themselves by the highest standards of ethics. And I insist on that. The rules and regulations are very strict. The level of conduct here, I think, is exemplary. *New York Times,* February 10, 1997

The mayor said
three different times that he and others in his administration always strove to "dot every i and cross every t."
New York Times, February 10, 1997

I don't think that there's been an administration in this city in a long time that tries as hard as our administration to meet every ethical standard that there is. . . . We meet them. We exceed them.   *N. Y. Times,* Feb. 10, 1997

To create the impression that there is something unlawful and unethical here is shameful. It also hurts public regulation of government. And this has been done according to every rule, every regulation. This city has never had an administration that bends over as much as we do to follow every ethical norm that there is.

New York Times, February 15, 1997

But if people did not believe him, the mayor had a simple solution: Ban all lobbying. That's right, just ban it.

As a practical matter, you do not need intermediaries to deal with the executive branch of government. People are turned down just as often when they have lobbyists as when they appear themselves.   *N. Y. Times,* Feb. 14, 1997

Nobody needs a lobbyist to contact the mayor. You call me on this radio show, other radio shows that I am on. I meet people in the street, I go to town hall meetings. I take notes from them, I try to deal with their problems. We don't need an intermediary to have our relationship. Nobody has to be making money off that. Whether they are advisers of mine, or friends of mine, or lawyers I know, or opponents of mine, or anybody else.

The people who are my advisers are following the law, the letter and spirit, in every respect. Each one of the articles says that, but then they stick headlines in the *Daily News* and the *Times* to try and create the other impression. They really shouldn't do that. If they were being fair with you, they wouldn't. But, as far as I am concerned, this shouldn't exist at all. There is not reason for it. The law should be changed for everybody. It should be banned, in terms of lobbying the executive branch of government.

Remarks on WABC radio show, February 14, 1997
New York Times, February 15, 1997

The idea of this proposal is something that is consistent with something that I have always believed. I don't believe that lobbying is necessary. It is not necessary to lobby my administration. I have gotten that message out many different times, including when the issue was presented before in the past. Lobbying is not necessary for this administration. There is no reason to do it. You do not get an edge. You do not get advantage. You can contact us directly. You do not need to pay a lobbyist to deal with the executive branch of government.

You [in the media] have created this issue. This is a created, false issue. I know about created, false issues. I have dealt with them before. The fact is that both Mr. Harding and Mr. Badillo have both undertaken to say that they will not lobby the administration during the course of this review that I am conducting. My advice to them would be never to do it.

News Conference, City Hall, February 14, 1997
New York Times, February 15, 1997

When the leading Democratic candidate for mayor demanded an investigation into lobbying of his administration, Giuliani dismissed her statement as a
political campaign document.   *N. Y. Times,* Feb. 16, 1997

By contrast, he said he had long held his belief that lobbying was unnecessary and should be prohibited—and his proposal was in no way an attempt at damage control while he campaigned for reelection.

It seems to me that the opportunity now presents itself.
New York Times, February 16, 1997

There was one little problem, however. The mayor, by his own admission, had gotten the idea only some fifteen minutes before announcing it to the public.

We don't know yet how it will work.
New York Times, February 14, 1997

[In a follow-up piece two days later, reporter David Firestone informed *Times* readers that the mayor's statement had "left the high-powered jaws of city commissioners and deputy mayors hanging open," that the mayor "offered no explanations of how such a ban would work," and that "even his senior aides conceded they had no notion of how to make it either practical or constitutional."]

In fact, several weeks later, the mayor confessed:

It is a more intricate matter than I realized when I first said it. . . . We are trying to come up with a proposal that is constitutional.   *New York Times*, April 3, 1997

He never did. And two years later, the issue of inside influence over his administration arose again when it was revealed that the investment firm of Goldman, Sachs had been granted special parking privileges by the city for its company limousines. Their lobbyist: the wife of one of Giuliani's closest, most powerful aides.

You don't need a lobbyist to deal with this administration. . . . I know the spin that happens here. This is a big business, so it has access to the Mayor. But the fact is I've done this for delicatessens. I've done it for candy stores. I've done it for people who call my radio show.
New York Times, January 20, 1999

The recipient of another special parking permit from the city: one of the mayor's fund raisers.

Oh, get out of here. No, I'm not going to comment on the Joseph Spitzer parking situation. It's the silliest thing. Oh, my God, he's got a permit to park in the city. Oh, my God. That's right, I'm a big crook.

New York Times, December 31, 1999

◆ On Public Servants Accepting Gifts (in the Form of an Apartment)

In the summer of 1994, when the New York media broke the story that William Koeppel—real-estate developer and major fund raiser in the mayor's campaign a year earlier—had offered vacant apartments in buildings he owned on Manhattan's very-desirable Upper East Side to staff members of the new administration, on terms that were (for the nation's tightest housing market) unusually favorable (including the introductory bonus of several months free rent), the mayor whose administration conducted itself according to "the highest standards of ethics," whose personnel strive to "dot every i and cross every t," reacted accordingly:

[A] cheap story. . . . If I find that anyone did anything wrong, I would be the first to administer publicly discipline that would be considered very harsh. On the other hand, if they haven't [done anything wrong], if in fact a mischaracterization is being created and kind of driven by the constant media attention to this, then I'm not going to just submit to that because people think that's the politically correct thing to do. . . . [The rents were] very comparable to what everyone else in the building is paying. . . . In each case, they are paying more than the prior tenant by a good deal. If anyone did anything

wrong, we'll take action. But I'm not going to submit to this kind of thing and create a further impression of wrongdoing. *New York Times,* July 16, 1994

I've thought of all different aspects of this. If anyone did anything wrong, I'll discipline them. In fact, concessions like this have been given to many people totally unconnected to my administration, and one like this was done just last month. Right now there is what has been commonly called a feeding frenzy going on. This is not the best time for decision making and in fact, I think, we're handling it very, very appropriately.

New York Times, July 16, 1994

(William Koeppel, Giuliani fund raiser and sweetheart landlord to so many of the mayor's most prized staff members, wound up pleading guilty to criminal charges that he illegally demanded contributions to Giuliani's campaign from tenants seeking rent-stabilized apartments in his buildings.)

◆ On The Evils of Patronage
(i.e., It's Evil If *You* Do It)

Mayor Giuliani, whose battle against corruption helped propel him to prominence as a prosecutor, called for a "dramatic break" with patronage in his first campaign for mayor in 1989. *New York Times,* August 8, 1994

From the day that I first started exploring running for mayor, I have made it clear to every political leader from the first discussion we have that there will be no jobs or patronage—only decisions made on the merits.

1989 campaign statement. Quoted in *N. Y. Times,* June 1, 1995

The former prosecutor sounded like a Democratic reformer of the 1960's and 70's as he repeatedly referred to political bosses and union bosses. Mr. Giuliani himself is supported by Mr. [Raymond] Harding, the Liberal leader, and State Senator Roy M. Goodman, who tightly controls the Manhattan Republican organization. Mr. Giuliani said he had told both that they could expect no favors from a Giuliani administration.

New York Times, September 20, 1989

There will be no Talent Bank operating in the basement of City Hall if I'm elected Mayor.

Campaign quip at expense of Mayor Ed Koch, who initiated a "Talent Bank" to enhance his administration's affirmative-action efforts, which was used instead to funnel jobs to Democratic Party regulars
United Press International, April 8, 1989

[Patronage is a] municipal plague. . . . Where government jobs are turned over in blocks to political leaders who have been in power for a long time, that almost always leads to corruption. I will create a Hiring Panel to get petty politics out of the City's hiring business. This panel will clear all high-level government appointments. It will work with DOI [the City Department of Investigation] to make certain hiring is being done fairly and based on quality. I am not just going to announce the end to system-wide patronage; I will investigate to make certain its corrupting influence is removed from government once and for all. There will be no patronage in my administration. Not under this Mayor's nose.

1993 campaign promise
Quoted in *Village Voice,* February 20, 1996

Ah, but in practice. . .

**All senior level appointments or reappointments (i.e.
Assistant Commissioner level and above, Chiefs of Staff,
Executive Assistants or Special Assistants to Commissioners, Press Secretaries, and any other comparable
senior level appointments) must be made in consulta-
tion with the Mayor's Office through me.**

> Memo to all City agency heads from mayor's Chief of
> Staff Randy Mastro, March 30, 1994

**In scores of cases, the Mayor has given jobs to campaign
supporters and officials of the parties that backed him.
He has hired at least three dozen members of his campaign staff, 16 district leaders from the Republican and
Liberal parties, assorted campaign volunteers, and relatives and in-laws of the Mayor himself or his political
allies.** *New York Times,* August 8, 1994

These hirings—many of them at stratospheric salary
increases—were *not* patronage, the mayor explained.

**To me patronage is—and I know it has lots of defini-
tions—is that some political leader has 20 jobs and gets
to fill those 20 jobs and there is not any thought being
given to qualifications and to the job. [His administration accepts résumés from political leaders but] we say
no as often as we say yes. [His Cabinet and administration are] so diverse that there's no danger of an outside
force taking over an agency.** *N. Y. Times,* Aug. 8, 1994

**They should be the best qualified person for the job.
[But] they certainly shouldn't be disqualified because
they supported me or helped me.** *N. Y. Times,* May 21, 1994

Of course we are hiring supporters. Who else would we appoint? Quote attributed to Mayor Rudolph Giuliani, *Village Voice,* February 20, 1996

City Hall patronage dispenser Randy Mastro told *Newsday* in early 1994 that the administration had only hired 500 from the 7,000 resumes sent to it, insisting that there was "a different order of magnitude" between Giuliani patronage and that of his predecessors.
Village Voice, February 20, 1996

People should understand that our public hospital system—while a wonderful concept and a good thing—very often is used by the politicians of this city as a jobs program for their favorites.
Defense of his attempt to hire someone recommended by a Republican state senator to run a municipal hospital; same man had been forced out of same job nine years earlier for misuse of hospital funds. *Newsday,* November 1996, requoted in column by former mayor Ed Koch, *New York Post,* November 15, 1996

The only thing that's being rewarded here is independence and qualifications. A lot of people supported me; not everybody that supported me was selected for jobs in the administration. It comes when there is a combination of general agreement on philosophy and a sense, if you are running city government, that this is the right kind of person for that job, that they can take it to a new level of achievement.
Announcing the hiring as commissioners of two supporters who had given up their legislative seats *New York Times,* December 31, 1997

Perhaps the most extreme example of the new mayor's elastic definition of what constituted "patronage" came at the City Department of Youth Services.

Mr. Giuliani said yesterday that he had not paid enough attention to personnel practices at the department, and that the lapse had resulted in the hiring of too many administrators at inflated salaries. The increase in salaries and staff, which left top officials receiving more than the Dinkins administration officials they had replaced, came even as the Mayor planned to cut the agency's budget by nearly $16 million and to eliminate thousands of jobs for teenagers. Over the last four months, his administration has greatly added senior staff, to the point that the Youth Services Department was spending at least $85,000 more for administrators than it had under Mayor David N. Dinkins, despite Mr. Giuliani's frequent assertions that he wanted to reduce layers of bureaucracy in the government.

New York Times, May 21, 1994

Not only was the Department of Youth Services turned into a patronage trough, the Rev. John Brandon, whom Giuliani had installed to run the agency (one of his few prominent backers in the African American community) turned out to have the same problem in his past that Giuliani had once lambasted David Dinkins for: nonpayment of income taxes. Brandon was forced to resign.

I regret very very much the events that have occurred. . . . This is our fault. He did not understand the downsizing process that we wanted. . . . [The department was] moving in a direction that's inconsistent with what we're trying to achieve in the entire administration. . . . You are not aware of everything that goes on. You're not and I take full responsibility for it.

New York Times, May 21, 1994

The mayor said he would personally review all résumés of job candidates for the agency **to make sure that they have substantive qualifications for the jobs for which they are hired.**

New York Times, May 19, 1994

But, in the midst of the furor over his hiring practices and the scandal at the Youth Services Department, the mayor's press secretary suddenly announced evidence had been uncovered that, under the Dinkins administration's last commissioner, the agency had overspent its budget and improperly approved service contracts—and that agency records had been destroyed and its computer system tampered with. Was he creating a diversion? Absolutely not, insisted Generalissimo Giuliani.

Allegations are facts. *New York Times,* March 24, 1995

One thing is not intended to obscure the other.

New York Times, May 19, 1994

The fact is that some of the programs [at the agency] are very valuable, some are average and some are totally unacceptable and have produced little or nothing. What I need is an accountable analysis of what's going on in there. *New York Times,* May 19, 1994

We're going to find out what the problem is and have it out in the open in a way in which people can have confidences . . . an honest, objective appraisal.

Announcing formation of commission that included city comptroller and private accounting firm to look into his allegations concerning department and Dinkins's administration commissioner
New York Times, November 11, 1994

The panel found nothing. There were no irregularities and the charge of destroying evidence was untrue.

◆ On the Exactitude of Family Ties

In 1968 Rudolph Giuliani and Regina Peruggi were married. In 1982 they were divorced. In addition, Giuliani obtained an annulment enabling him to remarry within the Roman Catholic Church. His grounds: He had not realized at the time of the wedding that his bride was also his second cousin.

This has been painted, as, well, something sneaky. But I was under the impression that we were third cousins because I never calculated the lines of consanguinity. I can't tell you what Gina thought. I don't think we ever discussed it in any great detail.

[He consulted Alan Placa, a childhood friend who had entered the priesthood.] He said, "You were related, you must have gotten a dispensation." I said, "Alan, I don't recall doing that. I don't recall realizing that I had to get one." He said, "Well, you know, the priest may have gone ahead and done it anyway."

New York Times, October 19, 1997

[Article went on to note that "as church experts confirm, approval would have been routine," but that "a search through church records found none of the required paperwork." Article also quoted the mayor's cousin saying "I knew they were second cousins. It seemed natural." And a May 13, 1997, profile in the *New York Daily News* reported, "Their fathers were first cousins. The wedding and reception . . . was as much a family gathering as a marriage celebration."]

But years later, responding to revelations that no less than four of his relatives had managed to find employment in his administration even as he was feverishly "downsizing government," the mayor said he had so many cousins—first, second, third and fourth—that it would be unreasonable to expect him to know all of those who may have been hired in his administration.   *New York Times,* June 8, 1994

At what degree of relationship should I know about? What about a second or a third cousin?
                    New York Times, June 8, 1994

And were there other relatives of his on the city payroll?
There could be; I would have to check.
                    New York Times, June 8, 1994

◆ February 1995: The Week of the Long Knives

Rudy Giuliani came into City Hall trumpeting his approach to "bipartisan" and "nonpartisan" government.
We haven't given in to partisan politics. I've appointed more members of the so-called opposition party than any mayor in history.   *New York Times,* February 10, 1994

But the last vestiges—or the last illusions—about that came to an abrupt end when a snowstorm blanketed the city one weekend in early February 1995. The mayor went out to pose for a photo opportunity with Department of Transportation workers who were removing snow from the Brooklyn Bridge. Because of a mix-up, he wound up having to walk from his car to where the work crew was—through puddles.

His feet were soaked, and the Generalissimo was furious. This had to have been done deliberately. Wasn't the department press aide responsible for staging the photo-op a holdover from David Dinkins? (Within two hours, the aide had been sacked.) And, while we're firing him, the Generalissimo reasoned . . .

In a new drive to tighten his control over city agencies, Mayor Rudolph W. Giuliani said yesterday that he was dismissing as many as 35 officials across the city government, some of them because they "had the agenda of the prior administration."

Some officials, he said, will not be replaced, while others would be replaced by people "who understand the philosophy, the direction of our administration."

New York Times, February 9, 1995

In some cases, it's to downsize. In some cases, it's in order to redirect the agency. In some cases it's in order to have someone who understands the philosophy, the direction and the agenda of the administration, as opposed to someone who's still carrying on the philosophy, the agenda of the prior administration.

New York Times, February 9, 1995

Overnight, some of the most experienced, knowledgeable, and trusted press spokespersons in city government were removed from their jobs. At the Police Department, the order came through that the size of the Public Information Office had to be reduced—until it was exactly one employee smaller than the Mayor's Press Office. And when the mayor's health commissioner was at first reluctant to dismiss her press aide . . .

At a news conference later yesterday, Mr. Giuliani was told of Dr. Hamburg's remarks and was later asked if he would order her to dismiss her aide. "Yes," he replied. Asked if he would relieve Ms. Hamburg of her job if she refused, he said, "She'll fire him." *N.Y. Times,* Feb. 10, 1995

The fact is that I'm entitled to have in these positions people that I have full confidence in. That is true of all administrations, and in certain cases we didn't have full confidence so we're making changes. We're continuing to make changes.   *New York Times,* February 10, 1995

The reality is that we want our own people in office that we have confidence in. We want to be able to put our own people in a number of these positions, because we have a lot of difficulties lying ahead over the next two, three, four or five months.   *N. Y. Times,* Feb. 11, 1995

The Mayor, his voice sometimes breaking, said that the dismissals would continue and that his main regret was that he had not carried them out earlier. "The only thing I would do differently, maybe," he said, "is having done what Governor Pataki did, which is to do a much heavier cleaning out when I first took office than we actually did."   *New York Times,* February 11, 1995

We're in charge. We know the direction we want to go in.
        New York Times, February 12, 1995

7

Rudy and the Police
("I Run the Police Department")

I believe there has never been a Mayor who has supported the Police Department more.
        Remarks at Police Department award ceremony
        New York Times, February 17, 1995

That statement by Rudolph Giuliani, at least, would seem not to be in much dispute. As mayor, he presided over a steep drop in crime that was without precedent in the city's annals, bringing relief to residents long resigned to living in fear.

Today, you take the first step toward becoming New York City Police Officers—members of the finest, best trained, best equipped, most restrained and most professional police force in the nation. . . . The Department's CPR program will teach you that professionalism and respect must be at the root of every interaction you have with the public. . . . From this day forward you will take on tremendous responsibilities to enable the people of the City to live freely and independently.

Address to new class of Police Academy recruits
Mayor's Office Press Release, July 3, 1998

But Giuliani's achievements in public safety were not an unmixed blessing; they came at a price. As mayor, he imposed his own iron control on the NYPD to such an extent that the city lost the most charismatic and successful police commissioner of modern times. Rank-and-file officers, who had overwhelmingly supported his election, came to loathe him. And in the face of increasing evidence that nonwhite New Yorkers had legitimate reason to complain that they were still living in fear—fear of the police themselves—Generalissimo Giuliani seemed absolutely unmoved.

Millions and millions of people have been liberated from the reality and the fear of crime.

Second Inaugural Address, *New York Times,* January 2, 1998

That was a far cry from the situation the Generalissimo described upon taking office.

Recently he [the Mayor] said the city's "future to a very large extent as a society" depended on New York's becoming safer. *New York Times,* July 8, 1994

It was amazing to me that people thought the squeegee problem [street hustlers washing windows of cars stopped at lights or intersections, without asking the drivers' permission, then demanding payment—Ed.] couldn't be solved. A civilized society can't let people go around the streets intimidating other people. But a weird philosophical thinking had emerged about these quality-of-life issues. If somebody was urinating in the street, the reaction would be, oh, we can't do anything about that. And then the idea would start to develop that there must be some inherent human right to urinate on the street. So the police started ignoring all kinds of offenses. They'd even stand by when drug deals were going on. The police became highly skilled observers of crime. *N. Y. Times Magazine,* Dec. 3, 1995

The turnaround actually had begun when, in response to a crime wave that terrified the city in the summer of 1990, Mayor David Dinkins launched—and lobbied strenuously for passage in the State Legislature of—a program called "Safe Streets, Safe City," under which local police strength was beefed up some 20 percent, to a total of nearly 40,000 officers. (In fact, the crime rate started to decline during the last two years Dinkins was in office, prior to Giuliani's ever becoming mayor.) In the highest traditions of bipartisan statesmanship, Giuliani thanked his predecessor's leadership and contributions to winning the war on crime thusly:

David Dinkins supported "Safe Streets, Safe City" because he was forced to do it. And he didn't fund the police officers. He was pushed into doing it. And in fact the Legislature was trying to take money away from him because he wasn't putting it into police officers.

Statement at mayoral candidates' debate,
New York Times, Oct. 30, 1997

And as for the strategy of "community policing" that had been implemented under the former mayor . . .

Police officers have to play the role primarily of preventing crime. Social-service aspects that were kind of added on to community policing, some of that has to be done but can't become a primary focus of all the police aspects in the neighborhood. The police officer's there to make sure the burglary doesn't take place, the robbery doesn't take place, a person can walk along the street safely. . . . Police officers were being given a tremendous amount of training that delayed their ability to get out into the community. The training was not preventing crime. The training was in trying to come to understand the whole social-service network [that even] social workers have a hard time understanding.

New York Times, January 25, 1994

One week into his mayoralty, Giuliani encountered the first test of his determination to distance himself from the way Dinkins had handled racial confrontations that involved the police. Officers, responding to what turned out to be a false report apparently designed to lure them to the scene, entered Mosque No. 7 of the Nation of Islam in Harlem—a designated "sensitive location" where, under similar circumstances in 1972, an NYPD officer had been killed in a case that remained unsolved. A melee ensued.

The law is violated. Now it's time for the people who were responsible to turn themselves in, and the courts can resolve what happened. We have a system of laws in this country, a system of laws in the city. I'm committed to them, and this is the same view that I would take no matter where it happened at any time it happened. . . . This is not the black community. This is about one par-

ticular mosque where several police officers were beaten and the officer's gun and another officer's radio was taken away. *New York Times*, January 13, 1994

Several weeks later he enunciated what would be his general attitude regarding such incidents.

My standard is support for the police unless the evidence demonstrated that the police acted illegally or improperly. I believe it's the way to create a civilized society and respect for the law.

State of the City address, February 10, 1994

And though in that same address the new mayor acknowledged that police "must be held to the highest standards" and that "we must act strongly" against illegal or improper behavior, when a commission chaired by respected former Judge Milton Mollen issued its final report on a resurgence of drug-related police corruption and brutality in the NYPD in the early 1990s, Giuliani did not endorse its call for a permanent outside monitor of the department.

[Police corruption is] a very important problem that the city must address [but it is] a part, not the only example, of corruption that exists in the government of New York City, the politics of New York City, or the way in which we conduct business in New York City.

New York Times, July 8, 1994

◆ "The Commissioner Is Looking for an Opportunity in Private Enterprise"

Incoming Mayor Rudolph Giuliani chose as his new police commissioner William Bratton, who had made his mark as a dynamic administrator—with a keen sense of public relations and a flair for self-promotion—as head of the police department in his native Boston and in an earlier stint in New York as chief of the transit police (where he had achieved major rollbacks in crime in the subways). Immediately Bratton set about reorganizing the NYPD and reenergizing its anticrime operations. And, aided by his press secretary, former local TV newsman John Miller, he began aggressively publicizing his efforts and cultivating the news media. Bratton quickly got results, on both fronts. He succeeded in raising morale—and his own profile. In the process, he made himself an implacable enemy: his new boss. Even before taking the oath of office, the mayor-elect had discussed with his inner circle the eventual necessity of getting rid of the commissioner he had just hired.

In February 1995, in the midst of purging press officers throughout city government, Generalissimo Giuliani made his move. The order was conveyed from City Hall to One Police Plaza: Employees in the NYPD Public Information unit were to be dismissed or transferred until that office was one staff member *smaller* than the mayor's Press Office. Rather than carry out the order, Miller publicly resigned. Bratton understood the message's meaning: If he didn't like it, he could quit too.

We essentially have police acting as budget analysts and public relations personnel. I thought it was best that they do jobs more related to police work.
> Statement by Mayor Giuliani on resignation of NYPD
> Deputy Commissioner John Miller, February 12, 1995
> Requoted in *New York Daily News,* March 17, 1996

Two weeks after the man in charge of public relations for the Police Department resigned under fire, Mayor Rudolph W. Giuliani said yesterday that the department's press operation had been "out of control" for several months. *New York Times,* February 24, 1995

I think the Police Department has lost some control over the way in which police activities should take place. I thought it did not present the correct impression of what my administration is all about, what we're trying to do and how serious we are about law enforcement. Some of the things I saw put law enforcement in a frivolous light.   *New York Times*, February 24, 1995

Bratton chose to stay on.

The Police Commissioner has twice in the last two days called me and told me he has no intention of resigning. . . . No one here is seeking his resignation.

Feb. 13, 1995. Requoted in *N. Y. Daily News*, March 17, 1996

Commissioner Bratton and I are moving in precisely the same direction. There isn't the slightest bit of difference in philosophy or approach.

Feb. 10, 1995. Requoted in *N. Y. Daily News*, March 17, 1996

The Police Commissioner has done an exceptional job. We've never seen such a substantial reduction in crime.

Statement at NYPD awards ceremony, *N. Y. Times*, Feb. 17, 1995

But there were ominous signs.

There may be some people that are uncomfortable with the changes that are being made in the Police Department. They're going to learn to be comfortable with it.

Statement after being unexpectedly booed by officers at
NYPD awards ceremony, February 17, 1995
Requoted in *New York Daily News*, March 17, 1996

There is no rift between the two of us. [But] at some point just about every commissioner in the administration is going to move on to something else.   July 10, 1995

Requoted in *New York Daily News*, March 17, 1996

I don't care if he leaves. I run the Police Department.

Comment attributed to Mayor Giuliani in conversation
with former mayor Ed Koch, Summer 1995. Quoted by
Koch in column in *New York Post,* April 6, 1996

When, in January 1996, *Time* magazine ran a cover story—
"Finally, We're Winning the War Against Crime"—featuring
Bratton's face (but not the mayor's) on the magazine, his days
in office were numbered. Shortly thereafter, in an extraordinary contravention of a commissioner's traditional prerogatives, Giuliani overruled Bratton on two major personnel
changes. One of the promotions vetoed was for the captain
who had led Mayor David Dinkins's bodyguard detail and
whose "loyalty" was questioned.

I go over promotions all the time.

New York Times, March 8, 1996

**I don't intercede with the Police Department. The
Police Department reports to me.**

New York Times, March 9, 1996

**[The Commissioner and I have a] very good, close rela-
tionship. . . . This is a situation where the Police Commissioner and I see eye to eye. . . . If you're talking
about the No. 2, No. 3, No. 4 position in the Police
Department, you're talking about someone who's going
to run a borough that's larger than the Police Department in most cities. Of course I'm going to have substantial involvement in that decision. That's what it
means to be ultimately responsible for the Police
Department. . . . I'm not going to take that judgment
and put it on suspension because I'm Mayor of New
York City. If I see something that's proposed that I dis-**

agree with, I'm not going to let it happen. If I see something that I agree with, we go forward with it.

New York Times, March 9, 1996

There's also an effort, and I think it's going on for a very long time, to separate Commissioner Bratton and me.

March 10, 1996

Requoted in *New York Daily News,* March 17, 1996

[This effort] is being done by people in the Police Department. Somebody wants to move, somebody wants a promotion, it doesn't happen fast enough, [so] they try and use tactics in order to achieve it.

New York Daily News, March 9, 1996

Next Giuliani publicly held up Bratton's formal reappointment, which was due, until Bratton turned over for review a contract he had received from a book publisher. Then stories began leaking about how Bratton's ethics would have to be probed, since he had accepted plane flights and the use of a vacation villa from an investment banker friend. Finally, the Generalissimo just couldn't wait—and did the police commissioner the favor of announcing his resignation for him.

The Commissioner is, in fact, looking for an opportunity in private enterprise. And he is looking for an opportunity that will enhance his career, help his family. He has made it very, very clear what he is looking for. I support him. I wish him well.   *New York Times,* March 25, 1996

The fact is that the Commissioner deserves great credit for the reduction in crime in this city, and for all of the other things I mentioned, and I left out probably 10 other things that he's accomplished, that will be part of what the New York City Police Department is now like. *New York Times,* March 27, 1996

[His leaving is] a perfectly normal thing. Like every commissioner, at some point he's going to move on.
New York Daily News, March 25, 1996

This is just the reality of what it's like in city government. And Commissioner Bratton, maybe because he's the police commissioner, is looked at in a different way. But commissioners come into city government, they stay for periods of time, and then they move on to other government jobs, or they move on to private practice, private enterprise.... He right now does not have a specific plan to leave, but it is no secret that Bill Bratton is looking for an opportunity in private enterprise, and if he finds one that fits, he is of a mind to take it. He's said that for over a year. When it happens, the department will be ready for the transition, but I'm not seeking to make it happen any faster than it would naturally happen.
New York Times, March 26, 1996

The Police Commissioner has said at some point he is going to leave for an opportunity in private enterprise.... So far the right one [offer] hasn't come along. *New York Daily News,* March 27, 1996

His position made untenable, Bratton quickly accepted a job with a private security firm. Now the question became: If it was simply an ego clash between him and the mayor, surely—for continuity's sake—Bratton's successor would be promoted from within his top management team. Wouldn't he?

Commissioner Bratton has built a very, very strong staff, which is the mark of a good administrator.

New York Times, March 25, 1996

In many ways, the very best indication of how good someone has administered something is if they can leave and things can function pretty much the way they would when that person's there.

New York Daily News, March 25, 1996

But Generalissimo Giuliani, seeing his golden opportunity to assert absolute control over the Police Department, was taking no chances this time. The new commissioner was to be Howard Safir, Giuliani's fire commissioner and longtime friend from their days in federal law enforcement. Irish-born career cop John Timoney, Bratton's No. 2 man and heir apparent, was bypassed for the top job. Timoney responded by blasting Safir as "a lightweight" and Giuliani as "screwed up." On reflection, he apologized for his remark—about Safir. Amid an abortive attempt by Giuliani to demote him in rank so as to slash his retirement pension—and threats from the Patrolmen's Benevolent Association that its members would march on City Hall if that was done—Timoney was banished from the premises at One Police Plaza, effective immediately. **John conducted himself in such a way that you could no longer allow him to remain during the transition.**

New York Daily News, March 31, 1996

[Timoney] should be finished in the Police Department today. I think he should not certainly be involved in the transition process, since he has publicly stated, unfortunately and unfairly, such a low opinion of the new commissioner. I've never been through a transition where

there wasn't one or two people, sometimes three or four, who get very, very angry and act very immaturely.
New York Daily News, March 30, 1996

Asked if more firings and resignations were in the offing, the Generalissimo answered:
If there are, it will be a positive thing.
New York Daily News, March 30, 1996

People are turned down for jobs all the time. . . . When Bill Bratton came in, 26 people left—boom, gone. So maybe a few more will leave; there'll be nothing like that kind of turnover. And we managed that, we got through it. What's happening here is minor in comparison to turnovers we've had in the past.
New York Times, March 31, 1996

A key departure in fact did follow—that of operations expert Jack Maple, the widely praised mastermind behind the department's new crime-fighting strategies. The Generalissimo had his wish; Bratton and his brain trust were all gone. The department—and the credit for falling crime rates—would now all be his.
We're talking about the kind of normal change that takes place when one commissioner leaves. The people personally closest to that commissioner usually go out.
New York Daily News, April 2, 1996

While still commissioner, Bratton had proposed a gala parade up Lower Broadway to honor the NYPD—timed to coincide with his birthday. The idea had been vetoed by Giuliani, and cited by the mayor and his advisers as a prime example of Bratton's terminal grandiosity. So how to give New Yorkers concerned about losing the popular Bratton a transfer of power that reassured them, while emphasizing the kind of refreshing, low-key, low-profile approach the mayor apparently preferred in a police commissioner? Why, by swearing in his successor at an outdoor gala ceremony at City Hall, complete with bands and bunting, such as are normally reserved for heads of state and sports champions, of course.

We think it's good for the people of the city to get a sense that the Police Department is having an important change that's being made. . . . We didn't think of it at the time [Bratton was sworn in].

New York Daily News, April 15, 1996

In private life, William Bratton continued to be a thorn in the side of Generalissimo Giuliani, who now taunted the man he had once praised. When Bratton was being mentioned as a possible candidate for mayor in 1997, he gave an interview belatedly giving credit to David Dinkins's "Safe Streets, Safe City" program for lowering New York's crime rate (something that, as commissioner, he had denied, in accordance with the Giuliani administration's official line), and criticized the mayor for race-baiting tactics.

I'd like to see Bill Bratton run. . . . When you know someone's strengths and weaknesses better from having worked with him, you sort of look forward to running against him. [He] should be ashamed of himself. And probably if he were a little more skilled and seasoned at this, he wouldn't have done it. *N. Y. Times,* Nov. 22, 1996

Later, in a swipe at Bratton's penchant for eating at a trendy Upper East Side restaurant frequented by celebrities:

You want a Police Department to be serious about itself. If you spend most of your time hanging out in Ellen's, or Elaine's, or whatever it's called, it's hard to do that.

New York Daily News, February 27, 1998

When Bratton endorsed Democrat Chuck Schumer for U.S. Senate against GOP incumbent Al D'Amato:

He's from Boston. What would he know?

New York Times, October 27, 1998

Actually, Generalissimo Giuliani did more than simply endorse the embattled D'Amato's ultimately failed bid for reelection or knock his own former police commissioner for supporting D'Amato's strongly pro-gun control opponent. He dragged his *current* police commissioner, Howard Safir, off to attend an election eve event at which D'Amato was "thanked" because he "delivered" a vacant U.S. Coast Guard facility for the NYPD's use—this despite a 1996 memo, from Safir himself, forbidding all uniformed members of the department from engaging in political activity. (As one police official explained to *Daily News* columnist Jim Dwyer, "Howard went because he was told to.") Ah, but you see, this event was entirely nonpolitical, explained the Generalissimo, its proximity to the election being purely coincidental.

It seemed to me and the Police Commissioner that we should express our appreciation to the Senator. We actually wanted to schedule it much earlier back in, I think in September, but the scheduling didn't work out. Today was a good opportunity to do it. . . . [Because of] a combination of the Police Commissioner, the Police Department, the Senator's schedule and mine, this was really the last opportunity we could do it.

New York Daily News, November 4, 1998

(This was not the only ethical quandary in which Generalissimo Giuliani's hand-picked police commissioner soon found himself. After Safir's wife's car was struck by the vehicle of a woman who gave a false name at the scene of the accident, the commissioner himself called the woman on the phone, NYPD detectives visited her, and the commissioner and his wife sued her for, among other things, "loss of consortium." It also developed that the commissioner's own detail of guards had been used to provide security at his daughter's wedding at taxpayer expense. And, on the eve of City Council hearings looking into a controversial fatal police shooting that he was supposedly not available—for business reasons—to testify at, Safir was photographed attending the Academy Awards in Los Angeles—courtesy of a private benefactor who flew the commissioner and his wife to the ceremony in a corporate jet. For these lapses, all of them at least as serious as the alleged transgressions used to shoehorn William Bratton into resigning, Howard Safir suffered no consequences.)

. . . It absolutely baffles me that you can't figure that out, or how you try to make that into something inappropriate. It's really, really strange.

Giuliani statement to reporters that he accepted Safir's rationale that he called woman whose car struck his wife's for security reasons, *New York Times,* April 10, 1999

. . . The Police Commissioner is not leaving. He is not going anywhere. The more unfair stories that you write about him, the more I am convinced that he is doing a really good job and people are threatened by it.

Giuliani statement that he found Safir's use of city detectives to provide security at his daughter's wedding "perfectly appropriate," *New York Times,* April 13, 1999

One of the main reasons I selected him was that I knew he had this ability to have tremendous command and organization of facts. Of how to analyze problems and to come up with solutions, and to make good personnel choices. . . . It's a professional relationship, but it's also a personal relationship. Howard disagrees with me fairly

often enough, and has, at times, been able to talk me out of things that he thought were the wrong approach.

Are there times when I would do something differently, or when he would do something differently? Of course. But I think he has excellent judgment.

New York Times, April 18, 1999

◆ On Police Brutality

The biggest beef New Yorkers have with the cops isn't that they're brutal—it's that they're rude.

Statement to *New York Daily News* Editorial Board, attributed to Giuliani by former Mayor Ed Koch. Quoted by Koch in his book *Giuliani: Nasty Man,* 1999

As for rising complaints in African American and Latino neighborhoods about police violence, false arrests, harassment, racial profiling, and other abuses of police authority under Giuliani, he urged New Yorkers living in those communities to look on the bright side of the situation:

There used to be 1,000 shootings in East New York a year. Now there are 200.   *N.Y. Times,* Nov. 1, 1997

◆ Police Brutality Crisis #1: Abner Louima

The Police Commissioner is making respect, ending brutality, violence, disrespect, as important a part of the evaluation of a police officer as reducing crime, and I know that will make a significant difference.

State of the City address, January 15, 1997

But, seven months later, ironically as NYPD officers were assisting the U.S. Government's effort to retrain and professionalize police in Haiti, a Haitian immigrant named Abner

Louima was arrested outside a Brooklyn nightclub, beaten in the patrol car on the way to the station, then taken into the stationhouse bathroom and sodomized with a broomstick. The incident seemed to crystallize what critics of Giuliani's law enforcement philosophy had been saying—especially since the victim initially reported being mocked "This is Giuliani time, not Dinkins time" while being tortured (a claim Louima later withdrew, admitting it had been made up to help get his charges taken seriously). It also came right in the middle of the mayor's campaign for reelection. Instantly, he was offering sympathy and healing insight:

That is not what happens with the vast majority of police officers. And I'm also aware of the fact that the police officers in minority communities are by and large doing an excellent job of saving the lives of people in the minority communities. *New York Times*, August 15, 1997

Attempts by his Democratic opponents to seize on this issue were "shameful."

[They] really should stay out of it. . . . All these people are doing—the candidates last night and David Dinkins—are seeking to divide for their own narrow political purposes, with illogical and irrational arguments. I think it backfires on them when they do it, because I think people want to see leadership, not negative attacks that divide people. *N.Y. Times*, Aug. 19, 1997

He urged NYPD officers to participate in "discussion groups."

Sometimes it takes tragic and difficult events to create openings and opportunities to change things. With the focus on this case, the intensity of feelings about it, there's a paradigm set up for other police officers and members of the community to do the same thing. I don't

think the atmosphere was there before. Both the police and the communities in New York City are suffering from the same kind of group blame. So we're essentially letting the worst determine the agenda, and the purpose of this is to find a way to crack through that.

New York Times, August 19, 1997

Then the mayor had an even better idea—he selected a blue-ribbon panel of prominent citizens to make recommendations for improving police-community relations. The panel included predictable allies such as Staten Island borough president Guy Molinari, a staunch conservative who had brought Giuliani to the infamous PBA rally in September 1992. But it also included police critics like Norman Siegel, executive director of the New York Civil Liberties Union.

That's the reason I put it together, because decent people will disagree with each other.

New York Times, August 22, 1997

I listened and talked. This is a process. There will be intensive discussions, and then we'll make decisions.

Statement after first meeting with panel, *N.Y. Times,* Aug. 27, 1997

But when the panel turned in its findings (the election being over by this time), it was not the kinder, gentler mayor who received its report. It was Generalissimo Giuliani, back in full roar.

With a tone of voice veering from annoyance to sarcasm, Mayor Rudolph W. Giuliani yesterday dismissed most of the recommendations of a task force he appointed last summer to examine relations between New York City's residents and its Police Department, saying that the panel had failed to recognize the Department's recent success in reducing crime.

His harsh comments disturbed task force members who had expected words of thanks other than insults.
New York Times, March 27, 1998

Some of the things we've already done. Some of the things I've opposed in the past, I'll continue to oppose them. And some of the things are unrealistic and make very little sense. *New York Times,* March 27, 1998

He went on to express disappointment that the panel "did not spend an equal amount of time on some things that are counter to the intuition of several of the police bashers that were on the task force."
New York Times, March 27, 1998

What does it say about my administration that something was leaked? It says that leaking all of a sudden happened and that people like Norman Siegel are actually looking for publicity for the first time ever. That's what it says. *New York Times,* March 27, 1998

He would agree to one proposal, he announced—changing the title of the Department of Community Affairs.
I think that's Recommendation 9B. So that's a good change. We can change it from Affairs to Relations.
New York Times, March 27, 1998

While he also stated at this time that he had not read the report "in great detail," and there was "nothing in it that changes my mind," one week later he granted an interview to one of the panelists, newspaper columnist Stanley Crouch:
I made the mistake of giving the impression that the task force recommendations with which I agree—somewhere between 60% and 76%—were of no interest to me.
New York Daily News, April 3, 1998

In the spring of 1999, Police Officer Justin Volpe—the perpetrator of the broomstick attack on Louima—was forced to plead guilty in midtrial after several fellow officers, in the most rare of occurrences, had broken cops' traditional silence in such cases and devastatingly testified against him in open court. (One codefendant officer was subsequently convicted by the jury of being an accessory in the attack.) Giuliani professed to see it all only as a bright new day for the NYPD.

I particularly want to congratulate the Police Department for breaking down the appearance that there is some kind of reluctance on the part of police officers to testify against other police officers when they have knowledge of serious criminal conduct. *New York Times,* June 9, 1999

It destroys the myth of the blue wall of silence.
New York Times, May 26, 1999

◆ Police Brutality Crisis #2: Amadou Diallo

On a dark night in February 1999, four members of an elite plainclothes Street Crimes Unit known for its aggressiveness were on the lookout for a rapist operating in The Bronx. Thinking he looked suspicious, they challenged Amadou Diallo as he entered the vestibule of his apartment. Diallo, originally from French-speaking Senegal, may not even have understood what the officers wanted. At any rate, in apparent response to a cry of "Gun!" the officers suddenly unleashed a fusillade of forty-one shots at him.

But Amadou Diallo was not the rapist they were looking for. He had no criminal record. He was totally unarmed. He was dead, shot nineteen times—and the four officers were indicted for murder.

In the wake of Diallo's killing, the Reverend Al Sharpton—a longtime flamboyant racial militant working at the margins of political respectability—seized his chance, organizing daily sit-in protests outside NYPD headquarters. As the demonstrations continued for weeks, the number of those arrested ran to the hundreds, and even mainstream political figures felt obliged to fall in with Sharpton's radical followers. (That included Giuliani's two predecessors: Former mayor David Dinkins underwent the indignity of being publicly handcuffed; former mayor Ed Koch, on the day scheduled for his arrest, was taken to the hospital with heart trouble.)

Generalissimo Giuliani? In this atmosphere of tragedy and polarization, he stood as a beacon of consensus, harmony, and conciliatory outreach.

I can understand the anger. I can understand all of it and I feel terrible that this happened as I have expressed on numerous occasions. . . . [But] there's a tendency of some people in our society to blame the police in broad strokes that is just as vicious a prejudice as any other prejudice.   *New York Times,* Feb. 11, 1999

Police officers are "second-guessed by some of the worst in society."

> Statement after murder indictments of NYPD officers
> in Diallo case, *New York Times,* April 2, 1999

Outrageous. . . . I know you'll attack me and you'll misinterpret it and you're going to do it in your own way, but I'm going to say this respectfully: the way you're attacking the Police Department is to the point of perversity, it really is.

> Attacking coverage given to former member of NYPD
> Street Crimes Unit, fired by department after giving
> negative testimony about unit to City Council committee, *New York Times,* April 27, 1999

Under him, Giuliani said, the NYPD had been "a model of restraint."

I know there are people in this society who bear the same kind of prejudices toward police officers that sometimes reflects itself in racial, religious and ethnic prejudices. I have to ask that they put those aside for the moment. When police officers do what we ask them to do, we really have to support them.

New York Times, February 25, 1999

If 70 percent or 80 percent of the people believe that police officers in New York City are brutal too often, that's a misperception. That's a false perception. It is driven by a very effective partisan political campaign, and the fact that there's been an obsessive concern in the media about it. . . .

Since the time of Mr. Diallo's tragic death, which was a horrible thing and a terrible thing—which I have expressed great remorse for and have done everything to try to rectify—there also have been 60 other murders in New York City since then, including a substantial number of murders in the minority community that I have to have an equal amount of concern about, and that I need this Police Department to interrupt, to prevent and to work on in order to protect people against the more realistic way in which they face danger in this city. . . . Speech given at Waldorf-Astoria Hotel

New York Times, March 17, 1999

Giuliani noted that the hotel where he was speaking had just had "a horrible, vicious murder" on its premises.

Look, we're in a hotel that two days ago, three days ago, had a horrible murder take place. A horrible, vicious,

awful murder. If you spent the next five weeks covering that murder, you would convince people that there was a murder problem in the city of New York, even though murder is down by 70 percent. Just think about that for a moment. If you spent the next five weeks—spent as much time on the murder that took place in this hotel for the next five weeks—had it on Channel 2, Channel 4, Channel 7, Channel Everyone, and all the newspapers for the next five weeks, you'd have people running around this city, 70 percent, believing that we had a significant murder problem in this city, even though murder is down 70 percent. That is essentially what has happened here. Speech given at Waldorf-Astoria Hotel
New York Times, March 17, 1999

If New York's police are not given credit for the things they do well, he warned, "it's very, very counterproductive—because I know cops. You're going to make things worse." *New York Times,* March 24, 1999

He complained that several protesters held aloft signs that compared him to Adolf Hitler and the Police Department to the Ku Klux Klan. "As the Police Department has made substantial changes in the way in which it behaves, not only in the last month or two but over the last five years," Mayor Giuliani said, "I'd ask people to acknowledge that and then to make the similar kinds of changes in their behavior. Not stand with people who try to pretend that the Police Department is the KKK, not engage in general bashing of the Police Department, stop the invocations of Hitler and Nazism and fascism, all this exaggerated hate rhetoric. It has an impact." *New York Times,* March 30, 1999

After in some cases years of not even meeting with African American elected officials, in the aftermath of the Diallo shooting the Generalissimo was finally moved to sit down with several. **Although he continued to defend the Police Department as one of the best in the country, the Mayor also said that "there is a reality" to the feeling "in the minority community that police officers are unfair to them."**

New York Times, March 25, 1999

What I did is try to explain why I have, as best as I can, tried to express my sensitivity, my concern, my regret over this situation—and at the same time not allow a Police Department to be defamed in the way in which it was being defamed, which could be easily destructive to the effort to save lives in the African American and other communities. *New York Times*, March 25, 1999

But the Generalissimo soon got his groove back. The protests at police headquarters, he said, have gone **way beyond the stage necessary to inform anybody about anything.** *New York Times*, March 26, 1999

Giuliani and his people stayed true to character, dismissing the demonstrations as "silly" and politically motivated. And in what seemed to be a not-so-veiled reference to race and class, the Mayor made the astonishing remark that the demonstrations were peopled by the "worst elements of society."

New York magazine, April 19, 1999

I think all of my views on it have been stated over and over again. There's nothing new that I would impart, and there were other things that I had to do.

Explaining refusal to testify before congressional task force on police brutality, *New York Post*, June 22, 1999

And in the face of proposals that one solution might be for the city to accept a federal civil-rights monitor of the NYPD, he would not yield an inch:

They can't do it. *New York Times,* July 13, 1999

My administration never compromises on matters of principle. Although the Justice Department has a role in investigating police departments, New Yorkers have certainly the right to ask, "What about all the other cities where police officers shot people two, three, four, five times per capita more than in New York City." . . . I think the bashing of the New York Police Department has been relentless for about four or five months . . . maybe, just maybe, the New York Police Department is doing something right and the bashing has created a wrong perspective. *New York Times,* July 12, 1999

At year's end, the trial of the officers was moved out of The Bronx, to upstate, heavily white Albany County. The Generalissimo was pleased that the case would not be decided by a jury in his city.

The rhetoric made it appear as if they were absolutely guilty, and there's no question about it. Whether that's true or not, you're entitled to a fair trial, and I think the judges said, "We're going to treat police officers the way we treat all other human beings. They're entitled to a fair trial also." I think a number of people do not treat police officers as human beings.
New York Times, December 17, 1999

What happened is, there was a concerted effort on the part of numerous people to make it impossible to have a fair trial in New York. When you start marching, demanding that people be indicted—you get in front of

courthouses and demand that people be indicted, that's like the Old West. I mean the reality is that the judges unanimously decided that, rendered a very, very wise decision. *New York Times,* December 20, 1999

Giuliani said his cops deserved the credit for another 8 percent overall drop in crime for the year 1999. . .

[Police officers] don't get the credit for it. . . . Police bashing wins out. . . . The Police Department in New York City is the most disciplined and the most monitored in the country. *N.Y. Daily News,* Dec. 30, 1999

. . . but the NYPD's critics deserved the blame for the murder rate going up 7 percent.

There was a substantial decline in police intervention after the [Diallo] shooting. In part because the police officers appeared to be concerned that their conduct would be questioned, that they would be put in jeopardy, that they would have problems.

New York Times, December 30, 1999

◆ Understatement on a Near Fiasco

There is no longer a sting; it is over. . . . It appears as if the execution of it was very different than the plan, and it appears that the execution had some mistakes attached to it.

> Statement on abrupt termination of plan to mail free
> MetroCards to the homes of wanted violent felons in
> the hope that the criminals would use the cards to ride
> the subway, where presumably they would then be
> overpowered and apprehended on crowded platforms
> or inside speeding trains; plan was withdrawn after

being leaked to negative publicity in media. In defense
of his actions in this instance, Police Commissioner
Howard Safir said, quote: "I had nothing to do with
that one." *New York Daily News,* November 5, 1999

◆ On Bordello-gate

**This thing was going on for a decade and a half, and it
was only the dogged efforts of the Police Department
that uncovered it. And for all we know, but for all the
increased emphasis on corruption in the Police Department, and the sophistication of the Police Department's
new techniques, nobody would have discovered them.**

Reaction to arrest of twenty officers and one sergeant
for protecting bordello that operated in their precinct
in return for free sex. Quoted by former Mayor Ed
Koch in *New York Daily News* column, July 24, 1998

◆ On Cops Who Don't Write Enough Tickets

One constituency that, surprisingly, took a dislike to Rudolph
Giuliani's policies in police matters: the police themselves.
The reason: money. Giuliani refused to give police officers any
better contract terms than he'd given to other municipal work-
ers, which included a pay freeze for the first two years of the
pact. The PBA and other cop unions, chanting "No Zeros for
Heroes," succeeding in getting several bills through a compli-
ant State Legislature in Albany in an attempt to get around
Giuliani, but he prevailed on Republican governor George
Pataki to veto all but one of them. So, periodically, to vent
their unhappiness, the cops resorted to a time-honored tactic:
They stopped writing the parking tickets on which the City of
New York depends for revenue.

I would like to fire one or two of them just to send a message.

Man, that really gets me angry. My contention, and it shouldn't be a contention, it should be a decision after all, I'm the M-A-Y-O-R, and I want them to write tickets.

On WABC Radio program
Requoted in *Washington Post,* June 30, 1999

8

Rudy and the Blacks (or, The Generalissimo, While on a Botany Expedition, Discovers an Exotic New Species— People of Color)

In 1964, several months after New York had been shaken by riots in Harlem, young Rudy Giuliani—as a liberal college student supporting Robert Kennedy's bid for a U.S. Senate seat in New York—had ridiculed Kennedy's opponent, GOP incumbent Kenneth Keating, thusly:

Was he able to use his authority to speak to the Negro youth in New York City to give them some hope of a bet-

ter tomorrow and in this manner prevent them from becoming victims of agitators?

Manhattan College *Quadrangle*, October 1964
wysiwyg://3/http://www.thesmokinggun.com/archive/
rudycolumn1.html

Twenty-nine years later, Rudolph Giuliani was elected mayor over the virtually united opposition of New York's black community, which supported its favorite son, David Dinkins. One of his first postelection stops was a church in Harlem.

I want the African-American community to know that irrespective of the vote, I want to serve all the people equally and fairly. You are entitled to exactly the same commitment, dedication, and zeal whether you voted for me, voted against me, or didn't vote at all. . . . I ask you to give me a chance to show in deeds rather than words my commitment to this community. . . . In a hotly contested election, the end result often can be that people feel wounded; they may feel disappointed; they may feel angry. But we have to come together as a city, and we have to work very, very hard to see the common bonds and interests we have as New Yorkers.

You really are basically all the same. That's the amazing thing you learn becoming mayor of this city. The people of this city—it doesn't matter what their race, age, ethnic background, gender, sexual orientation—they're basically the same in what they worry about. The people of Staten Island and the people of the South Bronx look at the world in exactly the same way. . . . In a very strange way, our problems unite us.

New York magazine, November 15, 1993

"The next step on the road," the Mayor-elect said, "is to begin the transition."

To select people of merit and quality who come from all the different groups in New York. The selection process has to first involve choosing the right person for each job, but after you've made 50 of those decisions, let's say, the pool of candidates has to reflect the city. I'm going to appoint people from all the communities of New York. That will be the next signal that this government is reaching out.   *New York* magazine, Nov. 15, 1993

But when that time came, the incoming mayor chose no deputy mayors of African American heritage and few black commissioners.

I don't play the game of symbolism.

New York magazine, May 7, 1994

He shut down the office of Special Advisor to the Mayor for African American Affairs (and similar offices catering to the Hispanic and gay communities).

He didn't want to balkanize the city.

Statement by Mayor's Press Secretary explaining decision, *New York Times*, February 11, 1999

And the man who had campaigned for office under the banner of "One City, One Standard" made a point of abolishing the city's racial-preference affirmative-action programs.

Indefensible . . . bad social policy. . . . The city is paying 10 percent more for a contract and it's going to have to pay damages to a company that should have gotten the contract in the first place. If you continue this for four, five or six years, you're now talking about another serious fiscal jeopardy for this city. . . . The theory of it is to remedy past discrimination. Now you can agree or dis-

agree with whether that is necessary. But the city has to present a program that is leading us to a remedy that is going to get us back to the day when we will no longer have set-asides and goals. *N.Y. Times*, Jan. 25, 1994

I've done away with a lot of that race-based analysis. Our analysis is, "How are we helping small businesses? How are we helping poor people in the city? How are we helping people who are poor, not people who are poor who are white or black?" *N.Y. Times*, March 24, 1997

Pursuant to that philosophy, Giuliani's deputy mayor for Economic Development, John Dyson, sought to end an arrangement under which part of the underwriting business for city bonds was given to an out-of-town firm owned by an African American woman—and clashed with the new city comptroller, who wished to continue the practice. Except that Dyson went further. The comptroller, he said, "ought to know the difference between a bid and a watermelon."

A *watermelon*? Hmmm. Now what could *that* be a code word for?

[Dyson] made a mistake.

Letter to New York State Comptroller H. Carl McCall
Quoted in *New York Times*, July 2, 1994

But in remarks to reporters, Mr. Giuliani dismissed calls for Mr. Dyson's resignation and criticized what he called a "piling-on exercise" by critics of Mr. Dyson and of the Mayor's administration. *N.Y. Times*, July 21, 1994

The first reaction to this was to demand an apology. There was an apology. Now the reaction is to demand resignation. I imagine tomorrow they'll be talking about execution. It seems to me that we're doing something that unfortunately we've done so often in this city. We're taking a comment that certain people found offensive, for good reason. And now the aftermath is that this looks like it is going to create more racial division or racial strife than the comment itself.

New York Times, July 21, 1994

Shouts erupted as Mr. Giuliani said he believed that Mr. Dyson had meant no harm. "The way in which we will become a better city is to respect each other," Mr. Giuliani said, fighting to be heard. "I didn't agree with all of your questions but I don't interrupt and yell at you."

The tone of the meeting, in southwestern Queens, was set when the first questioner asked the Mayor why he had not appointed any black members to the Board of Education.

"The mere fact that there isn't a person in a particular position who is Latino or African-American or white doesn't mean that people can't get the job done," Mr. Giuliani said.

New York Times, July 20, 1994

Ironically, when a Dinkins deputy mayor had made an inappropriate, racially charged remark about him in the wake of the PBA riot two years earlier, Giuliani's standard for how a mayor should handle such a situation was slightly different:

Calling Mr. Lynch's comments "a form of racial politics which is far worse than anything I've seen in this city," Mr. Giuliani said Mr. Dinkins had shown "abysmal leadership" by not rebuking Mr. Lynch. . . . "I think if the shoe were on the other foot, I would certainly be required to go a lot further."

N.Y. Times, Sept. 28, 1992

Giuliani continued to reach out from time to time—or at least to pay lip service to the idea of doing so.

I understand people's disappointment. But the reality is that I don't want anyone in the city of New York to feel that anyone has taken a step backward, because they have not. People in Harlem, people in the African-American community, made advances over the last three to four years. I don't want to see them diminished.

Speech to Harlem Chamber of Commerce
New York Times, March 22, 1994

Mayor Rudolph W. Giuliani worshiped with the black congregation yesterday after learning that there was a group of parishioners who pray for him, and, he said, "I want to encourage it because I need all the prayers I can get." . . .

"It's an effort to reach out to the entire community," Mr. Giuliani told reporters. He said recent polls had put his approval rating among blacks at 22 to 32 percent and he called that the biggest shift in support since his election, when he won 5 percent of the vote. . . .

Addressing the congregation, he said the job of mayor would be much easier "if I could figure out a way to get everybody on a Sunday or a Saturday or a Friday to go to a church or a temple or a mosque or to go to a house of ethical culture and to sit there for an hour or two and to figure out how to be better people."

New York Times, July 25, 1994

We all understand that we have to come to terms with the city's very serious budget problems. That's the reason I am re-structuring the city government. I don't want our city or its people now or in the future to be diminished, so we have to live within our means. My priorities are the same ones that I believe that you have.

Remarks at African American church, *N.Y. Times,* Nov. 14, 1994

The mayor exhorted his African American constituents to follow his example.

Speaking at a junior high school in the bleak streets of Brownsville recently, Mayor Rudolph W. Giuliani gave a conservative twist to the words of John F. Kennedy to preach self-reliance to the students. They should, he said to an audience of black and Hispanic teen-agers, ask "not what somebody else can do for you but what you can do for yourselves."

And ever since that Brooklyn school visit, Mr. Giuliani has repeatedly used a naïve question asked by one girl to build a morality tale of how students have unrealistic expectations of what government can, in fact, do for them. She had asked why there couldn't be scholarships granted irrespective of grades to allow people like her to go away to college.

"I thought it would be kind of useful, rather than kind of pandering to her, to get her ready for life," Mr. Giuliani said on WLIB, the black-oriented radio station. *N.Y. Times,* February 28, 1994

She was a teen-ager already and I said, you know, that other people won't pay for you. I couldn't afford to go away to college when I was your age. My family couldn't afford it. So I went to college in New York City. I commuted and got a very good education. . . . I didn't own my own textbooks—I had to borrow them. . . . You've got to talk to that young lady about realism, not fantasy dreams, because one of the things government does, we can realistically help, we can't provide fantasies. *N.Y. Times,* February 28, 1994

The woman, Giuliani noted, could go to the City University—though as mayor he derided CUNY defenders' "absurd" attachment to a city university that offers "make-believe" education. *Washington Post,* June 30, 1999

"I've washed dishes in restaurants," Mr. Giuliani explained in reference to his work in his father's taverns as he said squeegee men should find restaurant jobs. . . . Washing dishes 12 hours a day in a restaurant is "an honorable, decent, terrific thing to do," the Mayor says, and suggests that the squeegee men who wash windshields instead of holding a restaurant job are trying to avoid paying taxes. Of the high unemployment rate for youth, he says, "There are also jobs that don't get filled at the same time there's unemployment. So you push yourself a little hard, and you push yourself a little bit beyond, you're going to find a job."

. . . There can be a sense of time warp to Mr. Giuliani's comments as if Washington's debate of a decade ago has now come to New York. "In fact, there was just an article in one of the papers on how there were more jobs available in certain areas than people who want to fill them," Mr. Giuliani said last week in an uncanny echo of President Ronald Reagan when he was asked about black unemployment in 1982 and pointed to the help-wanted ads in *The Washington Post.*

New York Times, February 28, 1994

He invoked African American heroes in support of his agenda.

What Martin Luther King said about sweeping streets was, if you do it better than anybody else, then you're doing God's work, which is the way I look at it. So I think being into this philosophy that work is demeaning is very, very damaging. And it has a lot to do with what was wrong with our city. *New York Times,* March 20, 1997

He reminded them of the bad old days of high crime rates, before he became their mayor.

There used to be 1,000 shootings in East New York a year. Now there are 200. Those are things you feel in your life, and I think that that has created a certain amount of support and a relationship that wasn't there before. We have to build on that. So I don't think the barriers that we faced in the first two years will exist in the next four. *New York Times*, November 1, 1997

He even tried humor.

Have you been to one of these before? This wasn't as bad as last year. Everything is relative. The amount of booing last year was greater.

On being greeted with "boos and catcalls" as he marched in annual Labor Day West Indian Carnival *New York Times*, September 8, 1998

The applause is polite; but he's late and he's not staying long. "I want to apologize for leaving early. It's very, very hard for me to get a cab."

Dead silence.

"You think I'm kidding? Have you ever tried to hail a cab in New York?"

Deader silence. It's not clear that Hizzoner, who is engaged of late in a little recreational pounding of the taxi industry, realizes that most of the people in the room have been shunned by some cabby somewhere.

"I put up a finger to hail a cab and the cabby puts up a finger, too. But it's a different finger."

He waits for the laughs that aren't coming.

Remarks at Urban League gala, *Washington Post*, June 30, 1999

[Five months later, as the mayor was gearing up to run for the U.S. Senate, when actor Danny Glover went public with the fact that he too had been refused taxi service—a common complaint for years among African American New Yorkers—Giuliani was suddenly moved to initiate an overnight police crackdown on cab drivers who did so.]

Nothing seemed to work.

Mayor Giuliani, in asking Ms. [City Councilwoman Mary] Pinkett to come to the podium, called her "Councilwoman Fields," apparently confusing Ms. Pinkett with City Councilwoman C. Virginia Fields of Manhattan, who is also black. "We don't all look alike," Ms. Pinkett shot back. *New York Times,* June 2, 1994

The Generalissimo despaired that the situation would ever change.

I think I have a caring message, but it's very, very hard to convey that I'm trying to get people away from this sort of subsistence politics. Let's try property ownership. Let's try involvement in business. Let's try more personal responsibility. Let's try workfare. These are premised on a lot more history in the development of human beings than the things we have been doing.

This sounds really strange but I've thought through this a lot, and I think things are going to change very quickly, the way the destruction of Communism occurred in Eastern Europe. It came as a tremendous surprise to many people, particularly to Western intellectuals. Just as in Eastern Europe, there's a building sense in the minority community that the principles enforced by the so-called leadership aren't going anywhere—the battle over more entitlements and more welfare and more government solutions. When you find the right person who can connect to those feelings, you're going to see a major sea change.

New York Times Magazine, December 3, 1995

The Generalissimo admitted he was not likely to be that person.

I don't think the connection is there. The leaders that presently exist won't allow that to happen. They will try to demonize me. I can make marginal changes in people's thinking, but the major shift has to be done by someone they can identify with on a kind of intuitive level. *New York Times Magazine,* December 3, 1995

At the start of his second term, he expressed contrition— and hope.

We have to do a better job of serving all of you. We have to reach out to all of you. And if we haven't, I apologize. I'm sorry, and it is my personal commitment that we will try, endlessly and tirelessly, to bring all of you into the kind of success and optimism we have in this room. 1997 election night victory speech
Requoted by *New York Times,* September 8, 1998

The city is enormously successful right now. The vast majority of people have been affected by that and helped by it—but not everyone. So part of the resolution that we make for the rest of my term and next year is to try to reach more and more people.
Interview on day of second inauguration as mayor
New York Times, January 2, 1998

But things didn't change. In fact, they got worse.

◆ Khalid Muhammad

Khalid Muhammad was a follower of Louis Farrakhan so demented, racist, and anti-Semitic that even Farrakhan had felt obliged to purge him from the ranks of the Nation of

Islam. Farrakhan had led the Million Man March on Washington in 1995; in 1998 Khalid Muhammad announced his intention to top his old boss. He would stage a Million Youth March, bringing in young African Americans from all across the country. In the middle of Labor Day Weekend. In the middle of Harlem.

And, in the end, Khalid Muhammad couldn't have asked for a better press agent than Rudolph W. Giuliani.

Describing it as a "hate march," Mayor Giuliani yesterday accused organizers of a proposed Million Youth March in Harlem of "race-baiting" and being "out to divide people." . . . He called on New Yorkers to stand up against the march's "core of hatred."

New York Daily News, August 6, 1998

The city denied a permit for the march (but did offer Khalid two alternative locations outside Harlem).

From my point of view, this is a hate march. . . . The rhetoric is extraordinary. The attributions of the city's position [regarding the permits] to Jews in the administration doing this is mind-boggling in this day and age.

New York Times, August 6, 1998

It's really frightening to listen to what they're saying, particularly the leader of the group.

New York Daily News, August 6, 1998

I haven't heard this kind of language in a very, very long time or this kind of race-baiting and anti-Semitic rhetoric.

New York Post, August 7, 1998

He is not talking about a million kids; he's talking about gang members. [His speeches are] filled with hatred, anger, viciousness about the Jews, about Catholics, about the Pope.

New York Times, August 8, 1998

We're not going to allow a hatemonger to take over our city in any substantial respect. That just will not be permitted. *New York Post,* August 8, 1998

Then, in an about-face, the Generalissimo blamed the media for all the publicity the march was getting.

I think you've already paid way too much attention to it, way beyond what the facts indicate. This is a media creation more than anything else. *N.Y. Post,* Aug. 18, 1998

I've said everything I'm going to say about it. . . . The media . . . has given it far more attention than it deserves. *New York Daily News,* August 18, 1998

Moderates and elected officials in the African American community shunned Khalid but urged the mayor to be more cautious, warning that he was only building Khalid up.

Absurd. . . . We either had to just ignore it and pretend that a person who has engaged in the worst kind of rhetoric about Jews, about whites, about Catholics, about the Pope—that he should be allowed to carry a banner leading a lot of children. Or we could say something about it, which we did. . . .

You may have forgotten, but I don't, the hate language he used in reference to me. So I would expect that he would naturally gravitate toward a march that engages in this kind of hate rhetoric against Jews, against other people. *New York Times,* August 24, 1998

He publicly accused such blacks—who normally would have been a mayor's natural allies against the common threat Khalid posed—of a "failure of courage."

I would think that decent people would stay away from this because there's no point in supporting, encouraging

young people to hate. When good people do nothing about hatred and equivocate about it, it's a sad thing to see, and it usually indicates a lack of any sense of real leadership. *New York Daily News,* September 1, 1998

The permit for the march was granted, over the city's objections, by a federal court—but was restricted to a smaller area, with a 4 P.M. deadline. Only a few thousand actually showed up. But thousands more Harlemites felt put under siege by the lock-down-type crowd-control measures employed by the NYPD around the march area. And when 4:00 came—with police helicopters hovering and whirling directly overhead—officers literally stormed the stage and disconnected the sound system. Khalid used his remaining time to instruct his followers to "beat the hell" out of any cops "if they so much as touch you"—"if any of these bastards attacks you, take their nightstick and ram it up their behind. . . . [I]f they attack you, you take their guns"—but by the time chairs and bottles began being thrown and blows began being struck, he had conveniently departed.

They had their free-speech right. When it got to 4:01 P.M., it was over, and I'm very proud of the police in making sure it was over. . . . It was a pathetic showing, which may be the only good news that comes out of it. *New York Daily News,* September 6, 1998

The court order was "sacred," he declared.

If you want to know why the police came in at 4:01, go read the court order. This is all about creating a respectful society. The court said they had between 12 and 4; it meant exactly that. . . . They [the police] were quite prepared to be more flexible, but when the speech turned to incitement to riot and murder, they closed down the event. I had given them the discretion to make that determination. *N.Y. Times,* Sept. 7, 1998

The Police Department of this city acted magnificently.
New York Daily News, September 8, 1998

The police acted commendably. They listened to four hours of people, including women, who got up and talked about killing Jews and taking off their scalp and cutting off their heads. *N.Y. Daily News,* Sept. 7, 1998

Khalid, he declared, should face criminal charges.
I have no doubt about it. He called for the murder of police officers in a situation that easily could have led to [a] riot. *N.Y. Post,* Sept. 8, 1998

The police handled it superbly. They couldn't have possibly have done a better job. The lack of violence is really truly attributable only to the police, given the invocations to violence, the fact that it ended in the last 10 minutes with a call to kill police officers.
New York Times, September 8, 1998

Police actually did give Mohammad [sic] a grace period of about five to seven minutes. They didn't move in until 4:07 . . . and they moved in with great restraint. And before that, people were throwing chairs at them and attacking them. I have no doubt that the police did precisely the right thing, and you should have no doubt about it, given the result—no rioting, no destruction of property, no one seriously injured. When the police come out with that result, can't you have the decency to congratulate them? *New York Post,* September 8, 1998

Others, especially in the black community, reacted differently. They deplored Khalid's provocative swagger—but also what they saw as the mayor's equally belligerent response.

The most prominent clergyman in Harlem, the Reverend Calvin Butts of the Abyssinian Baptist Church—a leader who had become so Establishment that he was now an ally of Republican governor George Pataki—called Khalid a "disgrace" but labeled the mayor's military-style tactics "an insult." (However, the mayor and Butts were no longer on speaking terms. In early 1998 the pastor had called the mayor a racist under whom the city was becoming a "fascist state," and in October of that year the mayor called on Pataki to disavow Butts's endorsement for reelection. Though the two men publicly embraced in 1999, they were not reconciled; a state joint development project with Butts's church on 125th Street had to move forward without a city-owned parcel of land that stood right in the middle of the site, which Giuliani refused to allow to be included.) Harlem congressman Charles Rangel said the police had been "politically misused."

Geraldine Ferraro, onetime Democratic vice-presidential candidate running for her party's U.S. Senate nomination, was also critical. Generalissimo Giuliani had fun blasting her.

If they're in a primary, for example, they can get a group of voters to vote for them because they knee-jerk against the cops. I think they're really despicable when they do that. They realize . . . [that] you'll put them on camera and they can go home at night and watch themselves on television. You can figure out who they are.

New York Daily News, September 12, 1998

In the wake of the confrontation at the Million Youth March, the new Manhattan borough president, C. Virginia Fields (highest-ranking African American elected to office in the city since David Dinkins's defeat) led a call by black public officials for a meeting with the mayor. But, though they represented a community that constituted a full one-quarter of his constituency, the mayor said no.

The most important things are not make-believe meetings. The most important things are getting the truth out. *New York Times,* September 10, 1998

Ms. Fields said it was suggested to her that she should watch the videotape [of the disturbances that erupted as police broke up the Khalid rally—Ed.] and apologize publicly for her comments, and that then, "maybe," the Mayor would meet with her. To which Colleen Roche, the Mayor's press secretary, responded, "She was never told that if she apologized she would get a meeting." *New York Times,* February 13, 1999

By the time of the Amadou Diallo shooting in February 1999, the mayor had not met face to face with Fields—and some other leading black elected officials—for more than a year. Apparently, Generalissimo Giuliani felt such meetings would constitute, on his part,
kowtowing. *New York* magazine, April 19, 1999

He also saw only limited possibilities for genuine dialogue because of what he termed the tendency by Fields and other black politicians to put a "race overlay" on things.
When you start putting a race overlay on it . . . then everything starts getting explained by race, and it really is a form of racism when you do that.
Interview on WEVD Radio, *N.Y. Daily News,* Feb. 27, 1999

A week after Diallo's death, Fields was joined at a news conference by former mayor Ed Koch. Stressing that "I certainly am not blaming Mayor Giuliani or Commissioner Safir for the tragedy that took place," she pleaded for a meeting because the city needed to "move in a new direction."
Mr. Giuliani responded last night by impeaching the event's credibility, noting that Mr. Koch is a persistent

critic and saying that Ms. Fields failed to acknowledge the Police Department's accomplishments, including reduced crime in black neighborhoods. He maintained that he has working relationships with other black leaders . . . and tends not to deal with "highly partisan Democrats" who he said strive for headlines rather than for substance. "If you hold a press conference and attack me, attack the Police Department and completely discredit everything that's been done, and if you have somebody who is a persistent critic sitting next to you," the Mayor said, it suggests "no real willingness to work out a real solution. That happens in politics."

New York Times, February 11, 1999

Mr. Giuliani dismissed the news conference as a publicity stunt fraught with factual errors and devoid of any constructive purpose. He also portrayed Ms. Fields as one in a group of "highly partisan Democrats" who fall into a "certain category: partisan, political, with no real willingness to work out a real solution." He also said that he would meet with people "who want to work with me" in finding answers to problems. *N.Y. Times,* Feb. 13, 1999

But, after six more weeks of building tension in the city, the Generalissimo relented. He met not only with Fields but with State Comptroller H. Carl McCall, his frequent nemesis when it came to oversight of his Administration's financial and administrative practices.

The sudden decision to open his door marked a stark turnaround for the Mayor, who had previously dismissed Ms. Fields and Mr. McCall as being more interested in publicity than in substantive discussion. . . .

Ms. [Mayor's Communications Director Cristyne] Lategano suggested that the administration's shift was in part due to a change in attitude by Ms. Fields and Mr. McCall. Previously, she said, "there was a lot of public discussion for demands for a meeting. That tone has changed, and instead the discussion has been about productive private meetings." *N.Y. Times,* March 25, 1999

At the end of the summit, the article concluded, the mayor "broke in to offer the kind of perspective he has been promoting in recent days."

He said he looked forward to meeting with many people, although some seem to have "political aims, right or wrong." And he said, again, that he hoped those people would listen to "the other side of the story"—a reference to the achievements of the Police Department.

New York Times, March 25, 1999

9

Rudy's Report Card: "Works Well with Others"(?)

There is probably no other elected official in the country, short of the President, surrounded by as many monitors, auditors, oversight committees, second-guessers and back-street drivers as the Mayor of New York City. And it's hard to think of any mayor who has disliked someone peering over his shoulder with the intensity of Mayor Rudolph W. Giuliani.   *New York Times,* April 1, 1997

Nevertheless, power-sharing—and the separation of powers—is part of any constitutional government. And especially since its fiscal crisis and near bankruptcy in the mid-1970s,

New York City's mayors have had to expect that a great deal of fiscal scrutiny comes with the job.

Let us review Generalissimo Giuliani's work in this area, boys and girls, in order that we can better evaluate his performance in office. We already know how he has graded himself.
We see a tremendous amount of confidence in New York City. And a lot of it has to do with the fact that we have— in a very realistic way—straightened out the budget and financial plan of the city.
Comment on WABC Radio show, *N.Y. Times,* Aug. 10, 1996

He also questioned the political motivations of some of the monitors, including the State Financial Control Board, the State and City Comptrollers and Wall Street bond-rating firms. *New York Times,* August 10, 1996

◆ The Citizens Budget Commission

Founded in 1932 and supported by the city's business and financial community, the CBC operates as a kind of private-sector gadfly, offering its research and recommendations on the City of New York's budgetary practices. Mayoral candidate Rudy Giuliani, no less, found it a great resource.
I would go to briefings with the Citizens Budget Committee and some of the other groups. And they were clearly predicting then and exploring then both the fiscal problems of the city and the even worse ones of the state. *Barron's,* November 26, 1990

And, shortly after taking office, Mayor Rudy Giuliani even agreed to be keynote speaker at the commission's annual fundraising dinner. But traditionally the CBC eventually became critical of every mayor's policies, and every mayor (to varying degrees) became irritated by the self-styled good-government group. It was not long before Generalissimo Giuliani was grumbling about

so-called fiscal experts.   *New York Times,* March 29, 1994

But it quickly became clear that the new mayor had no intention of accepting his traditional role—or accepting the traditional criticisms of the commission.

Mayor Rudolph W. Giuliani sharply criticized a group of business leaders who have called for deeper conces- sions from New York City's labor unions as an alterna- tive to drastic cuts in services, calling their proposals "quite harmful" to his efforts to balance the budget.

Appearing before the trustees of the Citizens Budget Commission, a nonprofit watchdog group supported by businesses, Mr. Giuliani said he needed "realistic approaches" to help close the $3.1 billion budget gap for the fiscal year that begins in July. And he pointedly dismissed some of the commission's recommendations for changes in union work rules as "absurd."

. . . [The Commission's recommendation that the NYPD consider having one officer, not two, in some patrol cars was] "a terrible mistake" that would jeopar- dize officers' safety.   *New York Times,* May 4, 1995

I think it kind of moves the debate off in a very, very unhelpful and damaging direction.

New York Times, May 4, 1995

Lashing out at critics of his new labor agreement with the municipal unions, Mayor Rudolph W. Giuliani yes- terday denounced suggestions from fiscal monitors that he should have extracted more concessions as "outra- geous," "crazy" and "off the wall."

City workers, he said, had made more than their share of sacrifices to help balance the budget, and those who maintain otherwise have a "political agenda," though he did not spell out what the agenda was. . . .

Mr. Giuliani said that the budget commission and other critics had some kind of political agenda "that even I can't figure out." He suggested that the group was being critical simply to maintain its position as a critic.   *New York Times,* July 4, 1995

To criticize us for it, I think, indicates what their intent is, which is to kind of maintain their position by constantly criticizing.   *New York Times,* July 4, 1995

They should all calm down. They've got a year's experience with us now and I don't think this city has been managed from the point of view of fiscal affairs as responsibly as the way in which I'm managing it. And I'll take you back over 15 to 20 years.
                                                     New York Times, July 4, 1995

After the Generalissimo had been reelected, however, it was truly payback time for the gadfly group—when Giuliani's budget director began telephoning heads of Wall Street bond firms to offer his advice, as he put it, that "it would be in their best interest to know they could save money" by not buying a table at the CBC's upcoming annual dinner. The commission, as was well known in financial circles, depended on the dinner for most of its revenue. The message, as the worried recipients of these phone calls told the media (anonymously), was obvious: If your company contributes to the CBC by attending the dinner, you just might find yourselves on the losing end of the competition to market the next round of city bonds.

A stealth attack on a government watchdog? An act of intimidation and revenge against critics? No, no, no, said the Generalissimo.

My Budget Director was exercising his First Amendment rights to express his opinion, which he has an absolute right to do, and I would think all of you in the media would fiercely defend that right.

New York Times, December 20, 1997

I'm proud of him for doing it.

New York Daily News, December 20, 1997

Giuliani said that if anyone wants to support the commission, "there aren't any repercussions, nothing's going to happen to them." But the mayor was unrelenting in his attack on the panel.   *N.Y. Daily News,* December 20, 1997

We are sending exactly the right message. You want our opinion of the CBC? Their reports are pretty useless, they are a dilettante organization, and you are kind of wasting your money if you want to donate to them. If you want to do that, you have a perfect right to do that; it is up to you. If someone asked me about it, I would say, "You are wasting your money."

New York Times, December 20, 1997

[The Mayor] later added that he believed the Citizens Budget Commission was a "sacred cow" to the news media.   *New York Times,* December 20, 1997

With all the publicity over the implied threat to the organization's existence, the commission's dinner went on to raise a record amount of money.

We don't care.   *New York Times,* February 18, 1998

The Municipal Assistance Corporation

Formed in 1975 as an independent agency entitled to borrow money for the financially stricken city, MAC remained in existence afterward—and in control of substantial sums that it dispensed to the city, in return for an ongoing role as a financial adviser and sometime critic.

Mayor Rudolph W. Giuliani sharply criticized the chairman of the state's Municipal Assistance Corporation yesterday, saying he had overstepped his role in recommending that the Mayor include police officers, firefighters and teachers in an effort to reduce the municipal work force. *New York Times*, March 23, 1994

That really demonstrates a misunderstanding of his role. It isn't his role or MAC's role to be suggesting the budget priorities or political priorities of this city. . . . It's our money. It's not his. And nobody elected him to make decisions like that. *New York Times*, March 23, 1994

The Independent Budget Office

Created by the last major revision of the city charter, the IBO was set up to offer its own analysis of city spending, apart from either the Mayor's Office or the City Council. In 1998, in the midst of a fight between the mayor and the council over whether a new stadium should be built for the New York Yankees, the IBO proposed that noncity residents share in the cost of constructing any new ballpark.

This is, like, the stupidest thinking you can possibly imagine. Statement, September 1998

Quoted in *New York Post*, April 8, 1999

◆ The Bond Raters

An essential part of New York City's finances—the interest it pays on bonds for the money it borrows in the capital markets—is determined on Wall Street, especially by the universally respected firms of Moody's Investors Service and Standard & Poor's, with their all-important "creditworthiness" ratings. A rise or drop in the city's bond ratings can save it—or cost it—hundreds of millions.

Mayor Rudolph W. Giuliani defended his new preliminary budget yesterday against criticism that he had not done enough to address New York City's long-term financial ills. *New York Times,* February 1, 1997

The fact is that we have reduced the deficits that New York City faces by more than has been done in any recent year, more than has been done actually in any one of the last 10 years. Comment on WABC Radio show *New York Times,* February 1, 1997

Eighteen months into his mayoralty, after looking at Giuliani's first two budgets, Standard & Poor's lowered the city's credit rating—which it never did under the entire administration of David Dinkins, whom Giuliani had held up as an example of financially irresponsibility and incompetence. "The decision," noted the *New York Times,* was "clearly a symbolic blow to the Mayor's claim to be a financial housecleaner."

The Mayor denounced the action, saying no one would remember it by next week. . . . Mr. Giuliani, who said he has known since his inauguration that the downgrade was coming, angrily accused Standard & Poor's of cov-

ering up the real reason for downgrading by citing a series of "disingenuous" criticisms of his budget.
New York Times, July 11, 1995

The things they're picking on are small points to try to justify a decision that they can't really justify. In 1993, they wanted to downgrade the city, and they didn't do it because they felt it might interfere with the incumbent mayor's chances of re-election. There isn't a person in this city that doesn't know that. So that [press] release had to cover a lot of mistakes they made in the past.
New York Times, July 11, 1995

S&P wasn't buying it. Six months later, in the midst of a budget standoff with the city comptroller over Giuliani's intention to float a controversial refinancing of municipal debt and use other "one-shot" maneuvers to balance the budget, the city's rating was lowered again.

It's almost irresponsible not to take advantage of opportunities like that [the refinancing]. *N.Y. Times,* Jan. 13, 1996

For his part, the Mayor, a Republican who just last year said his budgets had "the least amount of one-shots and any form of gimmicks" in the city's history, dismissed the criticism by fiscal monitors. *N.Y. Times,* Jan. 28, 1996

There's only a certain amount of downsizing you can do. . . . We have been diligent in doing it. We have been progressive in the way in which we have done it. We have been disciplined. At the same time, you can't destroy the city. . . . Sometimes they just look at numbers. They don't look at people. I have to look at people. *New York Times,* January 28, 1996

◆ The New York State Financial Control Board

Another vestige of the 1975 fiscal crisis and New York State's rescue of the city at that time, this board consisted almost entirely of state and city chief executives (including the mayor himself) and chief financial officers, and its only function was to give a periodic review of the city's finances. Nevertheless . . .

With New York City's budget situation worsening, Mayor Rudolph W. Giuliani called the State Financial Control Board . . . "totally hypocritical."

New York Times, January 13, 1995

I actually think that the [State] Financial Control Board is an anachronism, and I think over the last year, year and a half, it's proved to be an anachronism.

New York Times, January 13, 1995

Calling the board "a partisan political operation," Mr. Giuliani added, "it was very supportive of the Dinkins budget that helped create the deficits that I have to deal with." *New York Times,* January 13, 1995

◆ State Comptroller Carl McCall

Comptrollers of the State of New York had long audited the city's books to examine the soundness and effectiveness of city policies and programs, and their authority to do so had never been questioned. But H. Carl McCall—first African American to hold the post, friend of ex-Mayor David Dinkins, married to a onetime deputy mayor in Dinkins's administration, open critic of the mayor, one of the black public officials Giuliani long refused even to meet with—was in for a surprise.

Stepping up his feud with State Comptroller H. Carl McCall, Mayor Rudolph W. Giuliani has barred auditors from Mr. McCall's office from evaluating City programs, a responsibility that the state office has carried out for decades.   *N.Y. Times,* March 28, 1997

Claiming McCall's civil-servant auditors were there on an intelligence-gathering operation for the Democratic Party in its race to unseat him that November as he sought reelection, the Generalissimo said:

This list [of City agencies to be audited] is a political list. This is not a list that has anything to do with the [financial] accounts of the city. So we are not going to roll over for him. We are not going to let him do it.
                    New York Times, March 30,1997

The way we see it, he was playing politics, and we don't want to let him get away with it.   *N.Y. Times,* Apr. 1, 1997

After two weeks, during which state auditors were ordered evicted from city agencies and the mayor offered to allow audits to be done if the comptroller "recused" himself, a truce was arranged . . .

Deputy Mayor [Randy] Mastro suggested that the Mayor had succeeded in teaching Mr. McCall a lesson.
                    New York Times, April 12, 1997

. . . and immediately broke down.

Mr. McCall seemed better able to support his position with the Friday letter from his counsel making it clear that the audits would continue.   *N.Y. Times,* Apr. 15, 1997

The matter went to court.
He has really no credibility.

New York Daily News, February 27, 1998
Requoted in column by former mayor Ed Koch, *New York Daily News,* January 22, 1999

(Generalissimo Giuliani's view notwithstanding, the courts ruled in favor of the state comptroller.)

◆ City Comptroller Alan J. Hevesi

Alan Hevesi and Giuliani were elected at the same time, and not even the Generalissimo could mount a case that it was illegal for the city's top financial officer to audit the performance of his administration. That didn't mean, however, that he had to like it. In late 1994, battling the City Council over whose plan to close a budget gap would be adopted . . .

Mr. Giuliani accused the Comptroller of criticizing his budget proposals while not challenging the Council's plan, which Mr. Giuliani contends would cut City revenue by $100 million. *New York Times,* November 29, 1994

It's an easy thing for him to say. But it's another thing to excuse responsibility. I think what I'm doing will keep the City's bond rating and those who evaluate the City much more confident. *New York Times,* November 29, 1994

Mayor Rudolph W. Giuliani dismissed the Comptroller's study, strongly suggesting that its findings were more political than empirical. *New York Times,* May 17, 1995

I have to emphasize that when you start dealing with secondary and indirect analysis, it very much is guided by the predisposition of the person who does the analysis.
New York Times, May 17, 1995

Mayor Rudolph W. Giuliani said yesterday he might have to make deeper cuts in spending in response to Comptroller Alan J. Hevesi's decision earlier this week to refuse to approve a plan to reorganize New York City's debt for an infusion of cash.

New York Times, January 13, 1996

When City Comptroller Alan Hevesi brought to public attention what he described as the "bizarre" awarding of a $43 million City contract to HANAC (the Hellenic American Neighborhood Action Committee)—a Queens organization which was neither lowest bidder (HANAC's bid was $8 million higher) or highest performer—Giuliani denounced Hevesi, defended his agency, and said the contract process had been marked by brave and heroic decisions. U.S. Attorney Mary Jo White has issued subpoenas and the Giuliani administration has belatedly canceled the contract, following further disclosures that HANAC hired the brother of a top mayoral aide.   Column by former mayor Ed Koch

New York Post, April 6, 1996

And in September 1996, when Hevesi released an audit that found nearly 1,200 drivers at vity agencies—and nearly 400 who worked at the New York Police Department—didn't even have a valid license . . .

It's a cheap-shot report, and a lot of the numbers are wrong. I don't at this point expect anything better from Alan Hevesi than trying to fudge numbers in order to get himself on television.   *N.Y. Daily News,* Sept. 7, 1996

Unfortunately, it [the report] frightens people.

New York Daily News, September 7, 1996

✦ McCall, Hevesi, and the Media
(Acting in Collusion, Of Course)

Often, the slant in The New York Times is their way. People don't get the actual and complete picture of the progress that we have made in straightening out the budget of New York City. *New York Times,* August 10, 1996

Mr. Giuliani's aides were asked on Thursday if the Mayor would be interviewed for an article on the fiscal monitors' evaluations of the budget, which the Council approved in June. But he used part of his radio program yesterday to criticize The *New York Times* before the article was published. *New York Times,* August 10, 1996

✦ Public Advocate Mark Green

Onetime Nader Raider, David Dinkins's crusading (and hardly camera-shy) consumer affairs commissioner, and confirmed liberal, Mark Green was not only sworn into office the same day as Giuliani, he stood to inherit Giuliani's job if for any reason it became vacant. You can imagine how delighted the Generalissimo was to have someone like Green aboard as a colleague in government.

Idiotic.

> Reaction to Green's first major cost-saving suggestion—a proposal to have Police Department custodial work and auto repairs done through private contractors
> *New York Times,* March 29, 1994

So far Mark Green plays the role of purely critic, and most often not in a way that's particularly constructive.
Statement on WABC Radio, *New York Times,* June 11, 1994

We'll look at his proposals. But I think Mark should wake up and realize the new world we're in and march ahead to the future rather than repeat all the mistakes of the past.

Reaction to "reinventing government" proposals offered by Green, *New York Times,* November 14, 1994

Actually, Generalissimo Giuliani had a "reinventing government" proposal of his own in mind—a whopping 23 percent "downsizing" of Green's office, cuts far bigger than that slated for any other city officeholder.

He even blamed the proposed cut on Mr. Green himself, saying the Public Advocate had not offered his own plan to trim his office's $2.7 million budget. Mr. Giuliani, who sometimes seems to bristle when Mr. Green's name comes up at news conferences, insists that the $600,000 cut for the office of the Public Advocate has nothing to do with punishing a foe and says he is making similar cuts in his own office. In fact, he likes to describe as a profile in courage his attempt to cut the budget of the man designated in the City Charter as the first in line to succeed him.   *New York Times,* June 11, 1994

I recognize the fact that that could be conceived as political, so I think it's quite courageous that I'm doing it, because it's quite substantive.

New York Times, June 11, 1994

The Mayor also read aloud choice lines from old newspaper editorials, written before Mr. Green started his term, that had called the Public Advocate's office: "A waste of taxpayers' money"; "A very dumb job"; "A post that has little meaning."   *New York Times,* June 11, 1994

When the attempt to kneecap Green with budget cuts did not succeed, the Generalissimo denied Green (and Mayor Thomas Menino of Boston) the use of a city building to hold a press conference.

"I know the mayors that were here came for a meeting that was sponsored by the Democratic National Committee to raise money," said Mr. Giuliani, explaining why the Mayors had come to New York in the first place. "So it would have been very hard to escape the fact that what Mark Green was organizing here was a partisan political event." *New York Times*, April 8, 1995

As the years went by, the Generalissimo, in his own way, mellowed toward Green.

This is another one of those guffaws by Mark Green. I guess he wants to position himself as the anti-police, anti-law enforcement candidate. . . . This is all about somebody running for Mayor by attacking the Police Department.

> Reaction to release of report by public advocate documenting major flaws in NYPD's internal disciplinary process and its cooperation with Civilian Complaint Review Board, *New York Times*, September 16, 1999

A typical pandering American politician of the latter part of the 20th Century. *N.Y. Times Magazine*, August 1, 1999

◆ The Great Charter Revision Hoax of 1999

Giuliani actually had once conceded that Mark Green
had all of the basic qualities to be mayor in terms of public service and level of intelligence, commitment.

> 1997 statement by Rudolph Giuliani
> Quoted in *New York Times*, June 22, 1999

But, as he prepared to run for the U.S. Senate, the Generalissimo surveyed the prospects of going off to Washington and leaving his legacy in Green's liberal hands. He did not like what he saw. The City Charter was clear, though: The public advocate becomes mayor if that happens. So the solution was simple: If you don't like the man who will succeed you, just change the charter.

Normally, city charters undergo revisions after long and painstaking efforts by blue-ribbon panels of distinguished citizens for such purposes as restructuring and updating the institutions of municipal government. But Generalissimo Giuliani was not a man to waste time with such frivolity. Why, only the year before he had suddenly appointed a panel of political supporters as a "Charter Revision Commission" to issue a set of minor, redundant proposals, purely to block the holding of a referendum that sought to block the building of a new Yankee Stadium in Manhattan that was supported by the mayor, the owner of the Yankees, and virtually no one else. (Whew! But that's another story; let's not get ahead of ourselves.)

Now, again, another charter revision panel—described by the *New York Times* as "a collection of Giuliani loyalists and campaign contributors"—was quickly assembled. Prime item on its agenda: requiring a special election for mayor within sixty days after the office becomes vacant, so that Green would be denied the chance to serve as mayor for a year after Giuliani's departure.

To the outcry, even from those who were by no means fans of Mark Green, that this was no way to treat the constitution of the City of New York, the Generalissimo had this to say:

I'm the Mayor of New York City, I hold a political office and the City Charter gives the Mayor certain powers, which I exercise. What I am doing is perfectly appropriate.

New York Times, June 16, 1999

This is politics. That's what I do.
New York Times, June 17, 1999

And his views on succession?
I'd certainly like them to take a look at it. I have lots of thoughts about it.   *New York Times,* June 16, 1999

Oh, God, is that a stretch! I'm not going to select my successor; the public is going to select my successor. That is about the worst kind of intellectual phoniness that you could possibly engage in. . . . How is it my own private good to have the public decide who the next mayor is going to be? This is the most hypocritical reaction.
New York Times Magazine, August 1, 1999

In the end, even Giuliani's own hand-picked charter-rewrite panel did not dare do something as blatant as alter the line of succession in the middle of a mayor's term; they made the change but delayed it for four years.
I think it's a shame that it can't be done right now. . . . For the future of the city, it should be done.
New York Times, October 26, 1999

The succession change was then mixed together with a batch of innocuous ideas that hardly merited the equivalent of convening a constitutional convention—and one thoroughly dangerous proposal, slipped into the package, that would have fundamentally altered the balance of power in city goverment by hamstringing the council's ability to raise taxes or fight the mayor in any future budget-veto impasses. Municipal unions, Green, and other Democratic opponents attempted to mobilize against what they called the mayor's "power grab," but amid a sparse turnout the vote appeared too close to call—until Giuliani's vaunted political operation began using its phone banks to broadcast a recorded message from Rudy himself to hundreds of thousands of New York households. The calls reached the homes not just of likely supporters but Giuliani opponents too. On Election Day, in a shocker, the mayor's charter changes were voted down—by a margin of 3 to 1.

An omen for the Senate race? Acknowledging "a mistake in presenting charter revision this year," the Generalissimo tried to put the best face possible on the debacle.

I don't think it'll have any bearing six months from now, much less a year from now. The turnout was so low it would be almost impossible to figure out what happened.

New York Times, November 4, 1999

[The opponents] did a much better job of pulling the vote. . . . When you make phone calls, sometimes you make to the right places, and sometimes you make them to the wrong places. The only solace in the election of yesterday is that when you lose 75–25, a few phone calls to the wrong place wasn't the reason you lost.

New York Times, November 4, 1999

The way I handled it was a big mistake.

New York Times, December 30, 1999

10

Rudy and His Predecessors

◆ Ed Koch

Rudy Giuliani's attitude toward Edward Koch, the Mayor of New York from 1978 through 1989, has always had a tendency to depend on the current political situation—and his immediate political needs.

For instance, when Koch was a beleaguered third-term mayor being buffeted by corruption scandals, and Giuliani's office was pursuing many of the investigations into those scandals, but the crusading U.S. Attorney—seeing the mayor's office as too long a shot to run for in overwhelmingly Democratic New York City—was looking to fulfill his ambitions elsewhere, he went on record saying this:

I think I know as much about these investigations as anyone knows, including a lot of confidential material, and there's not a shred of evidence or suggestion that Mayor Koch knew of crimes that were being committed by several of the Democratic leaders, and the Borough Presidents, or had any involvement in those crimes, or would have done anything other than turn them in if he had found out about them. Statement in *Newsday*, 1987, requoted in *New York Times*, December 30, 1998

When the poll numbers told him that Koch's office was, in fact, the one he should run for:

If you're happy with the way things are, re-elect Ed Koch. . . . But if you want to see real, honest, fundamental change in this city, then vote for me.

Formal announcement of candidacy, *N.Y. Times*, May 18, 1989

[Koch was] trying to make political points by using harsh words. *New York Times*, March 29, 1989

Rudolph W. Giuliani, the Republican mayoral candidate, spent the summer vilifying Mayor Edward I. Koch, saying that he had responded to corruption in his administration with "his eyes closed, his ears clogged and his mouth open." *New York Times*, October 28, 1989

If the Mayor had not turned over the Parking Violations Bureau to two of the biggest crooks in the city's history, there would have been $200 to $250 million more in revenue. Statement on campaign trail
Requoted in *New York Times,* October 28, 1989

But when Koch lost the Democratic primary, and winning meant getting "Koch Democrats" to vote for him against David Dinkins in November:
In Ed Koch's case, he worked hard on corruption involving the inspection services and the inspectors in this city. I know because I worked on those cases with him.
New York Times, October 28, 1989

On the stump this week, Mr. Giuliani lavished praise on Mr. Koch's budget modification, noting that several of the Mayor's proposals, like a hiring freeze and the refinancing of City bonds, were ones he had also offered. Mr. Giuliani . . . also went out of his way to commend the Mayor for putting forward the budget plan, and not leaving the chore entirely to his successor.
New York Times, October 28, 1989

When Koch (who campaigned hard for Dinkins after losing the primary) crossed party lines to endorse Giuliani four years later:
One thing about Ed Koch that I think everybody realizes is that he loves New York and that, for him, the best interests of New York are paramount.
New York Post, October 15, 1993

And as he took the oath of office, with Koch looking on:
The common sense approach of Ed Koch will echo again. First Inaugural Address
New York Times, January 3, 1994

But, while still supporting the new mayor, Koch began having some doubts. There were the violent personal attacks Giuliani unleashed on Ramon Cortines, a schools chancellor whom Koch admired. Then there was Giuliani's order that city workers begin tearing down campaign posters of Republican gubernatorial candidate George Pataki on city property after Giuliani had daringly broken party ranks to support the reelection of Democratic governor Mario Cuomo. As Koch later recounted it to the *New York Times,* when he suggested that Giuliani wait until after election day to tear the signs down, the Generalissimo said:

Don't interrupt me! *New York Times,* June 26, 1995;
New York Times Magazine, December 3, 1995

In the fall of 1995, Koch—a staunch proponent of Israel, but also a supporter of its peace process with Yasser Arafat and the Palestine Liberation Organization—publicly decried the "discourtesy" when Giuliani ordered the PLO chairman to leave a Lincoln Center gala that was part of the United Nations' fiftieth anniversary celebrations. Even more galling to the Generalissimo, Koch and David Dinkins appeared together to issue a joint statement of disapproval. Noting that Koch had once referred to the UN as "a cesspool," the Generalissimo shot back:

I think if we're going to take lessons in diplomacy and the way in which to express yourself, the last person in the world you should take it from is Ed Koch.
New York Times, October 26, 1995

◆ Judicial Appointments

Two months later Koch and Dinkins had reason to reassemble. As mayor, Koch had instituted a seminal change in the selection of city judges—he set up a professional panel to screen all judiciary candidates and recommend finalists to the mayor, ending the era of political appointments to the bench. Koch regarded the reform—which his successor Dinkins had maintained intact—as perhaps his proudest legacy.

At the end of 1995, Giuliani overrode the panel and refused to reappoint two judges for new full terms. Saying one judge "lacks the intellectual capacity to try cases" and that he wanted jurists only of the "very highest quality," the Generalissimo substituted two appointments of his own. One of his picks, it turned out, had flunked out of law school, never gotten a law degree, and been turned down by three other judicial screening panels—the Generalissimo compared him to Abraham Lincoln. The other had tried exactly seven cases in six years as an assistant district attorney in Brooklyn, never once as lead prosecutor, but had links to the Orthodox Jewish community in that borough, which Giuliani had assiduously courted. The process had been depoliticized; now, after two decades, it had been *re*politicized. No less than the top jurist in all of New York, Chief Judge Judith Kaye of the Court of Appeals, publicly expressed her dismay.

I don't think she should be writing articles lobbying for the reappointment of judges. I think the Chief Judge is stepping beyond her role here.

Interview on WABC Radio, *N.Y. Times,* December 28, 1995

But when the two former mayors joined forces to denounce what he had done, the Generalissimo went ballistic—even for the Generalissimo.

It's really unfortunate that former Mayor Koch and former Mayor Dinkins can get together over this, because this is really the height of hypocrisy. . . . So I think this attack by the two former Mayors is the lowest point they've reached, and it must be that they're just not getting enough attention. . . .

It's a consultative process. It isn't a game, it isn't a rubber stamp, it isn't a way for me to protect myself politically, which in fact the other Mayors used it for. Under the table and below the line, they would talk to the political bosses of this city and make sure things were engineered through this committee. I know that went on, any person who lives in this city knows that went on.   *New York Times,* December 23, 1995

Mr. Giuliani, furious, said that if anything he planned to remove more sitting judges from the bench when their terms ended, calling it his job to clean up the legacy of shady, politically motivated judicial appointments perpetuated by Mr. Dinkins and Mr. Koch.
New York Times, December 28, 1995

Had they the same standards as I have, I wouldn't have to be going through the problems of weeding off the courts some of the people that they put on, pressured by people like Stanley Friedman, Donald Manes, Meade Esposito.   *New York Daily News,* December 23, 1995

None of this is addressed by former Mayor Dinkins or Mayor Koch, both of whom perpetuated on the bench a significant number of Democratic machine politicians despite their hypocritical allegiance to some pristine process. I happen to know that process because I investigated that process.   *New York Times,* December 28, 1995

You can search our record over and over again, inside and out . . . and you can't find even the suggestion of a political appointment to the bench. Neither Mayor Dinkins or Mayor Koch can say that with any credibility.
New York Post, December 28, 1995

The Mayor has provided no specific evidence for the charge, beyond saying last week that both mayors' appointees to the bench were almost exclusively Democrats. *New York Times*, December 28, 1995

Soon after, several judges in New York—at the city and even the federal level—found themselves under fire, in the media and the political arena, either for misconduct or so-called junk justice rulings alleged to be soft on criminals and biased against law enforcement. Ironically, one of the junk-justice rulings was by a judge Giuliani had appointed—release without bail for one defendant accused of statutory rape, only $1,000 bail for the other. The Generalissimo paused from his attacks on other judges long enough to say, of his own appointee:

The judge made a reasonable decision. . . . This is an area in which reasonable minds can differ about the application of the law to the facts.

Quotation attributed to Mayor Giuliani in column by former mayor Ed Koch, *New York Post*, May 3, 1996

When the firing had stopped, Koch did not—as threatened—refuse to support the Generalissimo for reelection; in the 1997 campaign, he announced he would reluctantly vote for Giuliani over leftist Democrat Ruth Messinger, who had frequently vexed Koch when he was in office. However, he withheld an endorsement from the Generalissimo—and offered his assessment that, as a child, Rudy Giuliani probably tore the wings off flies.

I've been very nice to Ed Koch personally, and I don't understand the intensely personal nature of the attack. I remember the story in Koch's book about the fired Deputy Mayor who kneeled down and cried to keep his job. It's all in the eye of the beholder whether you're

**nice or not nice. My father used to say, "It's more impor-
tant that you respect me than that you love me. And
later on in life you can love me."**

Interview with columnist Maureen Dowd
New York Times, July 12, 1997

◆ Pornography

A year later, claiming he had rid the city of the pornography
industry that had once seemed to have a stranglehold on the
Times Square district, the Generalissimo could not resist issu-
ing a challenge:

**Former Mayor Edward I. Koch once bet us that we
would never win. He hasn't paid his bet yet.**

July 1998 statement attributed to Mayor Giuliani
Quoted in column by former mayor Ed Koch, *New
York Daily News,* February 5, 1999

◆ The Blue Room Portraits

By custom, former Mayors of New York pose for an official portrait, which is donated to the city and placed in City Hall. Also
by custom, portraits of the most recent mayors hang in and
around the so-called Blue Room, where mayors hold press conferences and other formal functions. In early December 1998,
the portraits of Edward Koch and David Dinkins were suddenly removed from the room. To Koch, "perhaps having the
faces of two mayoral critics staring at him from the walls of the
Blue Room was more disconcerting than we could imagine."

**Mr. Giuliani yesterday denied having had anything to
do with changes in the Blue Room. . . . He said it was
part of a refurbishing of the room, and that the portraits
would eventually be returned. . . . Mr. Giuliani said that
Mr. Koch was being "overly sensitive" . . . [and] sug-**

gested that Mr. Koch was simply trying to provoke a dispute to improve sagging ratings on his radio and television shows. *New York Times,* December 12, 1998

It wouldn't trouble me one way or the other if those pictures remained there, but it does make sense to have a rotation. *New York Times,* December 12, 1998

The Generalissimo did wax enthusiastic about the removals in one respect, though—they enabled him to move the painting of long-forgotten nineteenth-century mayor Edward Livingston, an ancestor of the incoming GOP House speaker Robert Livingston, into the Blue Room.

Edward Livingston laid the cornerstone of the building. That is a nice point I would like to make, maybe over and over again, for the next six months to the new Speaker of the House as we talk about aid to New York City. *New York Times,* December 12, 1998

If that was the Generalissimo's real motivation for disturbing the portraits (and mayoral tradition), he needn't have bothered. One week later, amid a "personal morality" feeding frenzy as Republicans forced through a party-line vote to impeach President Clinton, Livingston was outed for his own marital infidelity by right-wing members of his caucus—and was out of politics.

◆ Kackling as Koch Kanceled

At year's end, Koch suffered a setback in one of the several careers he pursued upon leaving City Hall—his daily call-in radio show was canceled to make room for the tough-love prescriptions of syndicated on-air therapist Laura Schlessinger.

After hearing about Koch's plight, Giuliani joked that he might want to be a radio talk show host himself when he leaves politics. "So my self-interest is in favor of him getting another show as quickly as possible." The Mayor added that he enjoys Koch's criticism because it gives him "something to talk about at a news conference."

New York Daily News, December 29, 1998

Giuliani also needled Koch—even to the point of mimicking the distinctive Koch voice—by claiming he "goes crazy" when someone calls in to proclaim Giuliani "the best Mayor in my lifetime." *N.Y. Post*, Dec. 29, 1998

Koch had just scolded Giuliani for an unfolding scandal at the largest union of municipal workers, where it turned out a controversial contract with the city had actually been turned down by the rank-and-file—and been "ratified" only because of massive ballot-stuffing.

You know why he's doing that? Because he's dying for a corruption scandal in my administration so that he doesn't end up with the most corrupt administration in the last half of the 20th Century.

New York Daily News, December 29, 1998

◆ David Dinkins

Mayor Dinkins, I salute your accomplishment for our city. Mayor Dinkins' special dignity and grace will also mark his governance of our city and it's something that we hope to call on in the future. And I know that we can and that we can count on it. First Inaugural Address

New York Times, January 3, 1994

But in fact, David Norman Dinkins—the 106th Mayor of the City of New York, who made political history as the first African American to govern America's largest, most ethnically diverse city—was never called on to do anything by his successor, Rudolph Giuliani, except perhaps be used as a whipping boy. If Giuliani's relationship with Koch had its ups and downs, his attitude toward Dinkins was quite consistent: unalloyed, undisguised contempt.

After three years of taunts, and an announced intention by Giuliani to link any Democrat who ran against him to Dinkins and the perceived failures of his administration, Dinkins briefly toyed with the idea of coming out of political retirement and defending his record himself.

I would welcome his candidacy.   *N.Y. Times,* Jan. 31, 1997

I feel sorry for Mayor Dinkins. I watched him on television last night and I saw a man who's very angry and very bitter, and I feel sorry for him.

New York Times, February 1, 1997

Mr. Giuliani said he felt no anger toward Mr. Dinkins, despite their two close races against each other, and said he "feels bad" that Mr. Dinkins still nurses animosity toward him. Mr. Giuliani said he did not know if Mr. Dinkins was serious about running but said he believed a rematch would be to his own advantage.

New York Times, February 1, 1997

I even think what he did in the last day or two is politically advantageous to me, and I question why he did it. I don't understand precisely what he's doing. But I don't have any personal animosity toward him.

New York Times, February 1, 1997

If I had his record, I'd be kind of embarrassed to show my face.

Comment attributed to Mayor Giuliani about former mayor Dinkins, made Winter 1998. Quoted in *New York Daily News*, February 27, 1998 and *New York Post*, April 8, 1999

◆ Arthur Ashe, a Study in Class; Rudy Giuliani, a Study in . . . ?

David Dinkins's great passion for tennis was well known. Almost as well known, at least among political and media circles, was that for two weeks out of every year the mayor of New York was basically governing the city from the stands at the U.S. Open, America's Grand Slam tournament held in Flushing, Queens. Indeed, while in office, Dinkins prevailed on nearby LaGuardia Airport—to the great relief of the players, the fans, and CBS, which televised the event—to divert incoming planes from their usual landing route, directly overhead the Open grounds.

Prior to leaving office, Dinkins also sealed a pact with the U.S. Tennis Association (USTA), guaranteeing the Open would remain in New York until well into the twenty-first century. The price: allowing the USTA more acreage in city-owned Flushing Meadows Park (home of both the 1939–1940 and 1964–1965 World's Fairs)—and agreeing that the city would be liable for fines, payable to the USTA, if an excessive number of planes flew overhead and disrupted play. Despite this highly irregular clause (Dinkins himself agreed to it with some reluctance), financial observers agreed that on balance, the contract was a bonanza to the city. The USTA built a sparkling new $254 million facility at its own expense, open to the public fifty weeks a year, while keeping a highly lucrative sporting event in town and paying almost as much in rent for a two-week tournament as New York's two baseball teams paid for using stadiums on city-owned land for an entire year. (To date, no fines have ever been levied against the city for aircraft noise.)

In August 1997 the main attraction of the new U.S. Open grounds—Arthur Ashe Stadium—was ready. The edifice was fittingly named for the classy, courageous, universally admired African American who overcame racial prejudice in his native Richmond, Virginia, to fulfill his dream of becoming a professional tennis player, won Wimbledon and the first U.S. Open, captained the American team in the Davis Cup, helped mobilize world opinion against apartheid in South Africa—and then became a model of personal dignity as he succumbed to a case of AIDS that he contracted from a tainted blood transfusion. The stadium was ready, a national televised gala featuring singer Whitney Houston and a constellation of past and present tennis stars was all lined up, Ashe's widow and daughter would be there to accept the honor. The only thing missing: the Mayor of New York. Four years earlier, Giuliani had said Dinkins should not sign the contract with the USTA (which Dinkins did in the last days of his administration, though it had been negotiated earlier). The Generalisssimo was invited; he had not replied. But surely he would not boycott an event like this. Would he?

A plane should not be re-routed because tennis players and spectators don't want to be bothered.

New York Times, August 22, 1997

I'm not going. . . . It really is outrageous that the City is put in the position of having to pay penalties if planes fly over the tennis stadium. *New York Times,* August 23, 1997

Giuliani, who has said that a jetliner could crash if diverted from the stadium, said he was insisting the USTA drop flyover penalties as "a matter of conscience."

New York Daily News, August 23, 1997

Someday who knows what could happen? I don't want myself associated with it. Even if you put the public safety issue aside, if the airplanes don't fly over the tennis stadium, then they fly over Mr. Smith's home or Mr. Jones' home, or somebody else's home.

New York Daily News, August 23, 1997

Mayor Giuliani said he would attend the event if the USTA agreed to renegotiate its contract with the City. . . . He said that if the provision was dropped before Monday night, he would attend the opening ceremonies.

New York Times, August 24, 1997

Mr. [USTA President Harry] Marmion said he was too busy to negotiate. I'm just as busy as Mr. Marmion. I have a few things on my mind, but I could negotiate with him. I can have this taken out in two hours.

New York Times, August 24, 1997

[The Mayor] cannot and will not look beyond that issue.

Comment by Mayor Giuliani's press secretary
New York Times, August 26, 1997

Mayor Giuliani yesterday blasted the head of the United States Tennis Association for "misrepresenting" its contract with the city and renewed his vow never to attend the U.S. Open until an "outrageous" and "stupid" provision is changed.   *N.Y. Daily News*, Aug. 25, 1997

"Waving a copy of the contract," the *News* reported, Giuliani raged:

Harry Marmion isn't telling you the truth about the contract, and David Dinkins stood there with him when he wasn't. It says right here that all the money [from

fines] will go to the tenant. The tenant is the USTA. . . .
If somebody was negotiating for the city who had the
kind of determination that I have in negotiations, [the
flyover clause] never would have happened. And I'm
not going to [the Open] until they remove it.

New York Daily News, August 25, 1997

News sportswriter Mike Lupica, surveying the public spec-
tacle Giuliani was creating, wrote a column likening the Generalissimo to Captain Queeg, the paranoid commander whose
behavior sets off *The Caine Mutiny.* In response, a fuming
Giuliani made Lupica's point:
You can get Mike Lupica to write the most illogical
garbage imaginable. . . . [This kind of column] happens
when people don't use logic or common sense.

New York Daily News, August 27, 1997

Giuliani did not go, the event was somehow a success without him, the U.S. Open continues to make huge amounts of
money for the City of New York—and the insult by the mayor of
New York to the family and the memory of Arthur Ashe, lingers.
But Generalissimo Giuliani wants everyone to know two things.
The tennis stadium is a good thing for the city, and it's a
wonderful sport. I actually play tennis, but I do it
secretly so nobody sees me.   *N.Y. Times*, Aug. 23, 1997

Arthur Ashe is a hero to me. Anyone who tries to make
this a racial issue is betraying their own desire to divide
the city for political purposes.   *N.Y. Times*, Aug. 23, 1997

◆ Crown Heights: The Apology That Wasn't

In August 1991 a caravan was following the automobile in
which Grand Rebbe Menachem Schneerson—spiritual leader

of the Lubavitcher sect of Hasidic Jews who lived in Crown Heights, Brooklyn—was riding as he returned from a visit to the grave of his wife. The caravan was accompanied by a police escort—part of special protection the politically powerful Lubavitchers had been receiving from the NYPD since the years of Mayor John Lindsay, in an effort to quell tensions that had long existed between them and the African American community they uneasily coexisted with in Crown Heights. Seeing that a red light would separate it from the police escort ahead, one car speeded up, ran the light, was hit by another car crossing the intersection, and in turn plowed into a nine-year-old black child named Gavin Cato, crushing and killing him.

Disorders quickly broke out in Crown Heights. Only a few hours after Gavin Cato's death, a Hasidic rabbinical student from Australia was randomly set upon by a mob and stabbed in revenge; he too died. For the next several days and nights, until the NYPD belatedly restored order, the Jews of Crown Heights cowered in fear and terror. Damage was estimated at upward of $1 million; 150 cops and at least 38 civilians were injured. For the Hasidim, the incident was chillingly like the infamous 1938 *Kristallnacht* that preceded the Holocaust back in Europe. Their fears, and rage, were only heightened when a Brooklyn jury not only acquitted the defendant accused of fatally stabbing the rabbinical student—but reportedly went out to dinner with him and his lawyer afterward. (After a long and arduous lobbying campaign, U.S. Attorney General Janet Reno agreed to a federal civil rights prosecution. The stabber was tried again and, this time, convicted; later on, so was an instigator who had stood nearby egging on the mob. The black community, meanwhile, nursed its own anger and fury, as the driver of the vehicle that struck and killed Gavin Cato flew back to Israel and never returned for questioning.)

The violence in Crown Heights was handled badly; an official report commissioned by New York Governor Mario Cuomo, and issued two years later, documented the many mistakes. But mistakes do not a conspiracy make—and a conspiracy by Dinkins and his administration is precisely what an aggrieved segment of the Hasidic community charged, in a lawsuit that somehow managed to reach the deposition stage (with Dinkins himself having to sit through a baiting cross-examination by the Lubavitchers' lawyer, and with transcripts immediately released to the news media) conveniently in time for the 1993 elections, in what struck many observers as suspiciously rapid progress through the court system.

Four years later Mayor Rudy Giuliani—who as a candidate had insistently used the loaded word "pogrom" to describe what happened at Crown Heights—announced he was about to make a healing gesture.

If the question is do I as the Mayor of the City of New York apologize to the people involved in that for the way the City acted during the Crown Heights riots, the answer to that is yes. . . . The City was wrong in the way it handled Crown Heights. . . . Whatever the outcome of the settlement discussions, [an official apology] would not be a part that I would have any difficulty doing for the city. *New York Times*, March 27, 1998

An apology and a financial settlement were made. But instead of closure for an unfortunate incident, the net result was this: The City of New York needlessly admitted to wrongdoing that plaintiffs in a lawsuit had never showed it engaged in, simply so that its mayor could win political favor with the ethnic community pressing the lawsuit. A legal precedent had been established that would invite similar lawsuits against the city in any future instances of ethnic or racial violence. And, under the guise of bringing peace and healing to the city, one mayor of New York had allowed a libel, and a lie—that the city's African American mayor had deliberately allowed Jewish constituents to be terrorized in order to play racial politics and show favoritism to his fellow blacks—made part of an official court record.

11

Rudy, George, and Al (or, The Generalissimo Learns— the Hard Way— Who's Top Dog in New York)

Alfonse D'Amato, former U.S. Senator, was for many years the most powerful Republican in New York. George Pataki, governor of the state, is the most powerful Republican in New York today. If Rudolph Giuliani is ever to become the most powerful Republican in New York, it will have to be over the dead bodies of these two aforementioned gentlemen. Here's how their relationship has evolved into the state of barely repressed mutual loathing that exists today—and that poses perhaps the biggest threat to Rudy Giuliani's ultimate political ambitions.

Once upon a time, Al and Rudy were best buddies. Al sponsored the nomination of Rudy as U.S. Attorney before the Senate in 1983. In 1986, for the cameras, they even dressed up as "druggies" and bought crack together. But—in conversations that neither party admitted to until several years afterward—in 1984 and 1985 Senator Alfonse D'Amato also made private inquiries about three prosecutions that were pending in Giuliani's office. Of even more concern (or what *should* have been concern): Two of the senator's three interventions concerned organized-crime cases.

"I didn't regard the communications in any way as improper or a suggestion what I should do." . . . [Giuliani] said that the three cases "couldn't have been prosecuted more." He also said such contacts did not need to be reported to superiors in the Justice Department unless there was something improper about them.

New York Times, October 26, 1989

(Giuliani's assertion that the cases "couldn't have been prosecuted more" requires a bit of a qualifier. In one prosecution, the defendants fled. In another, against alleged crime boss Paul Castellano, Mr. Castellano went to dinner one night in December 1985 at Sparks Steak House, stepped out onto the sidewalk, and *was* dinner—after which there wasn't enough *left* of him to prosecute.)

But apparently the contacts from the senator bothered Giuliani enough that, in 1988, when D'Amato was floating his name into the Senate race against incumbent Democrat Daniel Patrick Moynihan, Giuliani told D'Amato he would not resign his office unless he—not D'Amato—designated his successor.

We have so many important investigations of criminal activity now under way that I cannot leave unless I'm sure the right man succeeds me. . . . This is not something I should discuss publicly. We don't have a lot of time for transition and I need someone with a working, intimate knowledge of all the details of each of the cases we have been working on. Too much needs to be done. And unless someone is chosen quickly, I'm not sure I'll be able to run for the Senate.   *N.Y. Times,* Jan. 11, 1988

Years later he gave the real reason behind the double-talk: **Mr. Giuliani questioned as he left the job whether Mr. D'Amato would nominate a successor with enough integrity to pursue sensitive investigations.**

New York Times, October 26, 1994

Of course, D'Amato knew that was the reason all along—and did not appreciate the U.S. Attorney's chutzpah in seeking to usurp a senatorial privilege. He publicly warned Giuliani "not to threaten me." And the following year, when Giuliani did indeed resign to run for mayor, D'Amato decided to sabotage him. Saying "I certainly don't hold Rudy in any esteem," he recruited multimillionaire Ronald Lauder into the race.

February 1989. Mr. D'Amato endorses Mr. Lauder. Mr. Giuliani wonders who appointed Mr. D'Amato "political boss." *New York Times,* December 10, 1996

Lauder's television ads did not prevent Giuliani from winning the Republican nomination—but did succeed in creating a negative image of him that did not go away before election day. After his two-point loss to David Dinkins, Giuliani pointed the finger of blame at his onetime patron:

To the extent that Al D'Amato was a large part of it, then he has to take responsibility for that.

New York Times, October 19, 1997

Fast forward to 1994. With D'Amato staying out of the race this time, Giuliani has been elected mayor—though D'Amato pointedly is unable to attend the inauguration. Democratic Governor Mario Cuomo, his onetime presidential luster faded and his popularity plummeting, tries to hang on for a fourth term. To oppose him, D'Amato puts forth a little-known State Senator, George Pataki, whose campaign theme is deadly simple: I'm the one who's *not* Cuomo.

What is Giuliani to do? Even in heavily Democratic New York City, it presumably will be understood if he makes at least a pro forma endorsement of his own party's nominee. But what would be best for Rudy Giuliani? Cuomo serving out one final term, then stepping down to give Giuliani an open shot at the governor's mansion—without his having to risk running for reelection in the city? Or a puppet of his archenemy Al D'Amato entrenched in Albany, blocking him from moving up, perhaps forever? Confronted with exactly such a Machiavellian scenario by a caller to his radio program, Giuliani played coy:

Well, of course, that's a sucker question. The fact is that I don't know what I'll—I don't know if I'm going to run for re-election yet for Mayor of New York City. That's in 1997. That depends on my family, on the electorate, on. . . . What I've always followed in my career is: You do not rule things out that you cannot speculate about at this point. . . . I'd like to be a successful Mayor. And I'm not thinking beyond that.   Comments on WABC
Radio, *New York Times,* November 6, 1994

But the D'Amato-Pataki camp got broad clues to his thinking. And they did not like what they heard.

[George Pataki is] a candidate taking as few positions as possible, all of them as general as possible, taking no risks and being guided and scripted by others. . . . George Pataki's only essential characteristic is that he offers an alternative.

Comment during 1994 gubernatorial campaign
Requoted in *New York Daily News,* February 27, 1998

[Pataki has] no mind of his own.

Comment during 1994 gubernatorial campaign
Requoted in *Washington Post,* June 30, 1999

[Pataki has] a very right-wing voting record.
> Comment during 1994 gubernatorial campaign
> Requoted in *New York Times*, February 5, 1995

[Pataki has a voting record of] trying to deprive New York City.
> Comment on WABC Radio
> *New York Times*, September 24, 1994

George Pataki doesn't take positions that tell me what he's going to do as Governor of New York. I need to know; I'm not just a private citizen. . . . [He] has elected to have a campaign strategy that is to be nonspecific. . . . Essentially, the strategy is to kind of take up all of the vote that would be there, people who might be uncomfortable with Mario Cuomo. . . .

I think I'm exercising leadership by requiring the candidate to take positions that will help the people that I have the responsibility of serving. So far he hasn't done it. If he doesn't, my endorsement isn't there.
> Comment on WABC Radio, *N.Y. Times*, Sept. 24, 1994

The civics lecture continued with Giuliani scoring Pataki's votes to uphold a long-standing formula in state school aid that favored upstate areas, and shortchanged New York City by allocating it only 34 percent of education funding although it had 37 percent of the state's pupils.

Now he's a candidate for Governor. He has a right, as far as I'm concerned, to change his position if he wants. . . . He's now taking over broader responsibilities than just representing his district.
> Comment on WABC Radio, *N.Y. Times*, Sept. 24, 1994

A month later—after, among other things, canceling an appointment with Pataki while the nominee was made to cool his heels for an hour in the City Hall rotunda, in full view of the press—the Generalissimo dropped the hammer.

George Pataki's only essential characteristic is that he offers an alternative. Strangely, however, after lengthy analysis and a lot of soul-searching, I've come to the conclusion that it is George Pataki who best personifies the status quo of New York politics—a candidate taking as few positions as possible, all of them as general as possible, taking no risks and being guided and scripted by others. He has simply not made the case that he is the agent of change. . . .

I am well aware of the risk that I take as a Republican Mayor endorsing a Democratic Governor, but I've concluded that the risk is worth taking for the sake of the City of New York and the State of New York. . . .

[Pataki has] vacillated. See, Mario Cuomo is his own man. I prefer dealing with someone who is his own man, even if we disagree on some important issues. . . . I'm a Republican because I'm a Republican and I'd like to see my party produce candidates who can and will stand on their own.   *New York Times,* October 25, 1994

[It was] not a close choice.   *N.Y. Times,* October 26, 1994

The political world was momentarily turned upside down. Giuliani found himself standing under Cuomo's banner alongside liberal Democrats he had insulted and despised, while the national Republican Party, which had made so much of Giuliani's capture of City Hall, was appalled. But Giuliani made a point of noting that he was not switching parties (only putting his own personal agenda ahead of party loyalty).

I'm a Republican, I'm proud to be a Republican, and I support every other Republican candidate for statewide office other than the one for governor. And I support

Republicans in Massachusetts, in New Jersey. I've gone as far as Michigan to support Republicans.
New York Times, October 29, 1994

Pataki and D'Amato cried treason, and charged there was a backroom deal between the Democratic governor and the Republican mayor: more state dollars for the big Democratic city that upstaters love to hate.
There's never been a single discussion about anything in return. The suspicion of that comes from the way people view possibly the way Senator Pataki might operate, or Senator D'Amato. I operate differently from that. *New York Times,* October 29, 1994

Mr. Giuliani said it was Mr. Pataki who had struck a Faustian deal with his patron, Senator Alfonse M. D'Amato. The deal, the Mayor added, would turn a Pataki governorship into a shadow government for Mr. D'Amato. *New York Times,* October 30, 1994

By now not only endorsing Cuomo for reelection but hitting the campaign trail on behalf of the Democrat, Giuliani declared open war against Pataki and D'Amato—and began by burning his own bridges behind him.
Go ask Al if there were any deals, or did Al just do this because he's for good government? The reason that they're raising this is because that is the way they think. This is the way they operate. It's called projection.
New York Times, October 30, 1994

Mr. Giuliani criticized Mr. Pataki's proposal to cut taxes as "a shell game" that would hurt everyone in the state,

and he derided Mr. Pataki for showing a lack of leadership, even in the Republican Party.

New York Times, October 30, 1994

You have to be in some other state not to realize the Republican Party is in great dispute. That happens when there's a lack of leadership, or perhaps the wrong leadership. . . . [Pataki's campaign] makes people want to question those in the party who rammed him through. *New York Times*, October 31, 1994

In steadily escalating blows against Mr. D'Amato, Mr. Giuliani has taken to referring to the "D'Amato-Pataki" ticket. He has accused Mr. D'Amato of being a boss. And he has accused him of running a campaign of "hatred and anger." *New York Times*, November 6, 1994

Finally, on election eve, came the coup de grace—and the Generalissimo may have gone just a wee bit too far for his own good.

George Pataki is giving every indication that he will establish a government of D'Amato, for D'Amato, by D'Amato. If the D'Amato-Pataki crew ever gets control, ethics will be trashed. *New York Times*, November 6, 1994

Pataki had held the lead throughout the race, then faltered badly down the stretch—with Giuliani's attacks compounding the damage and sending his campaign reeling. The final polls showed Cuomo surging ahead. But a funny thing happened on election day: Upstate New Yorkers, apparently incensed by Giuliani's act of betrayal, turned out in numbers 13 percentage points higher than normal. When the votes were counted, George Pataki had won. Giuliani had not only failed to prevent

Pataki's victory; he may have caused it. Which meant that the new Governor of New York was not only a protégé of Al D'Amato, he was a man Rudy Giuliani had baited, taunted, demeaned, and publicly crossed. With the election over, New York City Democrats went back to opposing Giuliani. And Rudy Giuliani was alone and isolated, even in his own party.

George Pataki was the power now. Dogs instinctively understand what is to be done in such a situation. The smaller, lesser dog rolls over and bares its throat to what is thereby acknowledged to be the bigger, more powerful dog. Rudy Giuliani understood it too. He made a congratulatory phone call to Pataki. And was told the governor-elect would get back to him. And waited for the call to be returned. And waited. He waited four days.

Boy, they shouldn't make any mistake of the fact that I can be very, very outspoken and still have the opportunity to fight back very, very hard for New York City. If they try to hurt New York, they're not only going to be having to hear from me, but also all of the people who care about New York City. Once an election is over, well, my goodness. It's not enough having to go through it during election time. The very next moment you should get over it and then not worry about that stuff for four years. If they carry on with this partisan stuff, they're going to hurt themselves. *N.Y. Times,* Nov. 12, 1994

But he was unregenerate. The Republican National Committee announced it had dropped New York City from the list of possible sites for the next GOP National Convention.

The pettiest kind of partisan politics. . . . A lost opportunity. . . . This is something that would be good for the Republican Party, and here they're turning it down to make some petty point. *N.Y. Times,* Nov. 12, 1994

D'Amato announced he would fight to reverse the decision.

D'Amato would fight for the convention. Sounds like a big-hearted thing on the part of Al D'Amato—shows just how broad and big-spirited he is.
New York Times, November 17, 1994

(D'Amato, for his part, said of Giuliani on the Don Imus radio program, "I'm not going to squish him. He's going to squish himself. You leave the bug alone unless the bug is biting.")

Rudy Giuliani waited six days for his call to be returned.

The wonderful thing about following your conscience is that you can live with yourself however the decision comes out. . . . In my situation, a lot of people would say, the devil made me do it. I can't blame the devil. I did it myself. Remarks at Sunday services in an African American church, *New York Times,* November 14, 1994

Personally, I am not offended. But governmentally, when I called, I called as the Mayor of the largest city in the state and the economic engine that drives the state. *New York Times,* November 14, 1994

He waited nine days for his call to be returned.

Partisan political bickering in which they think they're hurting me, humiliating me, paying me back and all of those things which I think ultimately create a very bad impression of them in the minds of the public.
New York Times, November 17, 1994

And on the tenth day, he got a call—summoning him to be part of a public meeting with a dozen other elected officials. No private time with the governor-elect.

Mr. Giuliani . . . asserted today that Mr. Pataki's invitation was calculated to "embarrass the mayoralty." While accusing Mr. Pataki of "carrying on vendettas" and "political payback," the Mayor showed his pride. . . .

Mr. Giuliani said the only purpose of the meeting was to diminish the standing of the Mayor of the state's largest city. . . .

Mr. Giuliani suggested strongly today that Mr. Pataki was being manipulated by "the people around him."

New York Times, November 19, 1994

The fact is they've gotten away with one too many embarrassments, and I'm not going to let them get away with another one. So I'm not going to the meeting. And I'm not going to allow them to embarrass me or the mayoralty. It was done on purpose to do that.

New York Times, November 19, 1994

Mr. Giuliani said he had already made efforts to set up a one-on-one meeting with Mr. Pataki "in our own time and our own way." . . .

The Mayor alternately blamed Mr. Pataki for a failure of leadership, Mr. Pataki's aides for appearing intent on vengeance and the media for throwing fuel on the feud. If aides to the Governor-elect, rather than Mr. Pataki himself, were responsible for the slights, then Mr. Pataki should "discipline" them, Mr. Giuliani said.

New York Times, November 19, 1994

I want to get it over with. I want to move on and govern. I think the silly season should end, and we should all move on to the business of governing. I did that the minute the election was over.   *N.Y. Times,* Nov. 19, 1994

Mr. Giuliani said Mr. Pataki should agree to "a substantive, one-on-one meeting" with him to discuss issues, rather than continuing what the Mayor derided as "political shenanigans" and "childish behavior" by the Governor-elect and his aides.   *N.Y. Times*, Nov. 19, 1994

This is the silliest kind of political partisanship on the part of these people who are continuing to carry it on. And it's a little bit like bullies do: threat, threat, threat, threat, threat. They'll continue it until they realize it's hurting them more than it's hurting anyone else.
New York Times, November 19, 1994

And on the twenty-first day, it was decided that Generalissimo Giuliani's time-out had lasted long enough. He and the incoming governor had a meeting followed by what the *New York Times* described as a "coolly correct" appearance before the press.

The election is over. We both have very, very big responsibilities. I wished him the very best of luck and told him we wanted to work very closely with him to accomplish his objectives.   *N.Y. Times*, Nov. 30, 1994

In the aftermath of being made to contemplate political exile and oblivion, Rudy Giuliani got with the D'Amato-Pataki program. And, like a good Catholic, he made a heartfelt act of contrition. In fact, he made it so many times it began to sound like a mantra.

The alternative I was faced with was a very, very vague kind of program that didn't seem, at least then—I have different views of it now because I've been able to work with the Governor after he got elected—but didn't seem to understand the role that New York City plays.

Comments on *Firing Line*, PBS, *N.Y. Times*, Feb. 5, 1995

"No one lost out," . . . **Giuliani responded, saying that he and Pataki have established a "good working relationship."**
Response to query during on-line town meeting
New York Daily News, April 19, 1995

I think he is a hell of a Governor. If I had known George Pataki better, I would not have said those things. He is a very honest and independent person who is able to make his own decisions. He's handled his administration in a very honorable way. He's demonstrated right from the beginning that in making his decisions, he assesses the good of the entire state.
New York Times, February 2, 1996 (shortly after a joint appearance with Pataki on *Saturday Night Live*)

In fact, the Generalissimo became such a puppy dog to the new governor that, when Pataki came into office making huge slashes in the state's budget, Giuliani not only did not protest the cuts in spending on social services, he asked Pataki to cut make even deeper reductions in the Medicaid program than originally planned. And when Pataki began a shift of state agency offices (and up to 1,000 jobs) out of the city to Republican bastions upstate, he reacted thusly:

The Mayor and the Governor have probably worked out the best relationship that a Mayor and a Governor have had in a long time. We have worked very well together. . . . It really is the kind of thing you have to have the flexibility to do, if you run a state or run a city. I have to move jobs sometimes from one borough to another, because in fact you can save money, if it's more convenient and agencies are going to reorganize. And to pick on the Governor for this is not the best way to get the kind of help that the city needs. . . .

This is a Governor that has grown, I think, in office more than anyone I've seen in a short period of time. He understands what it means to be the governor of the entire state. . . . On the big issues, he came through for the city. . . . So on balance I would say he's been very fair to the City of New York. *N.Y. Times, Dec. 6, 1995*

And that business about "ethics will be trashed"?
That was an honest view I had at the time. Did it turn out that Governor Pataki was a better governor than I had expected? Yes. *N.Y. Times Magazine, August 1, 1999*

Mr. Giuliani said his 1994 remarks were "based upon a mistake I made in calculating how Governor Pataki would act, how Senator D'Amato would act."
New York Times, October 27, 1998

Well, gee, I was young. That was then and this is now. And I think Governor Pataki's done a terrific job. I think that the concerns that I had back in 1994, when I made that decision, turned out to be wrong.
New York Times, November 2, 1999

As for D'Amato, Operation Suck-Up pushed ahead on that front as well.
You have to be able to work with the people who want to work with you. Senator D'Amato has been very helpful to the City of New York. Every time I've called on him, in terms of our own personal relationship, in good times and bad, he's always been there for the City of New York. *New York Times, August 10, 1996*

But the senator, the governor, and the people around them had long memories. They would never turn their backs on Rudy

Giuliani again, they weren't buying his new apple-polishing act, and—especially when he got too fulsome about it—they did not bother to disguise their disgust. Such as the time when he took the podium at the 1998 GOP State Convention . . .

Now, I didn't get the relationship [with Governor Pataki] off to the best possible start. But he did. And that is to his great credit. This is a man who understands that public service is about improving the lives of people. *New York Times,* June 5, 1998

There hasn't been in the history of New York State a more effective Senator than Al D'Amato.
New York Times, June 5, 1998

Mr. Giuliani, who warned in 1994 that "ethics will be trashed . . . if the D'Amato-Pataki crew ever get control," yesterday described Mr. D'Amato as the most effective Senator in the history of New York, and said that Mr. Pataki had "more than earned my great admiration and respect." Many of the delegates sat in slack-jawed silence as Mr. Giuliani spoke. . . . Mr. Giuliani's welcoming speech was a minute longer than Mr. Pataki's acceptance speech. Asked how long Mr. Giuliani's speech was supposed to be, Zenia Mucha, the Governor's communications director, held up five fingers, and glanced with exasperation at the stage after the Mayor's speech. *New York Times,* June 5, 1998

. . . because, after all, the old Rudy was never far away. As in October, when a major campaign endorsement for Pataki—from the Reverend Calvin Butts, distinguished African American clergyman and community leader—was upstaged for twenty-four hours by Giuliani's demands that Pataki reject the endorsement because Butts had recently denounced Giuliani.

[Butts] plays the worst kind of racial politics. . . . If I were in Governor Pataki's position, I would refuse to take his endorsement. I would not take the endorsement of someone who throws the term "racist" as loosely as he does, and for such blatant political purposes. . . . [Butts uses] the word "racist" so loosely that it portrays something substantially wrong with him.

New York Times, October 12, 1998

A day later Rudy had been yanked back into line—again.
I think I'm entitled to my own personal view about somebody who viciously attacked me in a way that a minister shouldn't do. The Governor has a different relationship and a different set of views. . . . The Governor, I think, is doing a terrific job. I think Republican principles, both at the city and the state level, are responsible for the turn-around of the city and state. And I think that George Pataki deserves a lot of the credit for that. . . . There really is no question about the fact that I support the Governor. . . . You know, I speak my mind. It was that way yesterday. It's going to be that way today. It's going to be the same tomorrow.

New York Times, October 13, 1998

Pataki cruised to reelection easily. But D'Amato—despite Giuliani bringing his police commissioner to a last-minute rally on the senator's behalf, in violation of at least the spirit of NYPD prohibitions against political activity—went down to defeat at the hands of Democrat Chuck Schumer. D'Amato went into comfortable retirement as a quotable sage and lobbyist. Pataki—the protégé who had politically outlived his Svengali—remained. After the election, as both Pataki and Giuliani were mentioned as both presidential and vice-presidential timber on the 2000 Republican ticket, and Giuliani also began staking out a possible race for the U.S. Senate, the two men began getting in each other's way again. It seemed, up in Albany, that the uppity mayor had once again forgotten who was boss. And so the Generalissimo again had his attitude adjusted.

First, Pataki signed a bill pushed by the Patrolmen's Benevolent Association allowing state arbitrators, not ones from the city, to resolve contract impasses with City Hall, a bill the governor had vetoed as unconstitutional before and which had the potential to cost the city millions. Then he suddenly convened a panel to investigate construction problems in city schools, which were indeed in a scandalous state—thanks to a patronage-ridden public authority that was controlled not by the city but the state, whose Pataki-chosen chairman had just resigned under a cloud. Ah, but the power to create such a panel and make political mischief with it belongs to a governor, not a mere mayor.

I'm really at a loss to explain to you what the basis for it is. . . . Where does this go?   *N.Y. Times,* Jan. 24, 1999

O.K., have an investigation. But Buffalo's problems are significantly worse. Buffalo hasn't gone through any of the reforms we've gone through.
New York Times, February 3, 1999

Mayor Giuliani continues to slam Pataki's investigation as "destructive." *New York Daily News,* February 13, 1999

Then there was the matter of naming Joe DiMaggio Highway. The mayor wanted to give his friend, owner George Steinbrenner, a new Yankee Stadium on Manhattan's West Side. Pataki wanted that site for an expanded convention center and favored refurbishing the existing stadium in its historic Bronx home. After DiMaggio died in the winter of 1999, Giuliani immediately proposed renaming Manhattan's West Side

Highway—running right alongside his desired stadium site—for the Yankee Clipper. Pataki demurred, suggesting that the Major Deegan Expressway, leading to the *existing* stadium, be renamed for DiMaggio.

In the midst of this emerging Mexican standoff, a letter suddenly made the rounds in Albany, signed by the late DiMaggio's lawyer, claiming that DiMaggio himself had wanted the West Side road as his memorial and excoriating the governor for not agreeing to it. Pataki aides openly speculated that Giuliani was behind the letter.

It was all a misunderstanding, Giuliani said.

It baffles me to try to figure out why anyone would want to make this into a political dispute. There's no politics in this. This is out of respect for Joe DiMaggio, which the Governor and I both have. If someone got this confused, if someone tried to play into what they perceive as a political dispute, that's really very unfortunate. That was never my intention, nor was it the Governor's intention.
New York Times, March 17, 1999

Rudy got his way on renaming the highway, but when it came to the next tug-of-war he provoked, uh-uh. That was over who was supposed to contribute what to an expansion of the Museum of Jewish Heritage, a Holocaust memorial in Lower Manhattan. A press conference to announce the expansion had to be canceled at the last minute amid public accusations by Giuliani and his aides that the Pataki administration had agreed to split the $22 million cost with the city and had then backed out. (The state's version was that it was to donate the land for the expansion and the city the money.)

Whatever misunderstanding took place here, the end result is the State resents putting money in, will not put the money in, and the City is going to have to put all the money in. *New York Daily News,* February 5, 1999

Two months later, the Generalissimo saw the light.

In a statement released yesterday, the Mayor said he is "pleased to announce that the City will provide $22 million to fund the expansion of the Museum of Jewish Heritage."
New York Post, April 19, 1999

First and foremost, I want to thank Governor Pataki for his continuing commitment to this Museum and his support of the expansion project. *N.Y. Times,* April 19, 1999

Speaking at the [museum fund-raising] dinner, however, the Mayor made no mention of the Governor's contribution. *New York Times,* April 19, 1999

And so it goes. As Giuliani set his sights on the Senate, Pataki and D'Amato openly promoted the candidacy of a Long Island congressman as a rival to him in a GOP primary, then thought the better of it under pressure from national Republicans convinced that only Giuliani could beat First Lady Hillary Rodham Clinton for the seat—but not before D'Amato, now a lobbyist, was briefly barred from entering City Hall in retaliation. Pataki belatedly, reluctantly, warily endorsed Giuliani.

[I have] the utmost respect for Governor Pataki.
Letter to upstate New York GOP county chair
New York Daily News, March 20, 1999

I think he's been a very good governor.
New York Daily News, March 31, 1999

[Pataki is] a great governor.
Statement at GOP event where Pataki, with roughly equal sincerity, called Giuliani "the best Mayor the City has ever seen," *New York Times,* October 6, 1999

I think Governor Pataki is doing a good job in running not only the state but running the party. I think he has organized it correctly behind the candidate who has the best chance to win the Presidency.

> Statement at event at which Pataki and Giuliani both
> endorsed presidential candidacy of Texas Governor,
> George W. Bush, *New York Times*, October 19, 1999

And who did Generalissimo Giuliani suggest should be Bush's vice-presidential running mate? In an act of charity, he proposed none other than George Pataki.

I think Governor Pataki has the kind of record of leadership, the kind of philosophy, the kind of approach to government so he would be an excellent choice.

> *New York Times*, October 2, 1999

And what would that coincidentally do? Open the way for Rudy Giuliani to become governor—and finally become the most powerful Republican in the state. Which is where we came in. Stay tuned.

12

Rudy and the Press
("We Have the Most Open Administration in the History of the City"— and Other Howlers)

As United States Attorney, Rudolph Giuliani enjoyed an excellent relationship with the press. Indeed, for a prosecutor eager to make a name for himself, not overly concerned with ethical guidelines about prejudicial pretrial publicity, in sole possession of information that reporters craved, and for journalists desperate for a scoop, it was a match made in heaven.

But even then, some who covered Giuliani wondered if—with his near-obsessive determination to control his own image and everything that was written and said about him—he would be that eager to cultivate their friendship, or so forthcoming with answers to their questions, if he held another public office. A public office where he would find himself as often as not on the defensive, and where answering adversarial questions from prying reporters in front of glaring cameras came with the territory. An office such as mayor, for instance.

Within the first few months of Giuliani's administration, those apprehensions had been confirmed. Reporters accustomed to cultivating sources at all levels of city government and at various agencies were told that all statements had to come out of the mayor's Press Office. The Press Office began refusing to release even the most routine data—information that had historically been available as a matter of course to all those who worked in Room 9, the City Hall reporters' headquarters. The mayor, and his press secretary, directly intervened with editors to complain about stories, or to keep negative stories from being published, on a scale—and with an aggressiveness—the New York City media could not remember. And then there was the matter of the mayor's behavior at press conferences.

2 P.M. Time for the daily ritual in the Blue Room, which is crowded with reporters and 17 television cameras. "It's like going into the arena," Giuliani said. "I look forward to it." Today the reporters want to know once again why he is excluding [Cuban dictator Fidel] Castro and [PLO leader Yassir] Arafat [from official City ceremonies in conjunction with the United Nations' fiftieth anniversary].

"Some people," a reporter says, "think that if the party is financed by public money, then you have no right to exclude people, including Castro."

"Well," Giuliani replies, "some people think that, because you say that, but you're wrong."

"Why?"

"Why? Because you don't bother to check your facts, which is a very irresponsible thing to do."

"I'm asking you the—"

"Get your facts right in the premise of your question."

"I'm asking you to get the facts."

"No, you're not," Giuliani says, glaring at the reporter. "You asked the question, 'Some people think that'—the fact is, it [the event] is not funded by public dollars. The fact is that party is funded by private dollars."

Some of the foreign correspondents here for the celebrations appear startled to see the mayor lashing out at a mild-mannered reporter, but the regular press corps is nonchalant. It's used to much worse.

New York Times Magazine, December 3, 1995

Mayor Giuliani holds frequent news conferences. But he sometimes bridles when challenged by reporters. Once, according to reporters who were there, he walked out of a news conference after reporters pressed him about the administration's sensitivities toward racial minorities.

In what may be a classic example of the battle over how the Mayor's image is to be shaped, an aide later argued with one reporter whose article described the Mayor as angry, and Mr. Giuliani himself insists that he did not walk out. After a question had been asked three times, he said, he simply left. "I thought it was over," he said in the recent interview. "The question was asked a third time and I said, 'That's it.'" *N.Y. Times,* July 4, 1994

I've been accused of storming out of press conferences that I'd been at for 45 minutes. Maybe I just had to leave. Maybe I had to go to the bathroom. So I would say, "That's the last question," and walk out. The next day it would be written that I stormed out, or that I was bristling. It fits the stereotype.   *N.Y. Times,* Oct. 19, 1997

Daily News columnist Mike McAlary exposed possible shady dealings by a controversial Giuliani commissioner who, as a lawyer in private practice, had represented drug dealer clients.
Another scurrilous attack by a newspaper.
New York Daily News, April 3, 1996

The *Times* revealed that a neighborhood group with insider access to City Hall had been granted a city contract despite a spotty performance record and a proposal that was $8 million higher than the lowest bid.
That story is the lowest of the low.
March 1996 statement by Mayor Giuliani reacting to story. Requoted in *New York Daily News,* April 3, 1996

Even after being in power for six years, Generalissimo Giuliani still could not get used to the idea that, in a free society, a mayor—unlike a prosecutor—has to take it as well as dish it out. For instance, the opening question at his 1998 year's-end news conference was whether his administration had made New York "leaner and meaner."
I think that's an insulting question. Happy New Year. That's been a perception from the very beginning. It's something that you keep writing and I really don't give

a darn. I'm doing my job as well as I can do it. I think I'm taking New York City into the next century in much better shape than I found it. If people like my personality, thank you. If you don't, I really don't care.

New York Times, December 31, 1998

The Mayor went on to tell the assembled reporters . . . [that] "people don't care about a lot of the stuff you write about." *New York Times,* December 31, 1998

That is a terrible misconstruction of what I just said. And it makes the whole process of trying to communicate through you a very, very difficult one.

Statement to reporter at March 1999 press conference
New York Post, April 8, 1999

There's a difference between Khalid Muhammad and me, and if you can't figure it out, you probably shouldn't be in the journalistic profession. *Newsday,* Oct. 19, 1998

As Police Commissioner Howard Safir committed a series of ethical stumbles in the spring of 1999, Giuliani blamed the press for reporting Safir's transgressions:

I really do think that you are playing games with the Police Commissioner. I understand the game. It is a really cruel one and it's a nasty one and it's trying to go after somebody in public life. And it's really a shame that you do it and it's a shame that the media can't learn a little more discipline in the way they handle it. I am not angry, I am not lashing out. Somebody's going to write that tomorrow because no matter how calmly I say something, that's what you write. *N.Y. Times,* Apr. 13, 1999

And when, in the wake of the death of Amadou Diallo, a police officer was—with curious timing—dismissed immediately after testifying to a City Council hearing about abuses she said she had witnessed as a member of the Street Crimes Unit (four of whose officers had shot Diallo), the Generalissimo exploded:

The only thing suspect and outrageous here is the coverage in the newspaper that left out the background and facts about this particular police officer. I know you'll attack me and you'll misinterpret it and you're going to do it in your own way, but I'm going to say this most respectfully: the way you're attacking the Police Department is to the point of perversity, it really is.

New York Times, April 27, 1999

And why had not the NYPD itself released the "background and facts" the Generalissimo was complaining the story had omitted?

Because there's such a bias and prejudice in attacking the Police Department right now, they can't get information out that quickly. Because these reports are sitting in files, sometimes it takes a day or two to find them.

New York Times, April 27, 1999

Then there was the matter of his reaction to the State Legislature's overnight abolition of a commuter tax on suburbanites who worked in New York City—a minuscule sacrifice for the suburbanites, the repeal of which left a $360 million annual permanent shortfall in the city's budget. The Generalissimo was rightly infuriated at this blatant raid on the municipal treasury. But, months later, he was apparently no less irked by a headline (in his favorite paper, the *New York Post,* no less) that used the words "Rudy fumes" to describe his mood in the aftermath of the ripoff.

Stereotype! If you read the article, there's no quote attributed to me. I had no reaction. On Friday after-

**noon when this happened, I played golf with my son.
What happens here is they assumed my reaction,
because it's a stereotyped thing. Words like "fumed,"
"lashes out," "gets very angry," are applied when I
haven't any reaction at all.**

New York Times Magazine, August 1, 1999

And when *Newsday* noticed that a nonprofit fund that was
somehow run from inside a city office was featuring Giuliani as
the guest of honor at a number of its charity events just as
he was getting ready to announce his candidacy for the U.S.
Senate:

**It's probably one of the cheapest shots that newspaper
reporters can take . . . to tie everything into the Senate
campaign. . . . You know, every once in a while government does something good. This is a good thing. The
cynicism in this city should not overwhelm the holiday
season. . . . It's a shame to malign it. And when you lose
a sense of integrity, you lose everything.**

Newsday, December 28, 1999

The Generalissimo especially does not like it when members of the Fourth Estate engage in political "spin"—something, by the way, that he never engages in himself.

**The Mayor said that he felt no need to apologize "for an
unfair spin, or an erroneous spin, that somebody else
puts on the comments that I actually make. I learned a
long time ago in this business not to get spun into being
offended by the media when somebody didn't say or
intend what it is you're being spun around by."**

New York Times, January 20,1999

(Everybody get that? Good. Now, there will be extra points
on the exam for anyone who can successfully diagram that last
sentence.)

The Generalissimo attributed his problems with the press to their prevailing ideology.

I'm very different than they're used to. I'm the first Republican Mayor in a generation and a half and only the third or fourth in this century. That's really an unusual phenomenon. Many of the people in the press have a distrust of the Republican Party. Some of them have a hard time overcoming that. . . . Some of the criticism of my press and communications operation is that it is the press and communications operation of my administration, and not the press and communications operation of the administration they would like to have. *New York Times,* July 4, 1994

He attributed it to his preference for other than old-fashioned print-media technology.

The administration has also worked hard to find what Mr. Giuliani and his aides call "direct methods of communicating to the public." *New York Times,* July 4, 1994

In the past, the [Mayor's] Press Office was devoted to Room 9, but I ask something different. I pay significant attention to television and radio, and very often that may be the priority. For three or four minutes, people can see and hear me deliver my message, as opposed to reading "The angry Mayor said." They can see for themselves and decide for themselves whether or not I was angry. *New York Times,* March 24, 1995

Giuliani said yesterday he likes the electronic meetings because they are more "disciplined. You can actually get an answer out." Statement after holding first "on-line town meeting," *New York Daily News,* April 19, 1995

Or perhaps the problem was that the press simply didn't get it.

This administration, under this Mayor, is more open and accessible than any other. From his monthly town hall meetings to his weekly and monthly radio addresses to his daily visits to New York City neighborhoods, this Mayor is available to the people of the City of New York 24 hours a day, seven days a week.
Statement issued by Mayor's Press Office, *N.Y. Times*, Apr. 27, 1997

In recent weeks, the Mayor has described his administration as "an open book." *New York Times*, April 27, 1997

We have the most open administration in the history of the city. . . . The people of the city, I think, see a marked difference between this administration and the prior one with regard to the quality of life in the city. That happened because people working for this administration actually work. That requires not spending all of your time answering the press's questions. . . .

The commissioners speak to the press all of the time. But if they spent as much time speaking to the press as much as the press would like them to speak, the commissioners would not be able to do their jobs, and neither would anybody else in city government. . . . The Police Commissioner would spend all of his time answering questions and not reducing crime. The Parks Commissioner would be spending all of his time answering the press's questions instead of making the parks cleaner than they have been in the last 20 years, and so on and so on. *New York Times*, April 28, 1997

He said that most people would agree that his aides do a good job balancing their jobs and responding to

questions from news organizations. "The *Times* might not," he said with a laugh. "But I think the people of the city do." *New York Times*, April 28, 1997

This was around the time that, in response to all-too-frequent responses from Giuliani's administration that journalists should file Freedom of Information requests if they wanted to know the answer to even a basic question, the *Daily News* took the dare, took the mayor to court—and won, the first of many such losses Generalissimo Giuliani was to sustain in court over the next few years.

Mr. Giuliani asserted that his defeat was actually a victory, and he went on to rebuke in advance his critics in the news media. The press, he declared, "will undoubtedly report this story unfairly."

New York Daily News, April 28, 1997

Unfazed, the Generalissimo and his minions continued their pattern of forcing the media to sue under the Freedom of Information law, then appealing every defeat to the highest possible court, then finally obeying the court order and divulging the information—by which time, as they well knew when they adopted their strategy, the public's interest had frequently moved on to something else.

◆ The Cook, the Thief, His Wife, Her Lover, the Mayor, *His* Wife, and His Communications Director

If there was one decision that said everything about the kind of relationship Rudy Giuliani wanted to have with the news media, it was his choice of a press secretary.

Cristyne Lategano was twenty-nine, had worked on a handful of Republican campaigns out of state, and served as the backup press spokesperson during his 1993 campaign.

During her first interview with Giuliani in 1993, she is said to have impressed the future Mayor in part because of her firm grip on Yankee baseball trivia. "She is a real Yankees fan," Giuliani said last week, "and I can usually tell the difference." *New York Daily News,* June 6, 1999

Initially, she got the top job only because the No. 1 campaign press aide preferred to return to his native Philadelphia after the election was over. Even then, it was a month before she was confirmed in the post—and then only because she leaked the news herself.

The morning line on Lategano, among both reporters and coworkers, was: A novice in over her head. Way over her head. But their opinion, ultimately, was not what mattered. After a shaky shakedown cruise, Lategano's power suddenly began to grow. And her rep and persona underwent an almost-instant makeover—into that of a snide, cocky, snarling postadolescent fully confident that brashness was going to prove a perfectly adequate substitute for brains. And why not? After all, she was a snide, cocky, snarling postadolescent with power. Power in the form of a blank check from, and unlimited access to, Generalissimo Rudy Giuliani.

It was Lategano who gratuitously insulted, to their faces, reporters who had forgotten more about the news business than she had ever learned. No matter. It was Lategano who was caught red-handed planting a false story attempting to smear David Dinkins's last commissioner of Youth Services. No harm, no foul. It was Lategano who committed the ultimate no-no for a press secretary, bragging to *New York* magazine how she had gotten *Times* editor Joyce Purnick to kill a story—publicly embarrassing a veteran journalist who had done her a favor and who would have a myriad of opportunities to get even. No problem. It was Lategano who was the principal beneficiary of the wave of mass firings that decimated city agency press offices in February 1995, with all public affairs operations throughout city government now centralized under her direct authority. It was Lategano who was held in such low esteem by the press corps that, at their annual Inner Circle musical-comedy revue, she was lampooned as "Cristyne Lotta-guano, the Queen of Denial," only to have Giuliani take the stage for his traditional rebuttal and hold up the proceedings to deliver an emotional testimonial to her. If David Garth, the media consultant who had orchestrated Giuliani's winning race in 1993, didn't like the power she had acquired, he could quit—which Garth did. If Peter Powers, the mayor's lifelong buddy and first deputy mayor, didn't like it either, he could leave City Hall—which Powers did.

Mr. Giuliani defends his press secretary, saying that he doesn't care whether she pleases reporters, only "whether we are delivering our message to the people of the city. . . . I think she's doing a terrific job."

New York Times, March 24, 1995

The Mayor then offered a spirited defense of Lategano, starting with her development of a press strategy in the early months of his first term that allowed him to bypass the City Hall press corps by relying heavily on radio interviews. "That was all Cristyne," said Giuliani.

New York Daily News, June 6, 1999

For months, Cristyne F. Lategano, press secretary to Mayor Rudolph W. Giuliani, has shared the hard times with her boss, becoming an object of resentment by

**reporters and editorial writers chafing under her
intensely protective style. Yesterday, the Mayor provided
her with his response to the criticism: a promotion.**

New York Times, April 1, 1995

The promotion was to communications director, getting
Lategano out of daily contact with reporters while giving her
an office directly below Giuliani's—and a $25,000 raise. With
typical tackiness, Lategano explained—on the record—that
the city could afford her 32.5 percent pay hike during a time of
fiscal austerity because it was funded from the salaries of Press
Office employees she had fired.

**[She has] done a remarkable job in conveying the mes-
sage of an administration that, whether you've noticed
it or not, has made more change in this city in 16
months than I think has ever been the case before, with
the possible exception of the first 16 months of Fiorello
LaGuardia. The people of the city know that, and I
know that because I talk to the people of the city probably more often than any other mayor.**

New York Times, April 1, 1995

Meanwhile, there was another woman who, in the view of
many, had been of inestimable help to Giuliani in humanizing
his image and getting him elected—his wife, television
anchorwoman Donna Hanover. Hanover had, among other
things, made a particularly effective TV spot answering negative ads run by the Dinkins campaign against her husband in
the thick of the 1993 battle.

But, as the Generalissimo ran for reelection, his wife was
nowhere to be seen.

**She does a division that I think is appropriate. She acts
as the First Lady on things that have to do with chari-
ties, schools and hospitals, but she would not come to a**

Giuliani fund-raiser. It's not a big issue in the campaign. I think voters make common-sense judgments. The thing they should be concerned about is, are you doing the job? The rest is just background and general interest.

Interview with columnist Maureen Dowd
New York Times, July 12, 1997

I think people have a right to speculate, and I have the ability to conduct myself in a way I think is dignified. Exploiting my private life is something I've never done. You have to have part of your life that's private. That belongs to me. It doesn't have anything to do with my work. Interview with columnist Maureen Dowd
New York Times, July 12, 1997

Not unreasonable sentiments, except for the fact that once upon a time Rudy Giuliani had been willing to be quite frank about his private married life in public. Specifically, on the day he was inaugurated:

To my wife Donna, my partner, my inspiration and my lover. Donna is one of three people I believe most responsible for my standing here.

First Inaugural Address, *New York Times,* January 3, 1994

By 1997, however, he was no longer referring to his wife as "my lover." And she was no longer referring to herself as "Donna Hanover Giuliani"—on the air or off—let alone appearing at public events with her husband, political or otherwise. Finally, that summer, *Vanity Fair* magazine went public with the rumors that had been swirling through the media, and political circles, for nearly three years. Quoting anonymous sources from within the administration itself, it claimed the reason for Lategano's meteoric rise was that Giuliani's interest in her was not merely professional: It was also sexual.

The story is false, the story is insupportable, and it's patently based on unnamed sources, so I would expect that they're having real problems because they should never have written that story in the first place.

You have no decency. My private life is mine. It's mine.

Comments to press after publication of *Vanity Fair* article. Requoted in *Editor & Publisher*, October 25, 1997

The best thing for me to say about the article is, it's untrue, it's false, it's based on unnamed sources who are malicious, and I'm not going to say anything else about it. I think that to talk about it any more than that gives it a status it surely doesn't deserve. The best thing that can be done with this article, as far as I'm concerned, is that it can be thrown in the trash.

. . . I think people judge you on the kind of job you're doing. And there are people who think I'm doing a very good job, and people who think I'm not.

New York Times, August 5, 1997

In the end, the Lategano-Giuliani allegations were what gamblers call a "push"—no bets are paid, everybody gets their wager back. *Vanity Fair* failed to offer a clear and convincing case that Lategano and the Generalissimo had had an affair. And Rudolph Giuliani was never able to offer a clear and convincing case that Cristyne Lategano was in any way qualified—by temperament, experience, or intellect—for the unprecedented power she had been granted over the public-information apparatus of the largest municipal government in the United States of America. Donna Hanover did not divorce her husband—though she pointedly refused to tell reporters whether she had even voted for his reelection and stressed that they were staying together as "a family" rather than a couple. And in January 1999, Cristyne Lategano was given expanded duties, more power—and a raise to $130,000.

Then, a few months later, shortly after the mayor and his wife were noticed dancing in public together at a wedding reception (and as he readied himself for a U.S. Senate campaign that would not be helped with upstate voters if beset by rumors of marital woes and sex scandals), there emanated this sudden announcement from the Mayor's Office: Cristyne Lategano was taking a mysterious, indefinite leave of absence.

Her contributions to the Giuliani Administration have been immeasurable, and we respect her decision and welcome her back whenever she wants.

New York Times, May 28, 1999

Explanations were not forthcoming. Unlike in the late Soviet Union, Comrade Lategano was not promptly airbrushed out of all Giuliani-era historical photos—but neither did she return. Instead, she landed on her feet when, with Giuliani's intercession, the New York Convention & Visitors Bureau (to hoots of derision from a press corps no longer cowed by her) named her as its executive director.

This is an excellent opportunity for the Convention and Visitors Bureau to have the leadership necessary for marketing New York City around the world. Cristyne has demonstrated an extraordinary ability to communicate the renaissance of New York City, not just in New York City but throughout the world.

New York Times, August 25, 1999

Her new salary: $150,000 (or $15,000 less than her predecessor). "I could not live with myself making more than him," Lategano gushed, explaining that she had

once lived out of a suitcase while working as a Republican Party advance person. The experiences, she says, gave her insight into business travelers' needs.
New York Times, September 17, 1999

Mr. Giuliani said that thanks in part to Ms. Lategano, he is the "best-known Mayor in the world," credited with transforming a "basket case into the Renaissance city of the world." *New York Times*, September 17, 1999

I feel we're making a very strong appointment. . . . We're not making her the medical examiner.
New York Times, September 17, 1999

The pinnacle of Cristyne Lategano's prior experience in the private sector: shoe-store sales clerk.

13

Rudy on the Radio

Upon taking office as mayor, Rudy Giuliani was offered an hour-long call-in show every week on a local all-talk radio station, WABC. The show quickly became Giuliani's imperial chat room–cum–sounding board, in which the Generalissimo felt free to rap with his constituents, scold them, put them in their place, and offer them his advice (sometimes solicited, sometimes not) on what they had to do to solve their problems and make their lives better. Here are a few choice tidbits from Rudy's six years as a part-time "shock jock."

To Jim, who called from his car to protest his endorsement of Mario Cuomo for governor against his fellow Republican George Pataki:

JIM: First of all, I've got to talk for myself, but also a large contingency [*sic*] of my own people that are very disappointed in you for backing Mario Cuomo. But that's your business. I think you turned your back on some people who got you there in the first place. And you're, uh, I say we were very disappointed.

RUDOLPH W. GIULIANI: Well, I've got to tell you, you can be disappointed. You're entitled to that. But I haven't turned my back on anybody.

JIM: Well, you have—

R.W.G.: Well, you think I have—

JIM: Bob Grant. You have turned your back on Bob Grant—

R.W.G.: I haven't—

JIM: . . . who went out on a limb for you.

R.W.G.: But there are a lot of people who went out on a limb for me who support Mario Cuomo. And, and—

JIM: O.K., you think about it tonight.

R.W.G.: No, no, I want to answer the—no, wait, wait, you're not going to get to take that shot at me without my answer.

JIM: Yeah, fine.

R.W.G.: O.K. The fact is that when I ran for Mayor, including on Bob's show, I said over and over again that I wouldn't be the Republican or the Democratic Mayor of New York City—

JIM: (Laughs)

R.W.G.: You think that's funny? What I said is funny?

JIM: Yeah, I think it's very funny because—

R.W.G.: Well, I think you have to give—

JIM: You do a good snow job, Mr. Giuliani.

R.W.G.: Well, I think you're very disrespectful.

JIM: Listen, let me—

R.W.G.: So, I'm going to cut this call off. We'll talk to someone else who can act like a respectful person. I don't laugh at you. There's no reason for you to laugh at me. Thank you, Jim. Continue to drive safely.

Transcript released by WABC. Published in *N.Y. Times*, Oct. 29, 1994

To Bill from Manhattan, who wanted to know why it was illegal for private citizens to fly flags on city property:
Isn't there something more important that you want to ask me? *New York Times*, August 21, 1999

To Tony from The Bronx, who questioned his handling of the NYPD's fatal shooting of Amadou Diallo:
Either you don't read the newspapers carefully enough or you're so prejudiced and biased that you block out the truth. *New York Times*, August 21, 1999

To Margarita Rosario, whose son was shot and killed by NYPD detectives and who had continued to protest even after the police were exonerated, he offered these soothing words of comfort:
Maybe you should ask yourself some questions about the way he was brought up and the things that happened to him. Trying to displace the responsibility for the criminal acts of your son onto these police officers is really unfair. . . . Didn't your son have a criminal record of violence? . . . We have a real hard time in New York City and elsewhere asking these questions, so we displace responsibility to other things . . . escaping the more painful questions that need to be asked. Now, we are going to go to Meshulam in Brooklyn.

WABC Radio, July 16, 1999
Requoted in *New York Times*, August 21, 1999

To a caller who began by saying "I don't want to complain":
Ahhhhhhhh, come on: complain! That's what I'm here for.   *Washington Post,* June 30, 1999

To a caller who did complain—about the city's ban on people keeping ferrets as pets:
There is something deranged about you. . . . You need somebody to help you. I know you feel insulted by that, but I am being honest with you. This excessive concern with little weasels is a sickness. I'm sorry, that's my opinion. You should go consult a psychologist or a psychiatrist with this excessive concern—how you are devoting your life to weasels. There are people in this city and in this world that need a lot of help. Something has gone wrong with you.   *N.Y. Times,* Aug. 21, 1999

About Brooklyn Borough President Howard Golden, a former ally who had fallen out of Giuliani's favor and who was refusing to support the Generalissimo's plan to build a stadium for a low-level minor-league baseball team in Brooklyn (Golden was holding out for a higher-level franchise):
Can you believe that the Borough President of Brooklyn is opposing it? You gotta get your head examined (laughing). Man, am I going to get in trouble for that one. We're going to have all sorts of things now. . . . The whole etymology of the phrase will be examined now.
New York Post, June 19, 1999

Then there was the man who called Giuliani on the air one day after being acquitted of criminal charges (stemming from a bad habit of leaving threatening messages for the mayor's Press Office staff on the office voicemail overnight):
Get off the phone, you crazy nut! I don't like you. I think you're perverse. I think the jury made a terrible

mistake in acquitting you. And leave the women who work in this office alone. . . . I'm convinced there is something seriously wrong with him. Because a normal person doesn't do this. You don't start harassing somebody on the telephone and get involved in this kind of sick, compulsive behavior.

. . . [Juries] become delighted with perversion or irrationality. . . . If they weren't able to convict him in court, I'll do it myself in terms of a civil lawsuit. Sue me for defamation; sue me for slander. I'll prove that he's engaging in conduct that is really, really sick conduct. And now, let's move on to Ben in Brooklyn.

New York Times, September 17, 1999

To an argumentative caller named Anthony:
The problem you have is your view of the world is so prejudicial that the facts will not get in the way of it. . . . Ah, you just don't like me, Anthony, no matter what I did you'd be upset! Anthony, you are so filled with anger and hatred at me. Take some Valium, Anthony! Anthony, calm down, baby! Take it easy. *N.Y. Post,* Oct. 9, 1999

At times, the Generalissimo was willing to dispense the psychological counseling himself:
There is a lot of complexity here, a lot of deep psychological fears that people don't understand and therefore can't be put on the table. We have to be more open, we can't be so rigid. *Washington Post,* June 30, 1999

And one of those complex issues: doo-doo.
Mr. Giuliani recently began asking listeners to experiment with his brand of therapy on a particularly troublesome group of New Yorkers: the ones who don't clean up after their dogs. Such people tend to have "a

whole host of other problems that play out in their personalities," the Mayor said on yesterday's program.

New York Times, August 21, 1999

I get angry about this all the time. When I was a private citizen I would go up to people and tell them they were slobs. Actually, I think I've done it as the Mayor a couple of times. I would just walk up to them and say, "You're a real slob and you're disrespectful for the rights of other people, clean up after your dog, damn it." Now you know, I don't recommend this in all situations. You may walk up to the wrong person and who knows, you might get a punch in the nose or something like that. But if you feel capable of doing that, this is really something that people have to learn in society.   *New York Times,* August 21, 1999

And why did these lectures to his callers matter so much? In an interview, the Generalissimo offered some guidelines.

Having these conversations in private doesn't do any good in placing out there the other side of the story. If you believe in the search for truth, people have to be able to see the biases and prejudices and the irrational problems that are affecting somebody's point of view.

New York Times, August 21, 1999

14

The Generalissimo in General
(Rudy's Rare Moments of Introspection)

I'm a leader, not a follower. I can see, like, three steps ahead.   *New York Times,* October 9, 1998

People come to me and say—and it's probably exaggerated—you're the first politician who actually did what he promised.   *New York Times*, June 8, 1996

The Mayor insists that he rarely even thinks about partisan politics and that when he speaks out, he does so only in the interests of the city. [I] spend "99 percent of my time on the substantive issues of governing."
New York Times, June 8, 1996

When I'm there, I work 24 hours a day. I think my work week's gone from 90 hours a week to 85. I don't think there's any risk that the people of New York City are going to worry about how hard I'm working. You go find anyone who works as hard as I do and introduce them to me.   Statement made while on trip to Pennsylvania
New York Times, October 14, 1998

Even though he's very busy, Mayor Giuliani makes time to do the [weekly radio] show. . . .
    After all, he can't be everywhere all the time—even though he'd like to be! These [staff] meetings help Mayor Giuliani solve problems quickly and effectively [ih-FEK-tiv-lee]. . . .
    Mayor Giuliani won two four-year terms. In that time, he has worked hard to cut crime and create new jobs. He loves being Mayor and that he is able to make a difference in people's lives.
Reading aloud to class at P.S. 234 from *A Day in the Life of a Mayor*, a schoolchildren's primer by Liza N. Burby
New York Times, October 14, 1998

I like the idea of being a figure that is straight with people. I think that I play a useful role by being direct.
New York Times Magazine, August 1, 1999

I follow a very, very strict rule. I'll tell the people of the city what I believe is in the best interests of the city, what I think is the truth, rather than what I think people would like to hear. *N.Y. Times,* Dec. 30, 1994

I think that where political power remains in somebody's hands for a very, very long period of time, it's the rare individual who doesn't become personally corrupt. *New York Times,* January 16, 1988

People make the most mistakes sometimes when they feel too powerful and too strong and that they are kind of, like, on top of the world. *N.Y. Times,* Nov. 12, 1994

I'm not a politician by profession. . . . I have a theory that you should not get involved in politics until after you've done something else with your life. If you get involved in politics at a young age, you lose any sense of substance and can't accomplish anything except public relations. The city is used to politicians who submit to whatever is the safest thing to do or the safest way to say it. I think the city needs to be broken of that. *New York Times Magazine,* December 3, 1995

People elected me to change things. They didn't elect me to become part of the traditional apparatus of City government. *New York Times,* December 30, 1994

I got elected to be a leader, not a panderer. Associated Press, October 19, 1997

Leadership is not about polls. *New York Daily News,* May 3, 1999

I don't let other people set my agenda.
New York Times, December 10, 1999

I have a broad message for everyone. I don't believe in the philosophy of segmenting the city into this subgroup or that subgroup and some other subgroup, and having issues for this community and issues for that community.
New York Times, October 18, 1997

He says he is the only person in town willing to take on the special interests. The words "courage" and "guts," applied to himself, have entered his vocabulary at almost every public appearance.

Every other politician in the city, he said, excepting no one, has gone "into the tank for the special interests."
New York Times, October 19, 1995

The biggest and largest special interest group in the city is the intellectual establishment. New York is a great intellectual center that has become one of the most backward parts of America—unwilling to think a new thought. I absolutely love, and maybe I overdo this a little, to suggest something new and then watch the reaction to it, but I love to watch the reaction from the so-called intellectuals. The thinking establishment goes into convulsions over the idea that we could ask people on welfare to work, or that we should fingerprint them to prevent fraud. It's almost as if a secular religion had developed in which these are the things you must believe to be considered an educated, intelligent and moral person.   *New York Times Magazine,* December 3, 1995

◆ On His Personality

If my city doesn't work, I don't like the Mayor. It doesn't matter if I like him or I don't like him, I don't want him as the Mayor. If my city is getting better, and my life is getting better, and my children's lives are getting better, then I don't really care whether I like the Mayor or don't like the Mayor, he's a good Mayor.

New York Times, January 14, 1999

It's all in the eye of the beholder whether you're nice or not nice. My father used to say, "It's more important that you respect me than that you love me. And later on in life you can love me."

Interview with columnist Maureen Dowd, *New York. Times,* July 12, 1997

My father used to say, "The first thing that's important— you respect me. The rest you'll understand."

New York Times, June 9, 1988

Don't interrupt me!

Statement made to former mayor Ed Koch during phone conversation, October 1994
New York Times, June 26, 1995; also December 3, 1995

In one of our conversations, I asked the Mayor if he had ever regretted any of the missiles he launched over the years. He pondered for quite a while, apparently running through a list that ran well into the dozens. Finally, he shook his head, and said, "No."

Writer James Traub in profile of Mayor Giuliani
New York Times Magazine, August 1, 1998

You weren't listening.

Giuliani to Traub, shortly afterward in same conversation, on being asked if his recent treatment of the city schools chancellor constituted bullying
New York Times, August 1, 1999

I try to be polite. I don't always succeed.

Associated Press, May 24, 1998

In New York, you have to be a fighter.

New York Times, October 19, 1997

Why am I a bully? I'm very passionate about the job that I do as Mayor. I expect very, very high performance out of people. Sometimes I get impatient when things aren't happening fast enough, and sometimes maybe I even require more of people than is realistic or more of myself than is realistic, but I think I'm a pretty nice guy. [General laughter.]

Transcript of statement made at candidates' debate
New York Times, October 30, 1997

◆ On Compromise vs. Confrontation

My administration never compromises on matters of principle. *New York Times,* July 12, 1999

I think I end up in more controversies because I have an agenda that is different than the political establishment of the city and the people who represent the city have had for a number of years. If you are proposing things that there are a significant group of political figures in the city who have consistently throughout their

career opposed, they're going to oppose you when you do it.
New York Times, April 1, 1997

There's no way I could have won most of these battles without being confrontational.
New York Times Magazine, August 1, 1999

Politics is not all about harmony. . . . In a negotiating process, you've got to be willing to take the heat for a while to get to the final result. . . .

I'm a Republican Mayor in a city that is heavily Democratic, and there is at least one house of the Legislature that's heavily Democratic. The fact is that at times, in order for me to build up public support, I've got to make an issue public. I've got to get public opinion to work on the people that oppose a particular change. . . .

Sometimes you have to let some of the battling go on. Then there's a time, when everyone's made their point, where you have to figure where are we going to agree on this, and what really makes sense. . . .

Maybe the style is a little different, but the results end up almost always happening. And almost always they end up harmonious. But not all the time.
New York Times, June 20, 1995

Almost everything that I've accomplished, I've achieved by getting other people to agree that this had to be done. I think sometimes there are confrontations. Most of them get resolved. And then nobody pays attention to the resolution of them.   *New York Times,* June 25, 1995

I don't know that I have a choice. The only way I could be less combative would be if I would compromise more. If I compromised more I would achieve less. . . . Well, maybe sometimes I do it wrong. Sometimes you don't intuitively or rationally figure out exactly the right way to approach it.   *N.Y. Times Magazine,* Dec. 3, 1995

♦ On Freedom—and Authority

We look upon authority too often and focus over and over again, for 30 or 40 or 50 years, as if there is something wrong with authority. We see only the offensive side of authority.
Remarks at forum sponsored by *New York Post*
New York Times, March 20, 1994

Freedom is not a concept in which people can do anything they want, be anything they can be. Freedom is about the willingness of every single human being to cede to lawful authority a great deal of discretion about what you do and how you do it.
Remarks at *New York Post* forum, *New York Times,* March 17, 1994; also March 20, 1994 and October 19, 1997

♦ On Government

At the core the struggle is philosophical. There are many, many things that can be done with law enforcement to protect us better. There are many things that can be done to create a government that is more responsive and more helpful. The fact is that we're fooling people if we suggest to them the solutions to these very, very deep-seated problems are going to be found in government.
Remarks at *New York Post* forum
New York Times, March 20, 1994

On one side you have people who philosophically believe government has no role, and on the other side you have people who believe government should run people's lives. I try to fall somewhere in the middle. I try to figure out where government can be helpful. Sometimes government has to run people's lives because nobody will help them, but you should try to keep that to a minimum.   *New York Times,* July 17, 1997

◆ On the Use of Power

It was a calculated decision. I can't believe they won't go along because they can't live for the next year if they don't do the feast. I think they'll have to do it under our conditions.

> Commenting on his threat against Little Italy's San Gennaro Festival that he would shut the nine-day celebration down unless, as part of his effort to root out organized-crime influence on the festival, it agreed to outside fiscal monitors imposed by him
> *New York Times Magazine,* December 3, 1995

◆ On Criticism

As you get used to this job, you realize that some of the things that would get you upset when you started don't really matter. Maybe in 1994 I would have gotten really upset about it; I would think that this was going to form everyone's opinion about me forever. The only thing that still upsets me is when people question your integrity or your honesty; even there I've learned most people don't really accept it. So you end up having a much more philosophical approach. If I had known that five or six years ago, I could have spared myself a lot of effort.   *New York Times Magazine,* August 1, 1999

The perception [of him created by the media] often works to his advantage, the Mayor added, because when people met him, they say, "Oh my God, he's very different from what I thought."
                                   New York Times, October 19, 1997

I don't regard associations of my people that support me as fascists as a light matter. . . . But it's ultimately the results that matter.   *New York Times,* June 24, 1998

I take a different view of someone comparing me to Adolf Hitler than when someone calls me a jerk.
                              New York Daily News, October 25, 1998

◆ On Dissent (the In-Your-Face Variety)

Freedom isn't really very useful if people are yelling and screaming at each other and not listening to each other and not being respectful of the fact that we can completely disagree with each other.
     Comment about AIDS activist hecklers who disrupted Lower
              East Side town meeting, *N.Y. Times,* April 13, 1994

Now, you owe it to me to listen to my answers. You may disagree with it, but you've got to listen to the answers. Shouting and screaming is not the way for intelligent people to talk to each other.
        Statement while being shouted down at town meeting on
        West Side of Manhattan, *New York Times,* March 9, 1995

You should be able to march as the Mayor of New York City anyplace you want, and if people can't deal with their own anger over that, that's really something emerging from them, from inside them.

Comment after being booed at Gay Pride Parade
New York Times, June 28, 1999

Anger directed at public officials is really anger at yourselves. The kind of anger here is not really anger directed at me. Comment after being booed at Gay Pride Parade, *N.Y. Daily News*, June 28, 1999

Everybody is angry at me. That's why I'm a good Mayor.
Answer to heckler during public audience held at
Bishop Loughlin High School, Giuliani's alma mater
New York Post, May 20, 1998

Anyone who interrupts will be removed. . . . This tactic doesn't work with me. We really don't want to discuss a group therapy session.
Statement while public appearance is disrupted by AIDS
activists, *New York Daily News*, December 9, 1999

◆ On His Management Style

My theory of management is that for the first year you run as much of everything as you can, because you learn, and you learn not only your own strengths and weaknesses, but the strengths and weaknesses of the people around you. Then you delegate more once you know that. *New York Times*, December 30, 1994

- On His New Year's Resolution: Sharing the
Credit with Team Rudy

**"Some of those people don't get as much attention as
they deserve," said the Mayor, who is not known for
sharing the spotlight with members of his government.
"Maybe that will become my resolution: see if I can
have them get more attention. Because they deserve it.
They're doing an invaluable job."**

New York Times, December 31, 1998

15

Rudy's Rib-Ticklers
(or, The Generalisimo's Sometimes-Jarring
Sense of Humor)

Giuliani even produced a chart showing that prices at the
Fulton Fish Market have dropped an average of 6.5 percent—
bluefish, the mayor's favorite, was down 8.4 percent—since
the administration tackled the mobsters who once controlled
the market.
**"I didn't believe I'd ever do a chart on fish," the Mayor
chuckled.** *New York Post,* February 11, 1998

It has been said that people's sense of humor—what makes
them laugh, how they joke, and what they choose to joke
about—reveals clues to the inner workings of their minds. If
that is so, take a trip now into the deepest recesses of the personality of Rudolph W. Giuliani. And judge for yourselves.

For instance, there are the "Godfather" impersonations he never gets tired of doing.

He frequently entertains listeners with a less-publicized talent: a raspy-voiced imitation of Don Vito Corleone, the ruthless and brash patriarch played by Marlon Brando.

"It's nice of all youse to be here," Mr. Giuliani said, Brando-like, at a staff meeting in November. "Some of you come from the Upper West Side. Some from the East Side. We even got some people here from the Bronx." *New York Times,* January 1, 1998

Then there have been his performances at the annual Inner Circle show (given in rebuttal to the City Hall press corps' lampoon of him and others in officialdom), which have become increasingly weird and self-indulgent. In 1997, for instance, he chose to stage a skit with the cast of the cross-dressing Broadway musical *Victor/Victoria.*

. . . No one was fully prepared for the sight of New York City's brawling Mayor as he tottered onto the New York Hilton stage Saturday night in high heels, a full-figured spangled pink gown, a platinum-blond wig and several pounds of makeup. . . .

But in his newfound incarnation as Rudia, a transvestite nightclub singer, the Mayor even sang a falsetto version of "Happy Birthday, Mr. President"—a la Marilyn Monroe—and waved daintily at the crowd of thunderstruck spectators. . . .

It is believed to be the first time any New York City mayor has appeared in public in drag. (Historians are welcome to try to dig up other examples.) . . .

The audience of journalists, public officials and lobbyists greeted Rudia with a huge outburst of applause and hoots of sustained laughter, but when it became

clear that the Mayor was actually going to deliver a sustained performance in the outfit, members of the crowd seemed torn between being amused and being appalled.

When he pulled a huge cigar stock out of his sock, and later began dancing an intimate tango with the star of "Victor/Victoria," Julie Andrews (dressed as a man), several well-known audience members could be seen with their foreheads in their hands, open-mouthed.

The wonder only increased when Roxane Barlow of the show's cast sang a gyrating hymn to the sexual attributes of several recent mayors while watching Mr. Giuliani disrobe behind a screen.

. . . Mr. Giuliani remarked that he is "a Republican pretending to be a Democrat pretending to be a Republican." . . .

In a demonstration of their unquestioned loyalty to their boss, most of the Mayor's top staff members also appeared in drag. . . . But it was the image of Mr. Giuliani in lipstick and mascara that most people carried out of the room with them.

"I'm supposed to have a meeting with him in a few days," said one high-ranking City Council official. "I don't know if I can go through with it."

New York Times, March 3, 1997

Or how about the time he was addressing a fund raiser for the Urban League, and figured the way to break the ice with the African American group was this opener about a subject he was sure black people would find funny:

The applause is polite; but he's late and he's not staying long. "I want to apologize for leaving early. It's very, very hard for me to get a cab."

Dead silence.

"You think I'm kidding? Have you ever tried to hail a cab in New York?"

Deader silence. It's not clear that Hizzoner, who is engaged of late in a little recreational pounding of the taxi industry, realizes that most of the people in the room have been shunned by some cabby somewhere.

"I put up a finger to hail a cab and the cabby puts up a finger, too. But it's a different finger."

He waits for the laughs that aren't coming.

Washington Post, June 30, 1999

When his second inaugural address was briefly disrupted. . . .

The Mayor drew laughs from the crowd at the protesters' expense. "Oh, that's very nice," Mr. Giuliani said as police officers led the people away. "We'll find out exactly what they're protesting. Sometimes you don't find out until a day or two later." *N.Y. Times,* Jan. 2, 1998

When he began his second term with an all-out assault against "quality-of-life" offenses, which struck even some of his supporters as heavy-handed, he had a quick quip at the ready:

I have to leave here to give out some jaywalking tickets.

Associated Press, May 10, 1998

When he crossed a picket line while on a visit to Washington:

I felt right at home. *New York Times,* November 10, 1999

Ingratiating himself to an audience of pro-GOP conservatives, he brought down the house with:

We have 412 expressionless statues in Central Park. You have Al Gore.

Speech given at invitation of *American Spectator* Magazine, Washington, D.C., *N.Y. Times,* November 10, 1999

Conducting a briefing while standing before a slide-show screen chart as he pressed his case for an ill-fated revision of the city charter, he was struck by this flight of fancy:

I'm actually trying to create a shadow—that's the whole idea of this. *New York Times,* October 26, 1999

Nothing, however, stirred the Generalissimo's competitive juices—and his wont to yuck it up—than the prospect of taking on, and beating, First Lady Hillary Rodham Clinton for the U.S. Senate in the year 2000.

I spent a day today in Washington. I was on a listening tour. *American Spectator* speech, Washington, D.C. *New York Times,* November 10, 1999

I am also considering a new requirement in running for the Senate from New York. See if this would work. You have to demonstrate that you can get from LaGuardia Airport to your house, and that you know the way by yourself. What do you think?
Speech to Republican Washington Coalition, Washington, D.C., *New York Times,* December 2, 1999

The premise, you see, was that Washington–to–New York air traffic supposedly had been delayed to accommodate the First Lady's flight into LaGuardia on her most recent "exploratory" campaign visit to the state—an assertion that even the Generalissimo's ever-friendly *New York Post* found was false.

It was a joke! Gosh, you've got to lighten up!
New York Times, December 3, 1999

Thanks, Mr. Mayor. We needed the reminder.

16

Rudy on the Issues

♦ On Drugs—and Drug Treatment

I don't believe our drug problem is accidental. This is not a plague. This isn't something somehow one unfriendly foreign force created for us. This is something we created. This is something we created over many years, in our culture, in our thinking, in our failure to really be disciplined in our analysis of human health and morality and decency in the highest public sense. And if it's something that we've educated young people and others in society—by giving them the wrong messages about drugs in our movies, music, and indirect signals and direct signals and role models that we've permitted to create wrong impressions of what happiness is about—if we did all that, we can undo it. If we can educate people to do the wrong thing, we can educate them to do the right thing.

Speech to National Press Club, Washington, D.C.
New York Times, October 8, 1997

One little problem with that statement: While America's drug problem may not be something "one unfriendly foreign force created for us," and while it does indeed have its root cause in Americans' own demand for drugs, the facts remain that the two worst addictive drugs, heroin and cocaine, are not native to this country, that they must be imported, and that America's drug problem exploded in the 1980s—with huge shipments of drugs being brazenly smuggled across U.S. borders and dumped on the streets of American cities—during the very years that Rudolph W. Giuliani served as United States Attorney in New York and, prior to that, as the No. 3 official in the Department of Justice in Washington.

If I go out and buy cocaine and contribute my money to this deadly business, I'm going to get arrested.

New York Times, September 20, 1989

Another little problem here: In July 1986, in the company of U.S. Senator Alfonse D'Amato, Giuliani had in fact bought crack in a staged event for the media. Obviously, he and D'Amato were not arrested. More to the point, the seller was not arrested either (part of an intelligence-gathering operation, federal agents said).

As a prosecutor, Giuliani took credit for a policy known as "Federal Day"—meaning if you were selling drugs in a certain place on a certain day, even if you were only a low-level dealer, you would be picked up and prosecuted in U.S. rather than state or city court. Some critics questioned whether the strategy—besides being arbitrary—clogged the federal court system with minor cases.

I conceived of the program, because I know we had limited resources, and I said, "What kind of contribution can we make?" What we can offer to drug dealers, I decided, is a Russian roulette kind of deterrence. I cannot think of anything we could do that would be more positive for the twelve largest cities than to cut down the heroin traffic by a substantial amount. The quality of life is going to change, and it's *attainable*; it's not impossible.

American Lawyer, March 1989

As a candidate, Giuliani was similarly tough.

If I could select some areas in which my election or Dinkins' election would make the most dramatic difference in New York City in the next few years, on Day One, the

rules change for drug dealers in this city in a way that is going to shock them, in the same way I shocked organized crime, the white-collar criminals and the corrupt politicians in this city. *New York Times,* September 20, 1989

But even in those days, this hard-as-nails law-enforcement man had a soft spot in his heart on one point: that treatment for addicts, rather than imprisonment, was the ultimate solution. It's ridiculous to turn a heroin addict away from treatment, especially at the moment when he asks for it. That is when you are most likely to get a cure.

Village Voice, January 24, 1989

Warming up for the next mayoral campaign, Rudolph W. Giuliani criticized Governor Mario M. Cuomo and Mayor Edward I. Koch yesterday for "playing Ping-Pong" with drug treatment programs as drugs became a crisis.

. . . "Thousands and thousands of lives were destroyed and hundreds of thousands of crimes committed in the time they were dillydallying." As Mayor, Mr. Giuliani said, he would emphasize treatment programs. . . .

New York Times, March 29, 1989

I think drug treatment is very effective. There are programs, like Phoenix House and Daytop Village, Project Outreach, that I'm familiar with that have two-decade-long histories of rehabilitating drug addicts. So the notion that a drug addict cannot be rehabilitated just isn't true. That's a cynical and repeated phrase that ends up costing us the kind of support you need for heroin addicts, even cocaine abusers, who have been off the substances for five years, 10 years, 15 years, 20 years, and leading very productive lives. So there are programs that work and they are not getting the support that they deserve. *Barron's,* November 26, 1990

But, as mayor, Giuliani abruptly announced a change in his views in the summer of 1998: Methadone, a synthetic substitute that blocks an addict's craving for heroin and had been a key component of many drug treatment programs for more than twenty-five years, was henceforth to be banned from all treatment programs run by the city (which turned out to be those in the Rikers Island jails only; state- and federal-funded programs, by far the majority, were not affected by Giuliani's order).

Mayor Giuliani considers abstinence the more morally acceptable approach to curing addiction.

New York Times, August 18, 1998

Experts in the field were appalled.

I don't get offended any longer when people call me crazy. But I wonder about a doctor running a methadone program who, when a Mayor raises the idea that we should end methadone, which is a way of keeping people dependent, describes my idea as crazy.

New York Times, July 22, 1998

Even the chief of national drug policy, Barry McCaffrey, himself a retired Marine Corps general with impeccable hardline credentials, questioned what Giuliani was doing. But that was OK. To the Generalissimo, McCaffrey was just

a disaster.   *New York Times,* October 2, 1998;
                                           Washington Post, June 30, 1999

◆ On Labor (and the Sanctity of Labor Contracts). . .

In the winter of 1996, Rudy Giuliani achieved a signal success—District Council 37 of the American Federation of State, County and Municipal Employees (AFSCME), the largest union of nonuniformed city workers, ratified a controversial five-year labor contract under which, in return for no layoffs, members would get no pay raise for the first two years of the deal.

The pact brought labor peace to city government and helped contain costs. It was also the most bitterly contested contract in city history, ratified by the closest vote ever among the rank-and-file amid charges of tampering by dissident factions. Giuliani was jubilant.

This goes a long way to setting the pattern for the city because this covers virtually half the work force of the City of New York. *New York Times,* February 9, 1996

And indeed, it did set the pattern—firefighters, teachers, and sanitation workers had to accept the District Council 37 precedent; police officers had to work without a contract (and no raises at all) for refusing to accept it. District Council 37's president, Stanley Hill, endorsed the mayor for reelection a year later, defying pro-Democratic traditions by his union. Other labor leaders allied with Hill made commercials for Giuliani.

Just one little problem. It turned out—nearly three years later—that the union dissidents had been right all along. The pact was never approved. It had been voted down, but ballot boxes had been stuffed and the results falsified. The great centerpiece of Mayor Rudolph Giuliani's labor-relations policy rested on a massive conspiracy of criminal fraud.

At this moment of moral crisis and potential labor unrest, the Generalissimo kept his focus on what was truly important: **There are a lot of allegations going on now about DC 37, so we've got to wait and see what the outcome it is before we jump to any conclusions.**

New York Post, November 21, 1998

Mayor Giuliani said he is "disturbed" by the ballot-stuffing charge, but said it should have no impact on the legality of the contract. *N.Y. Daily News,* Nov. 21, 1998

As far as the city's labor relations are concerned and the contract itself, it would have no impact because so many other unions also supported it, and finally, the contract is now two, two and a half, three years into actual practice. . . . And as a matter of labor relations law, you would not be able to undo that contract.

New York Times, November 24, 1998

It's a contract that I'm sure lots of people would like to undo. They're going to find that, legally, they can't undo it, no matter what happens with this investigation. That's sort of a no-brainer, legally.

New York Daily News and *New York Post,* Nov. 25, 1998

Mayor Giuliani insists that the Council's contract remains valid because duly authorized union leaders had signed it. *New York Times,* November 30, 1998

Mayor Giuliani said yesterday that it would be "the worst possible thing" for City workers if he is forced to reopen a fraud-tainted contract with District Council 37.

In his strongest remarks to date on the issue, the Mayor said union officials pushing for the reopening are leading their members down a perilous path because he's prepared to block hefty raises if the 1995 contract is voided.

"We're not going to reopen it," Giuliani declared.

"And, I mean, the fact is if it did get reopened— which it wouldn't—then the City would be entitled to get a lot of money back, which nobody would like very much." *New York Post,* December 1, 1998

If you want to take us to court, God bless you, we'll see you in court and we'll seek sanctions from you for doing it. *New York Daily News,* December 4, 1998

An embarrassed Stanley Hill was forced to ask for the resignation of two subordinates who had engineered the vote fraud. An even more embarrassed AFSCME national headquarters forced Hill out, put District Council 37 into receivership, and brought in new leadership from Washington. Giuliani, invoking his crusader prosecutor roots, scoffed.

It's a problem for the present leadership of the union as well as the old leadership of the union, because— make no mistake about it—they were all on the same side as of a week ago. If there was any knowledge of this, they were standing next to the people who were doing it, and I've investigated enough cases to know on what side you have to look for obligation. They've got to clean themselves up, and frankly, I don't know who's going to be left standing a year from now for us to negotiate with. . . . The moral obligation is for those labor leaders to tell everything they know. . . . [The union's current leaders] are close associates of the people that are being named as possible defendants in this situation. Statement on WABC Radio
New York Post, December 5, 1998

More disturbing than Giuliani's self-serving slant on the whole mess, however, was the degree to which a onetime U.S. Attorney who had employed the racketeer-controlled-enterprise statute with pathbreaking gusto, who had attacked organized crime without mercy, who had driven a corrupt politician to suicide and even had stockbrokers hauled out of their offices in handcuffs, had himself developed such cozy relationships with labor leaders later stained by charges of corruption or tolerance of corruption. One of the two ballot-stuffing union chieftains, for instance, was a man whom Deputy Mayor Randy Levine, Giuliani's chief negotiator, had described as "a dear friend and a great union leader" only the year before, when he endorsed the Generalissimo's reelection. When Stanley Hill took a leave of absence from District Council 37 (a prelude to his permanent departure), Giuliani issued a statement that was anything but outraged:

In the Mayor's experience, Stanley Hill has been an effective leader who has always worked hard to resolve difficult problems and for the good of the city. This is an interim step, and we would all be best advised to await the final outcome. *New York Times*, November 29, 1998

And then there was the strange case of Charles Hughes, president of Local 372 of school luncheon workers and a major backer of Giuliani among the city's labor leaders. Even before the contract ratification was exposed as a fraud, Hughes had been ousted by his union, charged with racking up $1.6 million in bogus overtime and expenses. Giuliani's response: He kept Hughes on the city's fair-employment practices panel. And when a year later a criminal indictment was handed down against Hughes, the Generalissimo—who had handed down so many similar indictments in his time—had only this to say:

He's a very religious man, he's a very nice man.
New York Daily News, May 14, 1999

♦ . . . and On Pay Raises for Public Officials

There's an awful lot of populist nonsense about salaries for public officials. There really is.
New York Daily News, October 18, 1995

Indeed, there is—and only a few months before making that statement, Rudy Giuliani had engaged in a bit of such "populist nonsense" himself. When, upon taking office, Governor George Pataki had installed new leadership at the

Metropolitan Transportation Authority that promptly raised mass-transit fares (and raised them disproportionately higher on Democratic New York City subway and bus riders than they did on train commuters from the Republican suburbs), Giuliani essentially rolled over—his four appointees on the MTA board voted no, but did not speak out against the hikes. Instead, Giuliani said to avoid a fare increase the MTA **could actually discipline their executive salaries.**

New York Daily News, February 23, 1995

But when it came to executive salaries in his own administration, Giuliani took a less "populist" attitude.

You can't withhold a raise for 8, 9, 10 years, indefinitely, and expect that you're going to attract and keep the highest quality people. Because I'm going to end up losing them. I can't do magic, ma'am.

Statement at town meeting on Staten Island
New York Times, October 19, 1995

In my search for the very best, I lost, two or three times, the people I thought would have been the very best people to run certain agencies, because they had realistic problems, like children with special needs. A difference of $20,000 or $30,000 would have been a difference in getting that person.

New York Times, November 17, 1995

So he took the plunge—and implemented, by executive order, salary increases of up to 28 percent for himself and top city managers, as recommended by a blue-ribbon citizens' panel that had studied the issue. (Those salaries had been frozen since the Wall Street crash of 1987 forced the city into a period of prolonged austerity.)

For political reasons, I could have put it off. I could have played games with it, I could have said "Oh, let's wait." But if we did that, we'd have eight years of a pay freeze, compounded by four more years, and really very serious problems in managing our agencies, and it's the right thing to do. And over a period of time, people will understand that the City is being managed now with fewer people who are doing considerably more work. *New York Times,* November 16, 1995

All that is happening with elected officials, commissioners and mayors is to make them in some way equal to everyone who works for the City of New York.
New York Times, November 17, 1995

There was a certain problem of timing, however. Teachers' union leader Sandra Feldman had just gone out on a limb for the mayor, recommending her union rank-and-file ratify a labor accord with the city containing the highly unpopular two-year wage freeze. Now she complained that the mayor had sawed off that limb behind her. The Generalissimo was unsympathetic about the predicament he had put Feldman in. **I think that this is a question of who spins what. And she's got a ratification issue that she's nervous about.**
New York Times, November 17, 1995

Indeed, Feldman lost her vote—the contract was voted down by her own union. To the Generalissimo, ever gracious, it was all her fault.
Part of leadership is to deal with emotion and explain it accurately. If the president of the UFT had accurately explained this, you would have a very different reaction.
New York Times, December 9, 1995

The City is not in a position to offer anything more. The City made its very best offer, and things will have to move in the other direction, unfortunately. . . . There's no way they're going to get a better contract.

New York Times, December 8, 1995

In the end, the Generalissimo got his way. The teachers wound up accepting the two-year pay freeze. And three years later he wound up accepting another pay increase for himself, to $195,000.

◆ On Welfare

If I had said, five years ago, I promise there will be 350,000 fewer people on welfare if I'm elected to office, I guarantee you half the newspapers in this city would have predicted the destruction of the City of New York.

New York Times, February 11, 1998

We have done more in two and a half years for the poor of this city than they did in 20 or 30 years of consigning them to dependence. Remarks at reelection fund raiser

New York Times, May 15, 1996

The Mayor said that he had "turned around welfare" in New York City even more than he had reduced crime, but that he did not get credit for it because of a rigid, "politically correct" thinking in the city that prefers government programs—including the City's community colleges, with their low graduation rates—to hard work.

New York Times, March 20, 1997

Ultimately, he added, the city itself will be better off by ending a tradition of uncurbed generosity. "I think it

would be a city that loved people more and cared for people more. Because I don't see any value in continuing programs that take cycles of dependency and have them go on from one generation to the next generation to the next generation." *New York Times,* May 4, 1995

A city of 7.5 million cannot sustain a million people on welfare. You can't do it from the point of view of the amount of misery and hopelessness that it causes among a million people, and you can't sustain it because the number of people supporting the people on welfare keeps diminishing. Speech to United Jewish Appeal
New York Times Magazine, December 3, 1995

A society with more people on welfare is a society that is receding. Second Inaugural Address
New York Times, January 2, 1998

The Generalissimo's main tools used to cut the welfare rolls: Delaying the processing of welfare applications in the hope that would-be recipients would just give up. Verifying applicants' home addresses, fingerprinting them, and otherwise instilling fear in them that they had better not be cheating. And, through something the Generalissimo and his administration euphemistically labeled "Welfare to Work," requiring recipients to work for their benefits—even if they learned no marketable job skill by doing so, and even if their work duplicated that of municipal employees (whose own bargaining position with the city would be undermined as a result).

Giuliani gets his biggest round of applause when he moralizes about the workfare program. "In exchange for this benefit you have an obligation to give something back," he says. "That should be true for poor people,

**middle-class people, rich people. That's part of the
social contract that we were losing in this city."**

Speech to United Jewish Appeal
New York Times Magazine, December 3, 1995

The private sector was not particularly impressed with the
idea of hiring essentially unskilled ex-welfare recipients.

**One way in which you could help us is to expand the num-
ber of W.E.P. workers that you take in private business
and give them an opportunity and give them a chance.
We have had a tremendous amount of cooperation from
some corporations. We have had almost no cooperation
from others. And if we could get that kind of assistance,
you would help move this whole situation a lot faster. And
also help us deal with the tremendous mandates and bur-
dens that have been placed on us by the Federal Government, which I believe are too fast, too Draconian.**

Speech to New York City Partnership and
Chamber of Commerce, *New York Times,* March 20, 1997

But eventually—aided by a booming economy and the
abolition of welfare on a national level by a Republican-
controlled Congress—to the horror of traditional New York
liberals and the delight of the Generalissimo, his methods
worked. Or, rather, they *seemed* to be working. At any rate, the
welfare rolls continued to shrink.

**We've already transformed ourselves from the welfare
capital of the nation to the workfare capital of the
nation.**

Second Inaugural Address
New York Times, January 2, 1998

**Hundreds of thousands have been liberated from lives
of dependency on welfare. . . . And many more people
are now experiencing the very best social program any-**

one ever invented—much, much better than dependency on government. You know what that social program is called? It's called a job. . . .

In a few months we will no longer have welfare offices in New York City. When someone calls in for help, the sign on the door will not say welfare, but job center. If you need help, you will get help for as long as you need it. But you'll be as quickly moved back into the work force as we possibly can do. Work gives people self-worth. Dependency robs them of that. Never again will we repeat the mistakes of the past, with millions of people into the next generation in dependency.

It's not helping them. That's forgetting them.

It's not compassion. That's their [critics'] own guilt.

Second Inaugural Address, *New York Times,* Jan. 2, 1998

We're going to end welfare by the end of this century completely. We will replace dependency with work. . . . Everybody in this city will work.

Speech to business leaders, July 1998
http://eastvillage.miningco.com/library/weekly/a072198.htm

New York City, which used to be seen as the welfare capital of America, is now seen as the workfare capital, where we've put more people out of welfare, through worktry. . . . [Reductions in crime and welfare] are the two things that are at the core of the revival of the City of New York.   Speech to Republican leaders in Washington
New York Times, March 13, 1998

New York City will be the first city in the nation, on its own, to end welfare.   *New York Times,* February 25, 1999
[Part of article reporting that New York City welfare officials were seeking drug treatment records of welfare recipients and that mayor would veto a pending City Council bill that would provide an alternative to workfare]

Of course, beyond the numbers, there were still some doubters of the mayor's success story. Stanley Hill, shortly before the end of his tenure at District Council 37, momentarily abandoned his lapdog posture and, responding to his members' warnings that welfare clients were being used to replace municipal workers, called the workfare program "slavery." The Generalissimo tut-tutted:

I think this is a losing proposition for him. Workfare is happening all over America. *N.Y. Times,* April 20, 1998

When Generalissimo Giuliani took Texas Governor George W. Bush on a visit to a welfare-to-work office, he burst with pride to the man he had endorsed to be the next President:

This is an example of compassionate conservatism in action. *New York Daily News,* October 7, 1999

But the article went on to note that a federal judge had "halted any further expansion" of the mayor's "program of remaking welfare offices into 'jobs centers' until the City can prove it has stopped violating laws" that "guaranteed timely access to benefits" for those who filed applications for public assistance, including emergency Medicaid and food stamps.

And there remained the lingering doubts about the mayor's true thinking, and his ultimate agenda, in his war on welfare.

Saying it would be "a good thing" if poor people left the city, RG [Rudy Giuliani] said in response to questions about the effect of his welfare cuts: "That's not an unspoken part of our strategy. That is our strategy." Though this comment was reported by the news director of the City's own television station, the Mayor corrected it, saying an exodus "could be a natural consequence." The Mayor's favorite newspaper, the Post, cited one of RG's "chief policy architects" as say-

ing: "Then poor will eventually figure out that it's a lot easier to be homeless where it's warm."

Village Voice, November 4, 1997

In 1998 Giuliani had made this flat-out prediction:
By the year 2000, New York will be the first city in the nation, on its own, to end welfare.

Requoted, *New York Times*, December 29, 1999

So, with three days to go, he simply announced:
Several weeks ago we fulfilled that promise.

New York Post, December 29, 1999

Today marks the milestone of replacing the culture of dependency in New York City with the culture of work and empowerment. . . . The most important thing is we have every one engaged, either in working in the private sector, in the work force program or engaged in a process of being evaluated in order to work.

New York Times, December 29, 1999

What did that last phrase mean, exactly?
Mr. Giuliani said that all able-bodied welfare recipients without infant children were now either in jobs or taking steps to get them. *New York Times*, December 29, 1999

And what did *that* last phrase mean exactly? Thousands of welfare recipients who were in fact still on the dole but had received letters notifying them to report for a job-search interview were counted as being "off" welfare, just so the Generalissimo could claim victory.

◆ On Immigration (and Winnie the Pooh)

An example of the very best in immigration.
> Statement about children's literature character,
> Winnie the Pooh, *American City & County,* March 1998

[Context: member of British Parliament had called for return to United Kingdom of original Winnie-the-Pooh stuffed bear, which resides in a glass case in the New York Public Library]

◆ On Lingering Traces of Communism in New York City

Amid New York's budget problems during his first term, the Generalissimo analyzed the causes of the situation thusly:
He blames the City's bloated government and its many enterprises—vast real estate holdings, 500 gas stations, 17 hospitals, even radio and television stations.
> *New York Times Magazine,* December 3, 1995

The other governments that owned radio and television stations were on the other side of the Iron Curtain. The anomaly of this never occurred to anyone.
> *New York Times Magazine,* December 3, 1995

When he implemented a bitterly opposed plan to sell off for development neighborhood "community gardens" that local residents had planted on vacant city-owned lots, and that had become fixtures in many of those neighborhoods, the Generalissimo gave this advice to a caller who phoned his radio show to complain:
Welcome to the era after Communism.
> Statement on WABC Radio, *Washington Post,*
> June 30, 1999; *New York Times,* December 20, 1999

When a civic group cautioned against letting too much privately raised funds be used to maintain city parks:

That's the rich-and-the-poor knee-jerk reaction. It probably comes out of spending some time in school in the 40's or 50's studying Marxism or something. . . . [The group has] a very, very extreme radical political outlook on the world in which you were taught to look at things that way, and you just see them that way, no matter what the facts are. Statement by Mayor, October 1999
New York Times, December 20, 1999

When demonstrators disrupted the meeting of the World Trade Organization in Seattle, the Generalisssimo said it showed

the remaining damage that Marxism has done to the thinking of people. You know we have it in the city and the influence that it's had on universities and thinking and the idea of class warfare.
Remarks to business leaders, the 21 Club,
December 2, 1999, *New York Times*, December 20, 1999

The Mayor explained later, at a City Hall news conference, that his remarks . . . were meant to examine "the whole notion of class warfare, which really comes out of the teaching of Karl Marx, trying to divide people into different classes." He did not elaborate on his reference to the city's universities. *N.Y. Times*, Dec. 20, 1999

When the city narrowly avoided a walkout by its transit workers at the height of the Christmas shopping season, and the leader of a radical faction within the union urged a strike, saying it would shut down "an orgy of profit-making" by businesses:
There are people who want to cause anarchy. I know a week ago I said that Marxism unfortunately is still alive

in parts of New York City, even in the latter part of this century, even though it's been disgraced all over the world. . . .

The remarks by one of the leaders . . . is a perfect example of what I'm talking about, where he advocated taking away profits from business as being one of the really good side benefits of having a strike. . . . [That] means taking jobs away from people. It means seeing unemployment go up. It means really hurting people who need the most help. And it's a true misunderstanding of what America is all about. That comes from the influence of Marxism, and if you need any better indication of it, it was said at a Marxist study group.

New York Times, December 20, 1999

Philosophy is important. . . . The isms and ideologies of this century have cost an awful lot of human lives. . . . Just because we're in the latter part of the century doesn't mean the perversions of those philosophies don't affect it.   *New York Times,* December 20, 1999

♦ On the Middle East Peace Process, Yassir Arafat, and Diplomatic Etiquette

In 1964, when Giuliani was a student columnist at Manhattan College and the U.S. Senate race between Robert Kennedy and incumbent Republican Kenneth Keating was raging, Keating made an off-the-wall, loose-cannon charge that Kennedy had had secret dealings with Nazis. Young Rudy, an RFK supporter, leapt to his candidate's defense:

If one could add up all the times Sen. Keating has either mentioned this, or his love for Israel, or the many bar mitzvahs he has attended, it would outweigh all the other things or issues he has raised throughout this campaign. Sen. Keating is desperately trying to patronize the Jewish people.... Certainly, all of us have a stake in the protection of our firmest ally in the Middle East, but we do not go around wearing an "I Love Israel" button.

Column in *Manhattan Quadrangle,* October 1964, *New York Daily News,* May 13, 1997; *New York Observer,* July 12, 1999

Thirty-five years later, in a speech as a presumptive candidate for the very same Senate seat Keating (and, after him, Kennedy) had occupied, Giuliani expressed his philosophy toward Israel in these words:

My views are developed over 20 or 25 years of what I believe is in the best interest of the United States and my understanding of the history, background and the experience of the State of Israel. They are not developed for the purpose of one political campaign or another political campaign. . . . You have very, very few good friends in life. You know that, I know that. Nations have very, very few really good friends. Israel has proven its friendship with the United States.

Speech to Republican Washington Coalition
New York Times, December 2, 1999

Those are sentiments virtually all Americans, and for that matter all Israelis, would agree with. But the Generalissimo then elaborated on his thinking—and revealed just enough of himself to make it clear that, to him, certain kinds of Israelis are less fit to lead Israel than others. And that he, as an American, believes it is his prerogative to identify those Israelis whom he considers unsound.

The friendship between the United States and Israel means that peace and security are just as important for us as it is for the State of Israel. The peace process is important. I support it. I believe it should move forward. But it cannot be just a romanticized peace process. A romanticized peace process eventually falls apart, because it doesn't give at least an equal measure of concern to security. Speech to Republican
Washington Coalition, *N. Y. Times,* Dec. 2, 1999

Behind the code words, what that statement means is this: Rudolph William Giuliani is not just a supporter of the State of Israel *per se.* He is, to be exact about it, a supporter of the right-wing Likud Party of Israel, and shares its mistrust of any possible peace accord with that nation's Arab adversaries (especially with the Palestinians and their leader Yassir Arafat).

But in 1992, Israel's Labor Party, under the banner of General Yitzhak Rabin, mastermind of the nation's victory in the Six-Day War, won a landslide victory over Likud and returned to power. And Rabin—determined that young generations of Israelis should not have to endure the unending cycles of violence his pioneer generation had suffered—made a fateful, calculated decision to open up diplomatic contacts with Palestine Liberation Organization chairman Arafat, recognize the PLO, shake hands with Arafat at a public ceremony on the White House lawn, and begin peace negotiations.

It was a diplomatic coup that required Rabin to swallow his rage at the many acts of terrorism Arafat and the PLO had unleashed against Israel, and it earned both men the Nobel Peace Prize. It also earned Rabin in particular the sworn enmity of the Jewish religious right, both in Israel and in America, with some extreme rabbis even calling for the assassination of the war hero prime minister. As it happened, much of the U.S.-based hostility toward Rabin and his peace initiative was centered in New York City, within the Orthodox Jewish communities in the boroughs outside Manhattan, especially Brooklyn. And it happened that these politically conservative communities had split with the traditional establishment of Manhattan liberal Jewish Democrats and been avid supporters of Rudolph Giuliani in both his mayoral campaigns.

The peace talks dragged on for two years, pockmarked by a series of ghastly suicide bus bombings carried out by West Bank Palestinians influenced by those who refused to follow Arafat's lead and whom neither he nor Israel seemed able to stop. The shouts of "traitor" on Rabin's right became even louder. And then it came time for the fiftieth anniversary of the founding of the United Nations, with a week of gala celebrations hosted by the world body's host city, New York.

One such event: a concert of Beethoven's Ninth Symphony, with its "Ode to Joy," at Lincoln Center.

A UN official laid out the scene of the fateful moment. "The musicians and chorus were seated, and the concert hall was fully hushed," said the official. "Backstage left, Mayor Giuliani and [UN] Undersecretary [Gillian] Sorensen were waiting for the stage manager to give them their cues to come on and welcome the audience.

"Just then, the Mayor's aide rushed up. This is how the dialogue went:

"'Mr. Mayor, Arafat is here with ticket in hand.'

"The Mayor said, 'He was not invited; tell him to leave.'

"At that point, Undersecretary Sorensen spoke up. She said, 'Mr. Mayor, you cannot do that. Chairman Arafat is part of the UN commemoration and is here as an official observer. He is here with the approval of the

U.S. and has tickets for the concert.'

"**Then the Mayor spoke, addressing the aide: 'Ask him to leave.'**

"**When Undersecretary Sorensen tried to speak, he turned to her and said, 'Gillian, I don't want to hear it.'"**

New York Daily News, October 26, 1995

Deputy Mayor Randy Mastro was dispatched to order Arafat and his entourage to go. Even though it was unclear whether the city had the authority to tell a validly invited UN guest to leave the event, Arafat departed shortly afterward. The incident made international news. In Washington, the State Department issued a formal apology for Giuliani's conduct. And, even though Rabin brushed off the incident by saying "I don't pass judgment on others," anti-Rabin circles in America and Israel took heart. By his actions, Rudolph Giuliani had telegraphed this unmistakable message to them: Even I, the gentile Mayor of New York, can see that Arafat is evil. And I agree with you that your prime minister, in negotiating with him, has betrayed and endangered your country.

It was an unprecedented intrusion into the domestic politics of a friendly foreign nation on the part of an American politician, and—as quickly became clear—it had been done with apparently no thought as to the possible consequences.

I don't think we should be unrealistic about who Yassir Arafat is or what he stands for. Oct. 25, 1995

N.Y. Daily News

I would not invite Yassir Arafat to anything, anywhere, anytime, anyplace. I don't forget. . . . He has never been held to answer for the murders he was implicated in. The UN is one thing, the peace process is another thing. When we're having a party and a celebration, I would

rather not have someone who has been implicated in the murders of Americans there, if I have the discretion not to have him there.   *New York Times*, October 25, 1995

The *New York Times* noted that, as mayor, Giuliani had happily (and hypocritically) greeted Irish nationalist Gerry Adams—a convicted terrorist who had since become a key player in brokering a political peace settlement in Northern Ireland—at City Hall. Former Mayors Dinkins and Koch joined forces to deplore Giuliani's "discourtesy." Koch's criticism was especially stinging, not only because he reflected on a possible "behavioral problem" on the Generalissimo's part but because Koch was Jewish and ardently pro-Israel.

He [Koch] suggested that [the UN] be bombed and replaced with a parking lot. So I think that if we're going to take lessons in diplomacy . . . the last person in the world you should take it from is Ed Koch.
New York Daily News, October 26, 1995

I think maybe it's difficult for people to come to the conclusion nowadays that maybe somebody in public office would do something out of principle rather than whether you get so many votes here or so many votes there. . . . We thought it was the right thing to do. I continue to think it's the right thing to do.
New York Times, October 26, 1995

Giuliani stood defiant amid the firestorm, even scolding the U.S. State Department to "face up to the fact that they are negotiating with a murderer and a terrorist."
New York Daily News, October 26, 1995

Nine days later, the worst fears about the climate of hatred stalking Yitzhak Rabin came true. He was shot and mortally wounded while singing a peace song at a mass rally in Tel Aviv. In New York, the mayor mourned:

He invited me to Israel.   *N.Y. Daily News,* Nov. 12, 1995

Briefly, there appeared a glimmer of awareness that his own actions had—symbolically but recklessly—helped feed the ugly environment that struck Rabin down.

We must do all that we can to live up to his legacy of peace.   *New York Daily News,* November 12, 1995

Boarding an El Al flight to Jerusalem, where world leaders are gathering to grieve for Rabin, Giuliani called Rabin's assassination "an attack on all peace-loving people." Rabin was a friend of New York, the Mayor added, and his death "affects the people of New York in particular. He told me himself how he loved the city, and obviously the ties between Israel and New York go back to the foundation of the State of Israel. . . .

"Anybody who would express satisfaction at this is a very sick person, a very dangerous person. They encourage other people to do sick things."
     New York Daily News, November 6, 1995

But, after the funeral, touring Jerusalem (on his first visit ever to the Jewish state) in the company of the city's Likud mayor, he was back in the saddle.

Not that Giuliani ever felt he made a mistake [in his actions ousting Arafat at Lincoln Center]. "I'm very comfortable with my position."
     New York Daily News, November 7, 1995

When, a month later, the street in front of the Israeli Consulate in New York was renamed Yitzhak Rabin Way, Giuliani attended in the company of Rabin's widow, Leah. But he agreed to attend a subsequent memorial tribute to Rabin at Madison Square Garden only after what the *Daily News* called "several days of indecision," in deference to the views of his anti–peace process Orthodox supporters. And when he visited Israel again a few months later, in the midst of an election campaign, he embarrassed Rabin's successor by publicly offering him some condescending counsel:

The Mayor advised Prime Minister Shimon Peres not to "go romanticizing" Mr. Arafat. "Don't forget who he is," the Mayor said in an unsolicited pep talk.

New York Times, November 26, 1999

Amid a renewed spate of suicide bombings, Peres lost the election by an eyelash to Benjamin Netanyahu of the Likud. The ferociously demagogic Netanyahu—who had openly pandered to the Rabin-is-a-traitor element prior to the assassination—proceeded to spend the next three years polarizing Israeli society, obstructing the peace process at every turn, nearly wrecking Israel's relationship with the United States, and virtually emptying the Jewish state's moral bank account in the international community. On the other hand, he and Rudy Giuliani got along just fine. Finally, in 1999, a protégé of the late Rabin, Ehud Barak, another former general turned peace advocate, decisively unseated Netanyahu. Shortly afterward, he made the politically obligatory visit to the United States, and had his first courtesy call with the Mayor of New York.

He was especially interested in how we brought about [lower crime rates], so that they could apply some of the same practices in Israel. I'm a very strong supporter, always have been, of the State of Israel. If he needs any help or assistance, he should call on me.

New York Post, July 19, 1999

Perhaps the young Rudy Giuliani said it best back in 1964: **Let us hope the Jewish people, who have always been noted for their good common sense and their civic dedication, can see through this sham.**

N.Y. Daily News, May 13, 1997 and *N.Y. Observer*, July 12, 1999

◆ On Fidel Castro

Yassir Arafat was not the only controversial Third World political figure who was in for rough treatment at the hands of Rudolph Giuliani during the United Nations' fiftieth anniversary ceremonies. Even more of a no-brainer vote-getter in the ethnicity-driven politics of New York City, Giuliani calculated, would be an attack on Cuban dictator Fidel Castro.

Why, just the mention of Castro's name had the Generalissimo rhapsodizing back to his youth, when in 1960 Soviet premier Nikita Khrushchev had momentarily lightened up the Cold War by making a perfect spectacle of himself during the UN's General Assembly opening session, taking off his shoe and thumping it on the desktop in front of him during speeches he didn't like.

1:45 P.M. . . . Joseph Verner Reed, an under secretary general at the United Nations, comes in to lobby him to attend the world leaders' speeches at the United Nations on Sunday.

"I have the two best seats in the house for you," Reed says. "You can listen to President Clinton, and when Castro gets up to speak you can walk out."

"I can bang my shoe," Giuliani says. "I'll bring my spikes." *New York Times Magazine*, December 3, 1995

And even after Castro left. . .

Fidel Castro may have returned to Cuba, but Mayor Giuliani kept his notoriety alive for Cuban New Yorkers yes-

terday with another withering attack at an anti-Castro rally held in the Mayor's honor at City Hall.

Wrapping himself in the adulation of 250 pro-democracy Cubans and other Hispanics, the Mayor beamed as he was presented with a Cuban flag, an icon of the Virgin Mary and chants of "Bravo Rudy" and "Giuliani for President!"

The Mayor did not disappoint, chastising Castro for maintaining "a failed, horrible, oppressive system."

New York Daily News, October 29, 1995

Four years later, relations between the United States and Cuba hit a tragic snag when a refugee drowned trying to make her way to the shores of Florida; her six-year-old son miraculously survived; family relatives in Miami wanted to adopt the child, Elian Gonzalez, and win him asylum; but the boy's father, back in Havana, insisted on the return of his son, with the loud backing of Castro himself. The Generalissimo's contribution to a solution of this international and family crisis: He not only announced young Elian should stay (in violation of the precepts of U.S. family law), but floated the idea that the boy should come to Times Square and lower the ball signifying the start of a new millennium at midnight on New Year's Eve. A day later he retreated from his trial balloon.

[It] may or may not be a good idea. . . . No one would want to do anything that would hurt the boy. It would be up to the family, up to the committee. . . . I think that's something I should reserve decision about.

New York Post, December 17, 1999

The suggestion was worthy, but probably not a good one for the welfare of the boy. Involving him in this celebration would probably have created a lot of confusion.

New York Times, December 18, 1999

In a lengthy and at times rancorous exchange with reporters at City Hall, Mr. Giuliani said the question of whether the boy, Elian Gonzalez, should be returned to Cuba—as Fidel Castro and the boy's father have demanded—"plays out in a very dramatic way the purpose of America."   *New York Times,* December 18, 1999

[Elian] should be allowed to grow up in freedom, democracy, under the rule of law.
                                    New York Daily News, December 17, 1999

"My views are that he should be given the benefit of asylum protection, and whatever argument his father has should be made in an American court. The very dramatic act of his mother, in giving up her life in order to obtain freedom and democracy for her child, is a very powerful thing."

Mr. Giuliani appeared angered when a reporter suggested that he might be ignoring the rights of the boy's father. "That is the most simplistic, silliest thing."
                                    New York Times, December 17, 1999

I think, unfortunately and tragically, Castro has become a romanticized figure in America.
                                    New York Times, December 20, 1999

♦ On the United Nations (and Diplomatic Parking Tickets)

Rudy Giuliani took office declaring his strong support for the United Nations.

We've never effectively utilized our unique position as the home of the United Nations. The politics of the

Cold War and strong disagreements over past policies prevented it. But that's behind us now. That's the past. It's time to enhance our relationship with the United Nations and to build on it. Think of this: Albany, the capital of New York State; Washington, D.C., the capital of our nation. And New York City will again be the capital of the world.

First Inaugural Address, *New York Times,* January 3, 1994

Sometimes, leadership means taking unpopular positions, rejecting harmful political fads. Sometimes leadership requires challenging myths. That's the kind of leadership we need in defining our relationship with the UN. The UN provides a crucial forum for international debate and cooperation.   *N.Y. Times,* Sept. 20, 1995

But, along the way, the bloom fell off the rose, as it were, vis-à-vis his honor and the world body. It seems to have begun the night two thoroughly inebriated diplomats from the former Soviet Union—one representing the Russian Federation, one from Belarus—parked their car illegally in front of a fire hydrant, emerged to find two NYPD officers ticketing their vehicle, and duked it out with the cops. (Just a couple of Russian social drinkers out for a good time!) And the pair had racked up nearly four hundred outstanding summonses for illegal parking, all of them unpaid by virtue of their diplomatic immunity, to boot.

The Generalissimo was not amused.

To have them also hit a police officer and now start to lie about it, as if they were abused by the police officers: Well, we have enough real problems to deal with in New York. We don't need this kind of behavior. . . . Their activities and their actions are against a backdrop of almost constant flagrant violations of a host country's

**rules and laws. .... They're not people that we would
like to have in New York any longer. They're not welcome here.** *New York Times*, January 3, 1997

So Giuliani embarked on a new crusade: getting foreign
UN diplomatic delegations to pay the roughly $5 million in
unpaid parking fines they owed. Now, mind you, the City of
New York had just published a brochure entitled "In Appreci-
ation of the United Nations." It contained the following data:
Total UN spending in New York City in a year—$1.4 billion.
Total spending in the city by all diplomats accredited to the
UN—$3.3 billion. Annual spending by visitors coming to New
York for UN business—$27 million. Total number of UN-
related jobs in the New York economy—3,700. The brochure
also contained these statements:

**It is largely because of the United Nations' presence
that we refer to New York City as the "Capital of the
World."**

Diplomats are not required to pay for parking tickets.
New York Times, April 18, 1997

The brochure was signed by Mayor Rudolph W. Giuliani.
But no matter. Under the Generalissimo's pressure, the State
Department announced it would enforce the policy that
applied in Washington: Foreign embassy scofflaws would have
their license plates removed. Unfortunately, overlooked in all
this was that the Washington arrangement was part of a bilat-
eral treaty between the United States and any nation that
wishes to establish diplomatic relations with it. The United
Nations is a sovereign entity (its grounds are international territory, not American), and such an arrangement cannot be
imposed on the members of a multilateral body. This was
quickly communicated to the State Department by the UN
diplomatic community—as was a threat to file a lawsuit over

the matter with the International Court of Justice. As was a much-vaguer threat that maybe it was time for the world body to decamp for more favorable shores, where it would be more welcome. The situation was getting just a bit out of hand. It was time for cooler heads to prevail. Unfortunately, the Generalissimo got to the microphones first.

We're hopeful the State Department won't back down. I don't think they'll back down, because they'll lose a lot of credibility if they back down. *N.Y Times,* Apr. 11, 1997

They are making a little bit of a joke out of the UN by threatening to take a parking violations case to the World Court. It was not put together by treaty to argue out special-interest parking situations for diplomats.
New York Times, April 11, 1997

Instead of settling wars and human rights violations, he said, the institution was "defining diplomacy down."
New York Times, April 11, 1997

The consolation prize, should they leave, would be a windfall for the United States, a tremendously valuable property to New York City and State. In a fairly short period of time, it would start to become profit-making property, because it would be back on the tax rolls.
New York Times, April 11, 1997

"As reporters were leaving his office, he let out a cackle," the *Times* noted.
If they'd like to leave New York over parking tickets, then we can find another use for that area of town. It happens to be just about the most valuable real estate in the world, not just in the United States. That is enormously valuable real estate, and with the vacancy rates

that exist in the city of New York, can you imagine what we could do with that?   *New York Times*, April 11, 1997

He said today that he was willing to discuss the possibility of bidding the United Nations good riddance not only to call the diplomats' bluff but to "buck up the State Department so they don't back down."
New York Times, April 12, 1997

I would like the UN to stay but also would like the UN and their diplomats to respect—and I underline the word respect—the laws of the City of New York, instead of trying to make a mockery of it. The most valuable real estate in New York City has been turned over to the UN. New York City does more than any city in the world could possibly do for the UN. And we are thanked in return by 30,000 tickets by the Russian Federation not paid.   *New York Times*, April 12, 1997

The brouhaha now thoroughly out of control, the Generalissimo vented his disgust at the State Department and announced he would cut back on the three hundred additional "diplomats-only" parking spaces that were to have been part of the new policy.

There is no question that we are going to take some of the parking spots away. If I make a deal, I keep it. If you make a deal, you have to keep it. And they haven't.
New York Times, April 13, 1997

How do I know what they are going to do? They keep changing their minds. What happens is that they are very strong and assertive when they meet with us. Then they go back, and somebody at the United Nations, like, yells at them, they change their minds. So there is no way to really be sure what they are doing. All I can do is keep the pressure on them. And I am good at that.

New York Times, April 19, 1997

In the end, State struck a compromise. For every diplomatic car in scofflaw status, a foreign legation would lose one plate permitted it at renewal time. The Generalissimo was furious.

If you don't take the actual license plates away, then someone can easily evade detection. . . . We disagree with them, we'll push them, but the fact is that I don't run the State Department. We're forced to be realistic. If we don't go along with this enforcement mechanism, you have none at all. This is better than nothing. It's not nearly as effective as what the State Department originally agreed to, but the State Department caved in.

New York Times, April 19, 1997

And the United Nations he had extolled as "a crucial forum for international debate and cooperation"?

[They are] acting like the worst kind of deadbeats.

New York Times, April 19, 1997

◆ On the Role of Religion in Public Affairs and the Separation of Church and State

Early in his tenure, Rudy Giuliani gave a speech ruminating on the role of Catholicism in American society—especially for Roman Catholics who hold public office.

As the Mayor of New York City, I will work as hard to protect someone's right to believe in God as he or she sees fit—or not to believe in God—because I realize that my right to practice my religion depends

completely on my commitment to defend someone else's right to practice theirs, or to practice no religion at all. . . . [Many Catholics] feel that in some intellectual or quasi-intellectual circles, they are damned. Catholic-bashing has become part of the dogma of what they regard as the politically correct. Indeed, I do detect among some who accept the most recent intellectual fads a disdain for those who share in the more orthodox faiths, whether Catholic or Jewish or Muslim. In my humble opinion—and this is meant as an observation, not a challenge—that disdain emerges from an almost subconscious conclusion that to believe in God too fervently betrays a certain intellectual infirmity.

New York Times, April 21, 1994

He compared such a view with the "difficult time that some believers have in drawing the line between belief in dogma and respect for those who disagree." He called for believers and unbelievers alike to avoid "the arrogance of having no doubts.". . .

In his speech, Mr. Giuliani noted that America had been founded on the concept of religious tolerance, that "people fled Europe to protect themselves from a society in which religious dogma could dominate civic life in very disagreeable ways." And he said that in New York today, believers and atheists alike must tolerate each other's views.

"The condition of diversity—the condition most obvious to any one looking at New York—mandates that we live in respectful disagreement," he said. "It makes that demand because the alternative is that we cannot live at all. We must be allowed to celebrate what we believe in."

Of his own Roman Catholic faith, Mr. Giuliani said it helped him wrestle with the great questions of human history: of mankind's destiny, of whether there is a God, of whether death is final.

"The Catholic religion provides me the structure in which to ask these questions," the Mayor said. "The church has built the road that allows my intellect to traverse to the outer reaches of what is comprehensible and, at that point, the church offers a leap of faith to carry me where my intellect cannot go. For me, being a Catholic is not limiting but liberating."

New York Times, April 21, 1994

Early in his first race for mayor, asked his views on a woman's right to an abortion, Giuliani clarified what he saw as the proper limits of his private faith in formulating positions of public policy:

I wouldn't express my personal views in a policy action as Mayor. *Village Voice*, March 7, 1989

But, in office, on issues ranging from what kind of art was appropriate to display in the city-funded Brooklyn Museum to the use of school vouchers, Mayor Rudy Giuliani did in fact articulate a Catholic religious component in announcing and defending his actions. (For a fuller airing of Giuliani's views on abortion, see Chapter XXV, "The Race for the Senate: Target Hillary," under the heading "Abortion—Campaign Flip-Flop #3?"; on the controversy over a Brooklyn Museum art exhibit, see Chapter 24, "'The Brooklyn Museum Had Lost Its Charm'"; on vouchers, see Chapter 22, "Rudy: The Education Mayor.")

For instance, in a 1995 speech on the woes of the public schools:

Saying the New York City public school system is close to collapse, Mayor Rudolph W. Giuliani yesterday demanded that educational officials begin a program of "radical reform" that he said should be modeled

on the city's Catholic school system, from which he graduated.   *New York Times*, August 15, 1995

Let me suggest maybe a model for the things that have to be done to turn around the school system. . . . Maybe we can look for a moment at the parochial school system and see if it can't be a guide for the way in which public schools should be revised and reformed.
                    New York Times, August 15, 1995

Not that even Catholic schools were what they used to be, the Generalissimo discovered to his consternation one day.

Two weeks ago, Mr. Giuliani introduced an honorable cabdriver to a group of parochial school students who had been invited to City Hall. He explained that the man had returned some $10,000 he had found in the back of his cab, and he asked what they would have done in a similar circumstance. "Keep it," they rejoined. And everyone laughed.

But at a news conference the next day, the Mayor expressed shock. "I can't imagine if I had come to City Hall when I was in the third or fourth grade, when I had nuns teaching me, and the Mayor of the city had said to me what would I do with $10,000 that was found," he said, his face etched in disbelief. "If I had said that I would have kept it, I would not have returned home that night looking the same as I did going to school in the morning."   *New York Times*, February 15, 1998

17

Rudy: The Education Mayor

Republicans, conservatives and others should not in any way be walking away from the education issue. We should be at the forefront of it because we have the better answer to it.

Speech given at invitation of *American Spectator* magazine, Washington, D.C., *New York Times,* November 10, 1999

Two remarkable aspects of that statement were, first, that Rudy Giuliani, after running three times for Mayor of New York as the candidate of the Liberal Party, was finally—as he made plans to run statewide, for the U.S. Senate—revealing that in fact it was "conservatives" whose ideas he shared after all. And, second, that Rudy Giuliani actually *had* ideas and answers on how to make the public schools better, which would have come as a surprise to most New Yorkers who witnessed his performance in that area. His education platform, from beginning to end, seemed to consist of three basic planks: Make public schools like Catholic schools. Give me the power over them. And, knowing he was not about to be granted either wish, endlessly bash whoever *was* in charge of the schools and cut their funding.

Just like we've become a national leader and model for the country and some of the rest of the world in reducing crime and improving quality of life, we have to do the same for education.

State of the City address, *New York Times,* January 15, 1997

[Do] not vote for me based on the schools. I don't control them. The Chancellor isn't accountable either. The system is designed to remove accountability.
Phi Beta Kappan, December 1995

. . . You should not hold someone [like me] accountable for a system they're not entitled to run. I've done as much with the system as you could possibly do.
New York Post, December 30, 1999

I believe that right now the New York City public school system has reached a turning point. And if we don't do something, and do something dramatic, it's close to collapse. If we fail to act now to bring the system under control, to guarantee the safety and the security of children, teachers, principals and staff, to insure that the $8 billion we spend on this system is spent on students, not on bureaucracy, and to raise educational standards, and restore sensible educational priorities to the classroom, if we don't do all of that and more and quickly, the entire system really is in great, great danger of collapse. . . .

To me it's a challenge, and it's a challenge to change the way in which we are doing things, to change it radically. But I'm afraid that the bureaucracy fears change so greatly, and is so afraid of it, that they will do everything possible to reject it, and to reject the kind of changes that are needed. . . .

. . . Maybe we can look for a moment at the parochial school system and see if it can't be a guide for the way in which public schools should be revised and reformed. . . . All of these things [done in Catholic schools] are things that we can apply to the public school system: high standards, the ability to do something with children who are disciplinary problems, to remove them from the schools, school-based budgeting, school-based management, these are all things that can happen in the public school system if we want to make them happen. Or we can continue to mindlessly defend it and keep it exactly the way it is.

Speech to the Wharton Club, *N.Y. Times,* August 15, 1995

The idea, as much as possible, is to crush the adminis-trative system.

Statement accompanying release of proposal for abolition of New York City Board of Education, *N.Y. Times,* July 13, 1994

So-called experts have been controlling it for 20 years. I guess if you're satisfied with the results, let them keep doing it. . . . Maybe if they focus on the fact that they may not be there forever, and that there is a difference of opinion, including public opinion, maybe some of them will think more long term about their own futures.

New York Times, June 20, 1995

At one moment he called it [the Board of Education] "about the largest and most labyrinthine bureaucracy that man or woman has ever been able to design." At another, he described it as a "trapped octopus," franti-cally spewing ink at its predators.

New York Times, August 15, 1995

Hey, get rid of another 1,000 people at 110 Livingston Street [Board of Education headquarters], and nobody will know the difference. . . . The way you do this—if I were controlling the budget of the Board, which is what I'm asking for—would be to take $30 or $40 mil-lion from 110 Livingston Street. Then take another fair

percentage of it out of the local boards, reduce their administrative staffs. They could operate with a smaller administrative staff—maybe get some volunteers to help out.   *New York Times,* July 15, 1995

Mr. Giuliani said City funds should no longer be used to pay bureaucrats who have "diverted" money intended for the classroom . . . [or] the many "hidden administrators" who are on the books as teachers but rarely enter a classroom. He gave no details on the size of the problem, saying it was a matter for an investigation.
                    New York Times, June 20, 1995

There's enough money in the school system. There always has been. Nine billion dollars is a lot of money. The problem with the school system was the need to restructure it. The money wasn't going to the students. The money wasn't going to the teachers. The money was going to the out-of-control bureaucracy.
    Statement at candidates' debate, *N.Y. Times,* Oct. 10, 1997

. . . When I went to grammar school and high school, I was in classes of 40 or 50. I think one class I was in had 52 students in it. And I think that what we've done with students is to sometimes give them excuses for not learning. . . .

    . . . What teachers should be telling students is not to complain about budget cuts, but to read, to learn. . . . What we've done is create a philosophy of excuses, as opposed to a philosophy of success.

    . . . The people who are blaming me for the facilities in New York City, totally absurd, this has been going on for 30 years. The fact is that we're getting more money to the schools than was the case before. . . .

Learning isn't about the number of children in school. It isn't about what the facilities are like. It isn't about space. It's about reading. It's about accessing knowledge yourself. It's about acquiring the desire to learn.

Statement of views on overcrowding in public schools and need for new facilities, *New York Times,* September 7, 1996

Every one of the things I'm talking about are things I've had to get the Chancellor and the Board of Ed to support by pulling them along kicking and screaming. It will not happen without the determination and a strength and a fighting that isn't there in the Board of Education. *New York Times,* June 20, 1995

◆ Death Watch #1:
Schools Chancellor Ramon Cortines

The first school official subjected to the Generalissimo's pull-them-along-kicking-and-screaming strategy for school reform was, ironically, the man whose selection as schools chancellor on a 4 to 3 vote by the Board of Education in the summer of 1993 was widely perceived as a victory for challenger Rudy Giuliani over incumbent Mayor David Dinkins.

But Ramon Cortines, former superintendent of schools in San Francisco, quickly erased any trace of partisanship. His hands-on style—taking command of a panic over asbestos deposits found in city schools, making visits to classrooms to raise morale among teachers and students alike—quickly wowed and won over New Yorkers, who realized they had a superlative educator on their hands. Only one problem: In immediately making peace with Dinkins ("he's my Mayor," said the new chancellor, understandably seeking to keep politics out of the school system), Cortines had, without knowing it, made an enemy out of Giuliani.

A month after taking office, the Generalissimo released his first municipal financial plan. In it was a $291 million cut in school funding—dismissing 40 percent of the Board of Education's staff. Cortines protested that a cut that steep would mean letting go school crossing guards, lunchroom aides, even assistant principals.

Mr. Giuliani said cuts in anything besides administrative staff "was never my intention." . . . While Mr. Giuliani said that Mr. Cortines had his full confidence and insisted the two men were "moving in the same direction here," it instead appeared that they were on a collision course over the budget.

The Mayor insisted that he still wanted nearly 2,500 administrative employees cut from the Board of Education rolls, and he called the Board a "bureaucracy way out of control." . . .

Mr. Giuliani said he had left the session assured that both he and Mr. Cortines "have precisely the same desire to trim the out-of-control bureaucracy at 110 Livingston Street and the district offices without in any way harming the children." *N.Y. Times,* Feb. 4, 1994

That was not Cortines's impression. He gave a memo to the school board calling the mayor's proposals more "than impossible to implement."

It has always been my intent and desire to cut administrators. That's what we asked the Board to do originally. The Board sent us back a plan in which they had us cutting back almost everything else but administrators. Then we sent a directive back to them. Then they sent a

directive back to us and we sent one back to them. **The Chancellor then agreed on 1,000 and I asked for 2,500.**
New York Times, February 4, 1994

The next day the two met again. The Generalissimo appeared to relent—provided that the chancellor make "an intensive good faith effort" to carry out the orders he had been given.
My position has always been that 2,500 is a goal. If we can get close to that, then there may be other ways to satisfy that. . . . I convinced him that we should move toward 2,500, that that should be our goal, that he should make a good faith effort to do that, and he will. And if we get really close to 2,500, then we probably will achieve what we want to achieve. *N.Y. Times*, Feb. 5, 1994

But any impression of a letup in the pressure was only temporary.
It is time for major surgery, to remove the blockage preventing our tax dollars from reaching our children. If it needs more cuts—and it probably will—we'll make them. *New York Times*, February 10, 1994

At a news conference earlier in the day, Mr. Giuliani was asked if tensions had risen between them. "I really can't tell," the Mayor told reporters. "He [Cortines] says one thing to you and something different to me."
New York Times, February 10, 1994

By April, Giuliani's cuts had risen to $332 million—but Cortines said he could not do more than cut 700 jobs and eliminate another 500 vacant slots. Otherwise, he warned, "we aren't going to have much of a school system."
There is no question that he can do better than that. And we're going to work with him to try and see if we

can focus on that overhead—the very famous, well-known, bloated overhead at the Board of Education. . . .

Maybe this is a day I'm particularly frustrated. I've asked the Chancellor to find 2,500 positions in a school system bloated with administrators. Give me a break, you can find that in the system.   *N.Y. Times,* Apr. 2, 1994

At a City Hall news conference, Mr. Giuliani said that what Mr. Cortines had done with his latest proposal was "kind of slide back" from earlier promises to cut 1,000 Board employees.

After all that, Mr. Giuliani said: "I think my relationship with the Chancellor is a good relationship."
                                        New York Times, April 2, 1994

The reality is that the Board is going to have to make cuts. There is no line in the sand. The only line in the sand is it has to be a very substantial reduction. . . . This is really an opportunity for massive reduction in overhead and we'll go through with it. Decentralization can often lead to much smaller bureaucracies. Decentralization can also lead to large bureaucracies. It depends on how you manage it.

> Refloating old proposal to break up central Board of Education into five borough boards, which critics pointed out would only lead to duplicative competing bureaucracies and would replicate problem-plagued community board system set up in city's school decentralization plan implemented in late 1960s
> *New York Times,* April 6, 1994

Escalating a war of words over New York City's school system, Mayor Rudolph W. Giuliani leveled an unusually personal attack yesterday on Schools Chancellor

Ramon C. Cortines, accusing him of "protecting the bureaucracy" at the Board of Education and hurting schoolchildren. . . .

The Mayor repeated his demand in sharp tones, calling Mr. Cortines' plan [for cutbacks] "an embarrassment."

New York Times, April 7, 1994

Look, I've lived in this city a lot longer than he has. Don't tell me that there are only six, seven hundred useless bureaucrats at 110 Livingston Street. I've been in this city too long. I know it too well. So you've got to be realistic with me. . . .

Sometimes if you get your head out of 110 Livingston Street and you get it into the real world, you stop protecting the bureaucrats there. . . . Part of the problem could be that coming from out of town, maybe he doesn't realize that he's been captured by the school bureaucracy.

New York Times, April 7, 1994

Cortines was invited—alone—to a midnight meeting at Gracie Mansion. There he was ganged up on by Giuliani and a bevy of six of his top officials and told that a fiscal overseer would be appointed to monitor all his actions—unless he agreed, on the spot, to fire his budget director. And, oh yes, his press secretary too, a veteran of city government widely respected by the press corps, but one who bore the mark of Cain—he had (among other things) worked in David Dinkins's administration. Cortines, saying "my integrity is not for sale," resigned rather than comply with the ultimatum. Public opinion in New York was dismayed at losing such a superb schools chancellor after only eight months in office. The Generalissimo was faced with criticism from all quarters, even from supporters, over forcing Cortines out.

The Mayor calls Mr. Cortines's resignation "peevish" and says, "It really does seem to me almost childish to resign over that."

Reaction to Cortines's resignation
Requoted in *New York Times*, June 16, 1995

I'm sorry he did this, but we really have to move on and reform this system. There are some people who are capable of doing it and some people who maybe won't make personnel changes for one reason or another. You can't reform the system by magic or all by yourself. . . .

He's had months to make internal changes. He's made no changes. . . .

He's sitting there with precisely the bureaucracy that brought the problem in the first place, and every time he takes two steps forward they take four steps backward, and he wants to do nothing about that.

So I had one of two choices: recommend to him changing the system internally, which he rejected—I can't do anything about that: he runs the board. Or have a fiscal monitor that would assure me that we were moving in the right direction, so at least I could be accountable to the taxpayers for the spending of money. It is not acceptable to be spending seven billion dollars and not know what you're spending it on. . . .

What we need is stability and direction in the Board of Education. Someone who is willing to take the bureaucracy and fight for the children. The budget proposal I got from him was one that protected the bureaucracy and took services away from the children. That was unacceptable.

I have not talked to him. All I've seen is a press release in which the words "resigned on June 30" are there. It seems to me I take him at his word, he's resigned, let's move on to the future of the school system. We can surely find someone who will both embrace the rhetoric of reform and in fact accomplish reform by being willing to take on the bureaucracy so the children don't get hurt.   *New York Times*, April 9, 1994

I can't sit by and continue to have numbers that indicate things totally opposite the reality. This is a $7 billion to $8 billion system and we have classrooms that are falling apart, school books that are 20 years old. This is a problem in which the old politicians of this city, and the people who are used to the old political solution are going to fight like hell to preserve the system the way it is. And I was elected to change that. I would welcome the Chancellor joining me in this, and I was disappointed that he didn't.   *New York Times,* April 10, 1994

After high-level intervention by Governor Mario Cuomo, among many others, a rapprochement was reached. Cortines did not have to fire his two aides. Herman Badillo, Giuliani ally (and 1993 running mate for comptroller), would be appointed as fiscal monitor—but would report to Cortines as well as Giuliani. And Cortines rescinded his resignation. Everything was patched up—for the moment.

I am very pleased that the Chancellor and I have been able to resolve this. We'll be able to move forward. I believe that the resolution of this is a metaphor for our city and how we can resolve differences and problems.

There were difficulties. There were problems. By meeting together and talking about them we were able to resolve them. If the Mayor is able to move forward with his responsibilities, and the Chancellor is able to move forward with his responsibilities, the two of us can

**work out an agreement which we both feel very com-
fortable will fulfill the important mandate we both have.**
New York Times, April 11, 1994

**It wasn't the smoothest way to get where we wanted to
go, but we finally got there. We finally got what we have
had to achieve.** *New York Times*, April 12, 1994

But there were obvious signs that Cortines had only gotten
a reprieve.

**The proposal for borough governance is the only realis-
tic proposal to shake up and to end 110 Livingston
Street. It's the only realistic way in which it's going to
happen.** *New York Times*, April 12, 1994

**Mayor Rudolph W. Giuliani refused yesterday to give
the New York City school system an extra $4.2 billion
that Chancellor Ramon C. Cortines said he needs to
build new schools to relieve overcrowding over the next
five years.** *New York Times*, May 4, 1994

The cuts reached $358 million. Then, in August 1994, Giu-
liani cut another $450 million more. In his first two years in
office, the Generalissimo cut a total of $1.2 billion out of fund-
ing for the school system.

**Life is difficult. We all have difficulties, the Board of
Education has difficulties. . . . By and large, my experience with the Board is that when you ask them for
budget cuts, the first thing they do—the first submis-
sion—is to frighten the living daylights out of you. I
don't feel particularly unusual as a Mayor. They've been
doing it for 20 years.** *New York Times*, August 3, 1994

I think there's a lot more room [to cut].
New York Times, November 22, 1994

The Mayor tells a college audience, "I am not afraid to kick the living hell out of" the size of the school board administration. The Mayor said, "The system that is there is not willing to do that."

Statement by Mayor Rudolph Giuliani, December 1994,
Requoted in *New York Times*, June 16, 1995

One day after taking a swipe at Schools Chancellor Ramon C. Cortines by offering to "kick the hell" out of the size of the city's Board of Education administration, Mayor Rudolph W. Giuliani yesterday accused the Chancellor of using "scare tactics." . . . Mr. Giuliani said he still has problems with "the game that's played at the Board of Education, which continues, which is to constantly, always, no matter what the request is, to make the cuts come out of the classrooms, schoolrooms, children as much as possible." *New York Times*, December 6, 1994

The Chancellor keeps making the point that he's independent. I think that's a mistake. I think the Mayor should have the authority and the responsibility and the accountability for the budget of the Board so we don't have the Chancellor continuing to frighten children by cuts that are not necessary. . . .

I'm not willing to say that we will seek no further reductions in the Board this year or next year, not until I have a much better sense of the actual spending in the Board. . . . [I] said yesterday that Mr. Cortines was trying to create "a kind of political momentum and a kind of fear" to keep the City Council from forcing it to cut back on the [school] administration bureaucracy.

New York Times, December 14, 1994

Cortines's contract was up for renewal by the board. Giuliani began a war of nerves with the chancellor.

Mr. Giuliani said his "review process" of the extension is not complete and that he would withhold any comment until then. "I will then have a position," Mr. Giuliani told a news conference at City Hall.

New York Times, December 6, 1994

If, in fact, the Chancellor chooses to leave, then what I would ask is that the Board work with me, but it would have to be at their discretion. You would think that wisdom suggests that they would do that, and City Hall and the Board, the Mayor and the Chancellor should have a close working relationship. *N.Y. Times*, Dec. 15, 1994

This has always been about issues for me. I never got angry at Ray Cortines, I don't dislike him. It plays out that way because of the public impression of the two of us— me being very strong and tough, him being easygoing and nice and friendly. . . . It plays into a certain stereotype that works very well for them—that I'm a very tough prosecutor, very hard, very difficult to get along with. I'm very tough but not difficult to get along with. And I'm very reasonable. *N.Y. Times*, Dec. 19, 1994

But he did not have the votes to stop Cortines from being reappointed. For all Giuliani's attacks on him, the chancellor had the support of the editorial boards, teachers, parents, business and educational organizations—not to mention five out of seven votes on the Board of Education (the appointees of the borough presidents, even that of Giuliani's erstwhile ally, Guy Molinari of Staten Island, who was temporarily estranged from the Generalissimo over his endorsement of Mario Cuomo in the governor's race). Consistently they [the board members] have been unwilling to work with me and rather try to undercut and misdescribe everything that we're doing. At least an equal obligation has to be placed on them to work with me and my administration rather than constantly try to undercut it. After all, I'm the Mayor of the city.

New York Times, December 15, 1994

If I were asked to vote now and say do I have confidence in his being able to make the changes that I believe people in the city want, I haven't seen that. . . . This is an acceptance of the reality that he has the votes to remain. My preference would be for a new Chancellor. But the reality is he has the votes to remain.

New York Times, December 19, 1994

If the decision was mine alone, I would say he's had his 18 months and not shown an ability to create the change the system needs. If I had my druthers, I would say we should find someone who wants to make changes, rather than someone who has to be forced into it.

New York Times, December 20, 1994

Mr. Giuliani said he was suggesting a one-year contract with conditions as a way to satisfy some of his own concerns about management and financing of the school system, "because there's a very good chance, if not an excellent chance, he'll be there anyway. If he is, we want the Board to hold him to a clear and public substantive agenda of reform so he can be measured by that progress. In other words, we want him to be accountable." *New York Times,* December 20, 1994

Since our desire to have a new Chancellor is not going to be accepted by the Board, the least the Board can do is to come up with a group of very specific things the Chancellor has to achieve in reforming the system so that in the future he has to be judged from a substantive background rather than a more romantic, emotional background.   *New York Times,* December 19, 1994

But the board rebuffed Giuliani, offering Cortines a two-year renewal—with no demeaning "conditions" attached. The Generalissimo was able to use his two votes on the board to keep the decision from being unanimous, but that was all. He had been well and properly rebuked.

If we can't do a better job with $8 billion than the Board or the Chancellor are doing, then they have to turn the movement of that money over to someone else. The Chancellor is largely held unaccountable, and what the Board apparently wants to do is to continue that.
                                        New York Times, December 20, 1994

Mr. Giuliani sounded dubious yesterday about the Chancellor's ability to implement City Hall's "agenda of reform."   *New York Times,* December 22, 1994

Mr. Giuliani reacted to Mr. Cortines' decision [to accept the contract] by vowing to "continue to press our agenda of reform. To the extent that the Chancellor adheres to that agenda, and hopefully does substantially better than he has up to now, and doesn't undercut that agenda of reform, then we will work with him. To the extent that he doesn't, we'll continue to raise criticisms. The agenda of reform is more important than any person."
                                        New York Times, December 30, 1994

I think the school board is engaging, unfortunately, in the reflexive conduct that it engages in all the time

unless leadership is exercised. And here's where the Chancellor is not exercising leadership. They will protect their turf. They're not going to give up anything. They're not going to give up a position. They're not going to give up a bureaucrat. They're not going to give up an administrator. They're not going to give up on anything unless somebody pulls it away from them. And that's unfortunate. Schools are in serious condition.

Statement, May 31, 1995.
Requoted in *N.Y. Times,* June 5, 1995

The Generalissimo simply found a new avenue of attack— demanding that school safety be turned over to the Police Department. And when Cortines and the board demurred, lambasting them unmercifully.

I think most parents and most teachers would feel far safer if this were in the hands of the NYPD rather than in the hands of the school board and the Chancellor, who has not shown a great capacity at management in general and certainly not in the area of law enforcement.

New York Times, June 1, 1995

When Cortines formed a committee to review the issue, the Generalissimo erupted:

We've got children that are getting beaten up in schools. We've got children that have been murdered in schools. We've got crime going up 25 to 30 percent, and we've got an essay exam here. . . . I think it is appropriate for me as the Mayor of the city, to be somewhat concerned that the Chancellor—who just a week ago said that he knew more about school security than anyone in the system—is now sending out a memo asking for a definition of it. Maybe I have some concern about the

safety of the children in the schools as the result of a Chancellor who needs a definition of school safety.

New York Times, June 7, 1995

But soon the issues didn't matter. The object became driving Cortines out of town by any means necessary. And the method chosen was to inflict a form of vituperation on him uglier than any Mayor of New York had ever used to describe another government official in public.

[Cortines] talks out of both sides of his mouth.

Comments about schools chancellor, June 1995
Requoted in Washington Post, June 30, 1999

[The Mayor] called Cortines "precious."

Comments about schools chancellor, June 1995
Requoted in New York Times, October 12, 1995

The fact is he spent yesterday whining, which he does all the time and you fall for it. This is not about personal attack. Do not be distracted by that. The Chancellor should stop it. He should grow up. And what he should do is understand that he's got to embrace change and stop whining about it and stop playing the little victim. Comments about schools chancellor, June 2, 1995

Requoted in New York Times, June 5 and June 16, 1995

Ramon Cortines, a sixty-something bachelor from San Francisco, knew what the words "precious," "whining," and "little victim" were code for. And he knew where this was going. He decided to get out with his pride—personal and professional—intact. Still, having already stooped as low as many thought it was possible to go, Giuliani kept taunting and baiting him.

I imagine that Mr. Cortines makes his own decisions. I know they've called me a bully. I know that they called me all kinds of names. You want my reaction to it? I won't quit. . . . I think I'd better wait and see if he actually stays with the decision to leave. This is like *déjà vu* all over again for me, and rather than react to it immediately as we did last time, we're going to wait a few days and see if this turns out to be his formal decision. *New York Times*, June 16, 1995

This [his comments] has nothing to do with forcing the Chancellor out. *New York Times*, June 16, 1995

In that case, would he ask Cortines to reconsider?
I think that would be rather unrealistic.
New York Times, June 16, 1995

Cortines, his reputation as a first-rate educator unimpaired in the eyes of those who knew best, moved on to the Department of Education in Washington and, in 1999, returned to California with a mandate to run—and reform, from top to bottom—the Los Angeles school system. Back in New York, meanwhile, Generalissimo Giuliani was finding new targets for his invective.

◆ Death Watch #2:
School Board President Carol Gresser

Any hopes that the announced departure of Ramon Cortines would satisfy Rudolph Giuliani were promptly dashed.
Mr. Giuliani spent much of the day continuing the drumbeat of criticism that many believe drove Mr. Cortines from office. Though he lightly praised Mr.

Cortines for having "done some good things for the system," he said the Chancellor wasn't willing to reform the school system and then "take the heat" from the educational bureaucracy.   *New York Times,* June 17, 1995

Now he was training his sights on the board members themselves.

When I first asked them to reduce the budget, they were going to take the money from classrooms, from schools. It was only after a lot of bickering and arguments, with me on one side and them on the other, that they agreed to make the cuts without affecting classrooms and schools.   *New York Times,* June 16, 1995

This was his demand—I must approve your choice of the next Chancellor.

It certainly makes sense for the Mayor to have a substantial role in the selection of a Chancellor, so that both the Chancellor and the Mayor can work together and have at least a group of articulated common goals that they're working toward.   *N.Y. Times,* June 16, 1995

What we're going to try to do is, right from the very beginning, try to impress on the Board the fact that it's counterproductive to select a Chancellor that isn't selected with significant input and approval by the Mayor and by City government, by City Hall.

New York Times, June 17, 1995

And if he didn't get that power, he made no bones about it: Cortines is gone; you're next.

Maybe if they focus on the fact that they may not be there forever, and that there is a difference of opinion,

**including public opinion, maybe some of them will
think more long term about their futures.**

New York Times, June 20, 1995

**He once again took aim at the Board's preference for an
educator [as the next Chancellor], saying their refusal to
consider an administrator was an example of "bureaucratic rigor mortis."** *New York Times*, August 15, 1995

**In a sweeping bid for power that roiled the search for a
Schools Chancellor, Mayor Rudolph W. Giuliani said
last night that he has decided to support only those candidates who agree that City Hall should control the budget of the school system and school safety.**

New York Times, September 12, 1995

Giuliani, in fact, had already called some prospective candidates in to interview them himself and convey that message.
Board president Carol Gresser, complaining that the board's
top candidate had dropped out as a result of Giuliani's
demands, scored the mayor's *sub rosa* interference with the
selection process. In standing up for the board's lawful prerogatives, she became the target of his next vendetta.

**Carol Gresser isn't going to stop me from talking to
people about being Chancellor. So she might as well
take her silly remarks and do something else with
them. . . . [These discussions with the candidates were]
beyond Carol Gresser's ability to carry on a substantive
discussion.** *New York Times*, September 12, 1995

Gresser was, among other things, sayeth the Generalissimo,

silly, outrageous . . . crass. *New York Times*, July 9, 1996

. . . Through a surrogate, [he] urged her to "lead, follow, or get out of the way." *New York Times,* July 7, 1996

And he vowed to continue meeting with candidates, whether the Board liked it or not.

If I can intimidate a candidate for Chancellor, then the person shouldn't be a candidate for Chancellor. You better be tough enough to be able to handle New York City.
New York Times, September 13, 1995

He went on to deride the Board's plan to interview so many candidates as a script for "a *Saturday Night Live* skit." *New York Times,* September 13, 1995

Giuliani then escalated the power struggle. Having struck an alliance with the Brooklyn borough president, Democrat Howard Golden, he attempted to isolate Gresser and swing a 4 to 3 board vote in favor of a Golden favorite, president of Kingsborough Community College Leon Goldstein.

We have somebody who obviously does understand the politics of New York City, understands the City of New York and understands how to get things done. From my point of view, that's a very positive thing. Other people see it as a negative, but that certainly is a fair part of the debate. *New York Times,* September 27, 1995

Unfortunately, among those who saw Goldstein's political background as a "negative" were the Board of Education investigators who vetted his application. Their background check turned up a platoon of inconsistencies and questions—about his age, his marriages, his health, the educational degrees he claimed to have, his ties to the Brooklyn Democratic Party, and allegations of patronage and favoritism in the campus administration he ran. For none of this did Mr. Goldstein have anywhere near persuasive explanations. And the reaction of former prosecutor Rudy Giuliani, the mayor who swore his regime was all about ridding New York City of old-style political wheeling, dealing, corruption, and cronyism?

Cheap shots and misinterpretations. . . . Any mistake that a person makes—if they say 3 instead of 4, or 7 instead of 10, if they get something wrong at some point—is blown up into some major catastrophe. . . .

That's McCarthyism of the worst kind. . . . From everything I've seen so far, the man has done an excellent job running Kingsborough Community College. Those are the things that we really should be focusing on.

New York Times, September 28, 1995

Describing as "silly" a growing chorus of criticism of Mr. Goldstein, the Mayor said Mr. Goldstein had done an exemplary job as president of Kingsborough Community College in Brooklyn and would make an excellent Schools Chancellor. *N.Y. Times,* Sept. 29, 1995

I do support him. I'm comfortable that he would move the school system in the right direction. Let's go forward. Let's put him in charge, and let's give my ideas for the school system a chance. That doesn't mean that he would do all the things that I would do, in exactly the way in which I would do it, but the general direction, the general philosophy, that he has, the general approach that he has, which is very much rooted in common sense, would be a very, very good one for the Board. *New York Times,* September 29, 1995

Then the board's investigative report on Goldstein was leaked to the media. Giuliani, who in his prosecutor days had frequently been suspected of doing the very same thing, huffed with self-righteousness:

The process has been seriously tainted. Handing a confidential document that contains raw allegations that haven't been analyzed and haven't been investigated and haven't been proven, to hand that over to the press, when the document says all over it confidential, it taints the process. It does more than taint the process. . . . It is insecure, it is unprofessional and it's one in which if you can't defeat a candidate in any other way, you'll defeat the candidate by attempting to destroy their character and reputation and by giving out confidential documents against any sense of ethics or decency.

New York Times, September 30, 1995

The information, I think, is largely exaggerated and taken out of context. If this is the best you can do to someone in public life for 20 or 25 years, we're not talking about serious allegations here. We're talking about things ratcheted up into serious allegations. Unfortunately, that unfair part of this process has worked.

New York Times, September 30, 1995

Goldstein dropped out. That was "unfortunate," the Generalissimo said.
"The information doesn't trouble me." . . . **He described the allegations as "largely exaggerated," although he felt it prudent to add, "I can't say we've looked at every one. I advised Mr. Goldstein to stay in it."**

New York Times, October 2, 1995

Giuliani blamed Gresser for the leak. She responded—plausibly—that she had seen the investigators' confidential report for the first time when it appeared in the newspaper. She then got the board to approve a chancellor of whom Giuliani did not approve. That nominee, Daniel Domenech, highly regarded schools chief of Suffolk County on nearby Long Island, never took office. Pronouncing Domenech "unacceptable," the mayor privately pressured the Staten Island board member to change his vote, reversing the 4 to 3 outcome. Three weeks into the academic year, with Cortines leaving and no successor in place, the school system was leaderless—and the board and Giuliani were at an impasse. Hastily, they compromised on Tacoma, Washington, Schools Superintendent Rudy Crew—whom Giuliani, after all his insistence on this point, had *not* interviewed.

Initially, at least, all parties were delighted with Crew, and peace seemed to be restored. But the Generalisssimo did not forget how Carol Gresser had dared to defy him. The following summer, her presidency of the school board was up.

In public, Giuliani had an open mind and at least some interest in healing the previous year's wounds by supporting her reelection.

I'm thinking about it and talking about it and discussing it. I really think it should be left confidential.

New York Times, July 8, 1996

As far as I know, there is no movement to anybody else.

Statement by mayoral education adviser
Herman Badillo, *New York Times,* July 7, 1996

In private, Giuliani did his ally Howard Golden the favor he had been unable to deliver the year before—and swung a board vote behind the Brooklyn representative, William Thompson, to unseat Gresser as president. A year later he struck another deal—this time with Gresser's borough president, Democrat Claire Shulman, who agreed to drop Gresser from the board entirely. (As for Thompson, he was reelected board president in 1999, but only after a scare that Giuliani was going to unseat him in the same way the Mayor had used

Thompson to knock off Gresser—the alliance with Golden having ended, and the mayor and the crusty Brooklyn borough president now loud enemies.)

◆ Death Watch #3:
Schools Chancellor Rudy Crew

Cortines's successor Rudy Crew, a burly, gregarious bear of a man, made a point of immediately cultivating the mayor. They shared a taste for fine cigars and baseball. They made a deal on school safety. They bonded. And the merciless attacks on the school system ceased.

My confidence level in Rudy Crew is very high. I think he is the kind of person that can accomplish the reforms we need. Statement on Crew's appointment, October 6, 1995
Requoted in *New York Daily News,* May 3, 1999

The Board of Education is moving in the right direction.
Statement by Mayor Giuliani, November 26, 1995
Requoted in *New York Daily News,* May 3, 1999

We will work with the Chancellor.
Statement by Giuliani press aide, March 12, 1996
Requoted in *New York Daily News,* May 3, 1999

As you know, we are working very fine with Chancellor Crew. Statement by mayoral education adviser
Herman Badillo, *New York Times,* July 8, 1996

We want the Chancellor to have this power.
Statement by Mayor Giuliani to U.S. Department of Justice supporting Chancellor's power to fire Community School Board superintendents, March 15, 1997
Requoted in *New York Daily News,* May 3, 1999

Giuliani even cited his desire to back Crew to the hilt as a reason for dumping Carol Gresser as school board president. (Crew complained to the mayor of friction between himself and Gresser.)

The Mayor . . . would say only that giving the Schools Chancellor, Dr. Rudy Crew, "the kind of support that he needed" was paramount in his thinking.

New York Times, July 8, 1996

The Mayor liked his chancellor so much, in fact, that after cutting school budgets by $2 billion in his first three years in office, he actually allowed an increase in education spending in 1997, as he geared up to run for reelection.

The reason I am doing this is my confidence in Rudy Crew. Rudy Crew has assembled a very good team.

Giuliani announcement that he would allocate an additional $70 million for new school textbooks, November 1996. Requoted in *New York Times,* March 5, 1997

And in that campaign. . .

When a mother comes up to me and says, "Thank you, Rudy, for fighting back to save our schools," I tell her, "You should thank another Rudy—Schools Chancellor Rudy Crew." Giuliani reelection radio/TV advertisement Broadcast July 1997

I think Rudy Crew is doing an excellent job as the Chancellor of New York. Statement at candidates' debate New York Times, October 10, 1997

We plan to continue what Rudy Crew has done in the school system. *New York Times,* October 25, 1997

Into the mayor's second term, the stream of praise continued.

As we enter the next century, we will once again be a city whose educational system is the best in the nation. . . .

Many students have experienced improvements in education and are beginning to feel the control of their own lives and the hope for the future that that brings. . . .

We must build on the great success that Chancellor Rudy Crew has had, and his fine team, and support them and complete with them the projects that they have already started.

Second Inaugural Address, *New York Times,* January 2, 1998, and official transcript released by Mayor's Press Office

In the area of education, the change is absolutely remarkable. It would be impossible to have achieved this much change, I think in most people's thinking, four or five years ago. What Chancellor Crew and his team have done within the incredible constraints of a system and sometimes a bureaucracy that resists change is absolutely remarkable. And as somebody who tries to study change and figure out how to bring it about, I'm a real admirer of what they've been able to accomplish.

State of the City address, January 14, 1999
Requoted in *New York Times,* April 28, 1999

Most of what we've accomplished are things that people thought we couldn't do. So there's no reason why we can't do more things that people thought couldn't be done.

State of the City address, *N.Y. Times,* Jan. 15, 1999

Chancellor Crew and I have spent literally hundreds of hours trying to put the Schools Construction Authority

back together again, and what we really need is help in that endeavor.

Reaction to Governor Pataki's formation of panel to investigate construction scandals in city schools, January 1999. Requoted in *New York Post*, May 5, 1999

I think the Chancellor of the New York City school system is the best we've had, in my experience. I think the man is phenomenal.

January 23, 1999. Requoted in *New York Daily News*, May 3, 1999; *New York Post*, May 5, 1999

I think the Chancellor is doing a great job. I think he's a great Chancellor, and I think we're fortunate to have him. And I am glad we made the choice to bring him here, because I think it made a big difference.

Presentation of the city budget, April 22, 1999
Requoted in *New York Times*, April 28, 1999

The only open disagreement the two men ever had was when Giuliani once proposed, during a school overcrowding crisis, to have the city put some students in Catholic schools. The chancellor made it clear that he could never be a party to the depopulation of the public educational system, and Giuliani backed off. But gradually the idea, or variations on it, kept creeping back into the Generalissimo's public statements.

For years, either in the form of tuition tax credits or vouchers, critics of public education had pressed for some form of government financial assistance to parents who put their children into private or religious schools. Most constitutional scholars agreed that in either form such assistance would violate the separation of church and state, and supporters of public education denounced what they saw as a scheme to create a tax subsidy so that more people could abandon tax-funded public schools. (An alternative reform offered by some defenders of public education was the establishment of "charter schools," independently operated institutions that set their own rules and standards while remaining part of the public system.)

The tuition tax credit/voucher dilemma was particularly hard on Roman Catholic politicians in multireligious constituencies, attempting to please their coreligionists without offending others. In 1989 first-time candidate Rudy Giuliani faced it too and modified his personal pro-Catholic beliefs in pursuit of elective office.

Giuliani has just made another move in [Liberal Party Chairman Ray] Harding's direction. . . . He now opposes tuition tax credits, concluding that they "would encourage people to take their kids out of the City school system." *Village Voice*, March 7, 1989

Six years later, as mayor, even while giving a speech arguing that public education should adopt Catholic schools as its model, Giuliani still refused to support a voucher system.

We're going to see increased calls for privatization and for vouchers for private and parochial school education. Alternatives which in my view will weaken if not create the collapse of the New York City public school system. . . . I believe the voucher system in New York City would be very, very troublesome. Our system is so large that making that kind of transition would pose tremendous difficulties. Not to mention the constitutional and legal difficulties that would be entailed in providing tax relief and tax dollars for religious education.
Speech to Wharton Club, *N.Y. Times,* Aug. 15, 1995

Vouchers would be "a terrible mistake" because they would bleed the public schools of needed financing.
New York Times, August 15, 1995

But, as his second term began, and he began to contemplate races for higher office outside of liberal New York City, Giuliani began dropping hints of a flip-flop in the making.

We must encourage public school choice, as well as charter schools.

. . . The Mayor's responsibilities go beyond only children in public schools. The Mayor is responsible for all of the city's children. We must continue to provide as much help for all children as is consistent with the limitations of the Constitution, including continuing to support the School Choice Scholarship Foundation, which is providing children and their parents who cannot afford it the opportunity to exercise freedom, the freedom to choose the school that they want to go to.

Second Inaugural Address, *New York Times,* January 2, 1998

A year later, an open U.S. Senate seat in his sights, the Generalissimo let the other shoe drop.

Mayor Rudolph W. Giuliani proposed such a [voucher] system yesterday for New York City, saying it might force failing public schools to improve. The Mayor said his inspiration was a program in Milwaukee that uses tax dollars to send students below a certain income level to private and parochial schools of their choice.

New York Times, January 15, 1999

It would make sense to do that experiment with a voucher system with a school district—one school district in the city, and see if it works. See if we give poorer parents the same opportunity to make choices about their children's education that the richest and the most affluent parents in New York City have—let's see if that doesn't work to really energize that school district and

help to create another alternative and more competition for the school system.

State of the City address, January 14, 1999
Requoted in *New York Times,* April 28, 1999

[School choice is] the most important thing that has to be done with education in America. We have too many children in New York and all throughout America who go to a school that they don't want to go. We are going to have a good public education system in America again, like we used to have 30 or 40 or 50 years ago, when children are in the school they want to be in. . . .

New York Times, March 1, 1999

Why should a parent who earns $20,000 a year and has two kids and has their kids in a school that they are very unsatisfied with, why should that parent not have the opportunity to make the kind of choice that I can make because I have a greater income and more financial resources? . . . If it works, let's expand it. And by work, I mean, if it educates children more effectively. If it does not work, let's stop it.

Comments on WCBS Radio
New York Times, March 5, 1999

We should take advantage of it to see if something good can come out of it.

New York Post, May 5, 1999

Don't listen to the special-interests, job-protection coalition. . . . Don't let the school bureaucracy and educrats determine which school your child can go to.

Comments on WABC Radio, *Washington Post,* June 30, 1999

He conceded that he had criticized vouchers several years ago, but said his position had since "evolved."

New York Times, April 28, 1999

Despite the fact that he should have known his about-face on the issue would drive a wedge between himself and his good buddy the schools chancellor, Giuliani professed shock when Crew announced he could not remain if vouchers were introduced.

I don't think the Chancellor is going to quit over the discussion of an idea like this. . . . But I don't think it's an appropriate way to have a public discussion. If I said I would quit every time somebody was discussing something I disagreed with, I would have quit the first day I was Mayor.   Comments on WCBS Radio
New York Times, March 5, 1999

I hope he doesn't resign over it, but I can't restrain ideas because somebody wants to resign over them. Maybe out of it something will emerge that's not exactly like this. But to kill the idea—pow!—is nearly like the Inquisition.   *New York Times,* April 23, 1999

Then, in late April, the Generalissimo took his philosophical disagreement with the chancellor—and his barbs about the public school system—to a whole new level, when he said this:

I think the Chancellor is working within a system that's dysfunctional. The system is just plain terrible. It makes no sense, and the end result of this system is, if this were a business system, it would be in bankruptcy. . . .

The whole system should be blown up, and a new one should be put in its place. . . .

. . . New York, because of the stagnant politics of the status quo and the fear of our politicians, is unwilling to do that.   Presentation of city budget, April 22, 1999
Requoted in *New York Times,* April 28, 1999

Just forty-eight hours before Rudolph Giuliani made his remark that the New York City school system "should be blown up," two disturbed teenagers had entered Columbine High School in Littleton, Colorado, armed with high-powered rifles and explosives, and proceeded to go on a killing spree, murdering thirteen students and faculty members, wounding and terrorizing many others. The siege finally ended when the two committed suicide—and only after their homemade bombs, with which they aimed to destroy their school, failed to work. These facts were well known, thanks to extensive live coverage at the scene and in the aftermath of the incident. The town was still in mourning; the nation was still in shock. In making the conscious decision to use those words in the wake of the carnage at Columbine, Giuliani had made perhaps the single most inappropriate comment ever to come out of the mouth of a Mayor of New York. All across the city, jaws literally dropped at the bloodcurdling tastelessness of what he had said.

In the face of withering criticism, the Generalissimo took the heat in a most honorable way. He attributed the choice of words to a man who was dead and conveniently unable to defend himself—former Deputy Mayor and School Board President Robert Wagner Jr.

That's an expression I've used at least since 1993, "blowing up the Board of Education." So this is not like a newfound position for me. I have not used any kind of destructive rhetoric. *New York Daily News*, April 28, 1999

Bobby used to say that as a metaphor for, you have to blow up the whole thing up in order to start all over again. I can understand why people pick on it, because they want to deliberately misunderstand it. . . . I've used it numerous times, including I believe once or twice even in State of the City speeches. So it's a common expression to me, and if anybody misunderstands it, they're honestly doing it on purpose.

New York Times, April 28, 1999

Former mayor Ed Koch, in whose administration the much-admired Wagner had served, spoke up to doubt the truth of Giuliani's claim. But far more worrisome to the Generalissimo was Crew's response. The chancellor faxed to dozens of leading New Yorkers a letter debunking Giuliani's voucher proposal and scorning his "reckless statements" and "rhetoric of destruction."

I don't understand it. I mean, the things that I've said last week, I've said over and over again, and I've said to Rudy Crew directly. *New York Times,* April 27, 1999

The Mayor said he was "baffled" by the Chancellor's reaction [to the voucher proposal], "because I explained all this to the Chancellor personally in a meeting. There's nothing that I've done that I haven't told him."
New York Times, April 28, 1999

But there were the same old signs that had presaged the departure of other talented but independent-minded people, such as Ramon Cortines—and, for that matter, William Bratton.

I am focused completely on how we can reform the school system. And so far, the response of the Chancellor and the school system has been a very rigid defense of the status quo. . . .

The ball is now in the Chancellor's court. What is the agenda for radical reform? Or is the agenda to keep the system exactly the way it is? *New York Times,* April 28, 1999

Suddenly Crew could go—if he wanted to, that is.
I wouldn't be responsible for it—nope. People have to make their own decisions about what jobs they want, what jobs they don't want. . . . [I must see an] impressive agenda of reform. . . . I am advocating for things, that's

**how you bring about reforms. No one person has the
power to bring about reform.** *N.Y. Times,* April 29, 1999

And, suddenly, all those good things Rudy Crew had
done—why, he hadn't done them at all. Rudy *Giuliani* had
done everything.

**Mr. Giuliani took credit for Dr. Crew's improvements.
"In fact, the amount of accountability that they now
have, that the Chancellor is very proud of and he should
be, are things that I originally suggested."**

New York Times, April 28, 1999

**The whole reason why the Chancellor is talking about
ending social promotions is because I stir things up. The
whole reason why there is a discussion of ending principal tenure is because I stir things up.** May 7, 1999

Requoted in *New York Times,* May 10 and 12, 1999

Why was vouchers even on the table for discussion?

Because I stir things up. May 7, 1999

Requoted in *New York Times,* May 10 and 12, 1999

Why was abolition of the Board of Ed even being debated?

Because I stir things up. May 7, 1999

Requoted in *New York Times,* May 10 and 12, 1999

**I am very happy that I caused this controversy. Other-
wise, you all wouldn't be writing about schools or talking about it and nobody would be writing Op-Ed pieces
about it. Do you think that the discussion of social promotion comes about other than the fact that I created
the agenda to make it happen? Or the discussion of the
Chicago system possibly being done in New York comes
about without my creating the controversy that makes**

that possible? So whether we achieve our entire agenda or not, we are certainly setting the agenda and I think that's clear to everyone.   *New York Times,* May 10, 1999

For his audacity, the chancellor was summoned to a meeting in the principal's—er, the mayor's—office.
I'm waiting for Chancellor Crew to explain his actions to me, and I think I have a right to that. And then maybe he can explain to me what he did and why he did it.
     May 1, 1999. Requoted in *New York Times,* May 4, 1999

But the meeting did not seem to heal the breach. Afterward, the Generalissimo was asked how his personal relationship with Crew was faring.
I'm not going to discuss my personal relationship. My personal relationship is personal, and if I start discussing it with you, it becomes a public relationship.
     New York Times, May 4, 1999

In fact, as Crew told associates, there was no personal relationship between them any more. There would be no more cigar-stoked, long, late-night conversations. The ties, personal as well as professional, were shattered. This could have been predicted from the moment Giuliani decided to change his position on vouchers, knowing they were a third-rail issue with the man he had hailed as the savior of the city's schools. Just as predictable was that Crew began entertaining job offers back in his native Washington State.
The City has not talked to anybody about being Chancellor. [But] when the Chancellor a month or two ago announced that he might resign, we obviously gave some thought to it.   *New York Times,* May 10, 1999

To give the chancellor a sense of urgency in his hunt, Giuliani worked the swing vote on the board—the woman who had been nominated by the mayor's ally, Queens Borough President Claire Shulman, as a replacement for the dumped Carol Gresser—to reverse the chancellor's capital-construction budget priorities in favor of her home borough, the first such repudiation Crew had received from the board. The 4 to 3 vote was a sharp reminder that the Queens representative would also break the tie on the board about whether to OK a voucher plan and on whether to offer Crew a new contract.

The fantasy plan. . . . They use Monopoly money. I have to use real money.

> Giuliani on Chancellor Crew's school-construction capital plan, which he had months earlier referred to as "realistic" and then later as "ambitious—but it should be,"
> *New York Post*, May 14, 1999

It was candidly admitted to me that there was money in the plan going to boroughs that didn't need that much money, that didn't have that much overcrowding, because they had to get the vote of that borough. And I said, "Suppose we just throw it all out and we just look at need? Suppose we look at a plan like that?" And I was told that that plan couldn't pass. *N.Y. Times*, Apr. 23, 1999

Rudy said, in effect, "Forget about the Senate race." . . .

Let's try to get the partisan politics and talk about the Senate and all this stuff out of here. This is a debate that I've engaged in for 10 years. It's about the good of the children, and it's only about the good of the children.

> *New York Times*, April 28, 1999

. . . until Chancellor Crew, in another display of what was taken as defiance at City Hall, appeared at an event with First Lady Hillary Rodham Clinton, the Generalissimo's opponent-in-waiting.

I don't know what's appropriate or inappropriate. Are you asking me do I think it's political? Sure.

New York Times, June 12, 1999

For which one of them, he was asked—or both?

I was being purposely ambigious. You figure it out. Did I think that was basically a politically motivated event? The answer is yes. *New York Times,* June 12, 1999

Did it bother him?

I didn't say that. In fact, maybe it doesn't.

New York Times, June 12, 1999

In an article that appeared over the summer in the *New York Times Magazine,* writer James Traub asked Giuliani specifically about Crew.

The Mayor made it clear that he would be happy to see Crew go. When I cited this to Giuliani as another case of calculated bullying, he shot back, "You weren't listening."

"Didn't you basically invite him to quit by expressing your lack of confidence?"

"Well, I guess you could put it that way; but it had its intended purpose. He's much more aggressive now."

New York Times Magazine, August 1, 1999

The Generalissimo's "psych-out" strategy on Crew apparently didn't work as well as thought, though. Three days after the magazine article appeared, a public letter from the mayor to Crew was released:

I am concerned that you have canceled our last six regularly scheduled weekly meetings on education. In light of the many challenges facing our public schools, regular meetings and communication are crucial. Whatever may be your reasons for canceling these meetings,

I hope you will be able to put them aside so that we can continue to work together to reform our school system. *New York Post,* August 4, 1999

Things limped along until the ultimate denouement. Crew plainly was fed up and had one foot out the door. Giuliani plainly wanted to be rid of him but was worried about the political implications of having to conduct a new chancellor search in the middle of his senatorial campaign. At year's end, opportunity knocked, twice, in the form of scandal allegations. One was genuine—the permanent schools investigator found that teachers had engaged in systematic cheating to help manipulate students' scores on state achievement tests and implied that Crew was aware of the situation. The Generalissimo played his cards close to his vest, practically talking about Crew's tenure in the past tense.

I think the Chancellor has done a good job in light of the powers that he has and the ability he has to affect them. . . . I think there are areas in which Rudy Crew should have been more willing to suggest destroying the system that he runs. That's a difficult thing to do.
New York Post, December 13, 1999

The other was a cheap shot—the panel George Pataki had formed to investigate problems in school construction, and whose formation Giuliani had protested, issued a report on a different subject, claiming city schools were falsifying and inflating attendance figures. (A lawsuit had been filed against Pataki and the state citing discrimination in state school aid to the city, based on the number of students in school there. The report, besides being irrelevant to the commission's stated purpose, was all too convenient for the defendants in the suit.) Again, Giuliani kept tongue in cheek, but noticeably failed to defend his onetime friend, the chancellor.

What they have illustrated, aside from the dramatic facts that are in there, is that this system does not work.
New York Post, December 14, 1999

On December 23, 1999, the Board of Education, in effect, fired Chancellor Rudy Crew—refusing to extend his contract and even moving to buy out his remaining six months so as to be rid of him immediately. The vote—4 to 3, with Giuliani's appointees and those of his two borough president allies doing the deed. It was a stunning fall from grace for the man who, less than a year earlier, had been Giuliani's confidant.

The Chancellor's been there a long time, much longer than average. Change is good.
New York Post, December 24, 1999

Mayor Giuliani said the Board made the "right decision."
New York Daily News, December 24, 1999

This is something that each of them [on the Board] freely and independently wanted to do. I did not ask them to do anything. I knew what they were going to do, but it's something they wanted to do.
New York Post, December 24, 1999

I'll work [to] select an outstanding new Chancellor who will work to reform the system.
New York Daily News, December 24, 1999

But when it came time to pick an interim replacement for Crew, Giuliani's fourth vote deserted him—and the board selected a candidate the mayor opposed.

She gave no explanation for her vote so, you know, in the absence of an explanation, we have to look for one. . . . They have selected the least qualified of the

two. I have to say to myself, there must be some other influence involved.　　　*New York Times,* January 13, 2000

The only reason for this choice is the worst kind of politics instead of the best interests of the children. [The interim chancellor] lacks not only the educational experience required by law but the administrative and management experience required by common sense.　　　*New York Daily News,* January 10, 2000

This is a step back into the 1970s and 1980s, in terms of machine political control of the system.
　　　New York Daily News, January 11, 2000

The board president was rhetorically indicted too—as was the teachers' union.

The pressure on him was enormous. The pressure was exerted both by Democratic politicians and by the union, and he caved in under the pressure and selected the less qualified of the two people.
　　　New York Times, January 11, 2000

Mr. Giuliani said Mr. [Board President William] Thompson had made "a calculation" that it would be better for his candidacy for [City] Comptroller if he went along with the desires of the United Federation of Teachers and with the Rev. Jesse Jackson. The Mayor implied that Mr. Jackson had lobbied Mr. Thompson to vote for Mr. [interim Schools Chancellor Harold] Levy.
　　　New York Times, January 11, 2000

This is a major political problem because often the Mayor is held accountable for a system that the Mayor is not allowed to run. . . . The system is a terrible, terrible system that dis-serves the children. Somebody has to say it. You can accuse me of playing politics saying it. I am saying it because I care about the children of this city.

New York Times, January 11, 2000

So, in what he billed as possibly his final "State of the City" address, the Generalissimo revealed his Doomsday device—ahem, his last-ditch strategy—for the public schools.

Things are slipping and getting worse under a Board system that makes no sense. . . . [Allow private companies to] compete with the Board and see who does a better job. *New York Times*, January 12, 2000

Privatize it. . . . Bring in competition. Don't be afraid. . . . We should be ashamed of ourselves that we don't have the political courage to take on the unions, the special interests and everything else holding our children back. State of the City Address

New York Times, January 14, 2000

As for the board . . .

Last year, I advocated burning it down. All right, well, I'm softening up. I'm becoming an easier guy. . . . It was a figure of speech. So now we won't blow it up, we'll sell it. We'll sell the building. . . . We're going to give them a more modern building. We're going to give them one of these smart buildings. That'd be good for the Board of Education, a smart building. State of the City Address

New York Times, January 14, 2000

But he added that "it's only going to be 25 percent of the size of the present building. Get it?"

State of the City address, *New York Times*, January 14, 2000

. . . and the schoolteachers . .

**The Mayor particularly singled out the teachers'
union . . . for what he called its "job protection
system." . . . [He] made one of his most aggressive
attacks yet on the City's teachers, saying they do not
deserve an across-the-board pay raise in coming negotiations, but rather salary increases based on merit. "The
ones that really stink don't get any pay raise at all," Mr.
Giuliani said.** State of the City address

New York Times, January 14, 2000

In the meantime, to read the Generalissimo's official biography, things are actually going quite well in the public
schools, no matter what you might have heard—and it's all
thanks to him.

**To turn around the nation's largest urban public educa-
tion system, Giuliani has worked tirelessly to restore
accountability and raise standards throughout the City's
schools—introducing innovative new instructional programs that improve reading skills, give all students
access to computers, and restore arts education as a
fundamental part of the school curriculum. As a result,
student achievement throughout the system is rising,
and New York City's children are gaining the skills and
tools they need to succeed.**

Official biography of Mayor Rudolph W. Giuliani
Issued by Mayor's Press Office, 1999

◆ Bonus: Rudy on Summer School

When it turned out that thousands of New York City youngsters were sent to summer school because of a computer
malfunction that gave them lower-than-actual scores, the
Generalissimo took it in stride:

If I were a parent of one of the children, I would say, "Thank you for having the child in summer school" because the child got more education. You got to understand, the alleged error is an error with the children at the lowest end of the score. In other words, they were children that had come very, very close to not making the, what was it, the 15th percentile. They are children who, next year, when the standards are just a little bit higher, would not be promoted. So these are children very much in need of additional educational help.

New York Times, September 16, 1999

18

Rudy's (Self-Graded) Report Cards

A record number of people visited New York City last year, and Mayor Rudolph W. Giuliani said yesterday that his quality-of-life campaign had played a crucial role. . . .

"You shouldn't minimize the importance of improving the quality of life," said Mr. Giuliani, announcing the tourism figures at a news conference in the Novotel hotel in midtown Manhattan. "When people come to this city and see it better than they saw it before, then this is a city they'd want to come back to."

He added, "Each one of the efforts may seem like a small one, but it has a tremendous amount to do with the overall revival of the spirit of the city."

New York Times, August 25, 1998

Rudy Giuliani has rarely missed an opportunity to give himself a pat on the back or to take credit for positive trends that are at best only partially his doing. This trait has been most noticeable in the periodic mayor's Management Reports. The Mayor's Office has been required to issue these twice every fiscal year—a preliminary report in the winter, a final one in September—since the city's fiscal crisis of the 1970s. Originally they were intended as a kind of self-auditing diagnostic tool, a means of reassuring Wall Street that the city was back on the road to administrative and financial soundness. But under Giuliani's administration, they have come to serve quite another function: propaganda (and, sometimes, self-amusement as well).

In 1995, making major cutbacks in city government in the midst of a severe lingering recession, Giuliani actually made this straight-faced claim:

I think the most remarkable thing about this report is how little effect that all had on services—not at all the level in which people opposed to those reductions claimed, suggested or argued.

New York Times, March 3, 1995

In 1998, flush with good times. . .

Continuing one of his favorite traditions, Mayor Rudolph W. Giuliani produced a stack of charts yesterday that suggested the city is ever safer, its streets ever cleaner and its citizens ever healthier under his leadership. . . .

"What this all adds up to is a massive change in the way people feel about New York City. . . . All of these things show what most New Yorkers believe when you poll them, but that people who want to be consistent critics refuse to accept." . . .

Mr. Giuliani was jubilant in his presentation of statistics on crime, welfare benefits and City responses to medical emergencies, calling the improvements

"astounding," "tremendous" and "remarkable." But his chest-pounding moment came with the unveiling of a new set of statistics: the number of wins by the Yankees and Mets, both of which have increased since the baseball-fixated Mayor took office. "This comes from having the most dedicated and knowledgeable baseball fan as Mayor," he said. *New York Times,* September 18, 1998

A year later, however, reporters noticed that the murder rate was up and that police response time to emergencies had slowed.
Picky, picky, picky. *New York Post,* September 23, 1999

But the technique was best on display in the year 1997.
By the time Mayor Rudolph W. Giuliani got to the 48th chart yesterday showing that New York City was somehow safer, cleaner, healthier, smarter and even drier than it had ever been, only one statistic from the torrent could still be remembered: the number of mayoral charts is now at least 30 percent larger than under any previous Mayor. *New York Times,* February 14, 1997

It's a far different picture than what the City was dealing with just a few years ago, in which most of the areas I'm now talking about, the City had a picture of dismal failure. Now the City, with regard to some of the most difficult and intractable social problems, has shown more progress than at any time in the recent past. . . .

This isn't a city that has solved every problem. There's no human being that can do that and no city that can ever do that. But I want to present them with a picture of a city that is improving, that looks a little better this time than last time. *N.Y. Times,* Feb. 14, 1997

With a pointer in his hand and a microphone clipped to his lapel, Mr. Giuliani spent an hour presenting 66 charts of City statistics—a record, up 37 percent from the 48 charts in February—and only one showed anything negative. *New York Times,* September 18, 1997

This is really a remarkable performance. It has been for four years, and each year you build on that. And a city government that was unaccountable, and was well known throughout the country or the world for being unaccountable, has been turned into a city government that is now considered to be one of the most accountable in the country. *New York Times,* September 18, 1997

. . . Mr. Giuliani declined to describe departments where there might be problems.

"For me to single them out would then have you all descend on them and give them a very hard time. And I think all of them by and large are doing a very good job. And I have been accused of a lot of things; I have never been accused of being a sucker." *N.Y. Times,* Sept. 18, 1997

After an hour of conveying the good news, he was asked whether there were any disappointing figures in the report. He responded, simply, "I am disappointed in any that haven't reached perfection yet."

New York Times, September 18, 1997

Why, if you didn't know better, you'd almost say that the mayor's 1997 Management Reports were campaign documents.

Which they were.

19

1997: The Race for Reelection, the Quest for Validation

Long before Rudy Giuliani had to face the voters at the polls in search of a second term as mayor, he was already testing his campaign themes.

This city was failing because it was being governed by the wrong ideas. *N.Y. Times Magazine*, Dec. 3, 1995

Rudy: He's earned our trust.
Slogan unveiled at fund raiser for
Mayor Rudolph W. Giuliani, May 14, 1996

With 1,300 of his biggest campaign contributors arrayed before him in a sea of candlelight and filet mignon, Mayor Rudolph W. Giuliani demanded an end to cynicism in New York. . . . He said his policies had transformed the city in just 29 months, breaking radically with the "old thinking" of his predecessors.
New York Times, May 15, 1996

Unlike the cynics, the pessimists and the defeatists who had been running New York City, and who would like to run it again, I believe in the indomitable spirit of human beings to improve things. . . . I believe there's something you can do about every problem. Maybe you can't find a perfect solution, but you can improve every time. . . .

I will not concede a single inch to the old politicians of this city . . . with their caring about the poor of this

city. We have done more in two and a half years for the poor of this city than they did in 20 or 30 years of consigning them to dependency.

Remarks at campaign fund raiser, *N.Y. Times,* May 15, 1996

You can't just ask people for their vote. You have to give them a format around which to make that decision. If you seek their trust, you'll get some to trust you, and you'll get some that have questions, but still reach out to vote for you. And I think we have the kind of record from which we can make that argument. . . . What we're going to do, to build up people's trust, is to show, here are the promises, here's the performance, and it's a good record.

Remarks at campaign fund raiser
New York Times, May 17, 1996

I think we've effected more changes than any administration in the history of New York City in three years. But I can assure you there's a lot more to be done. There's a tremendous amount of enthusiasm for doing it. And if you think that we've made a lot of changes in the last three years, just hang on.

State of the City address, *N.Y. Times,* Jan. 15, 1997

[New York is] a city today that has more compassion, more love, more understanding and more wisdom than the city we found three and a half years ago. The politically correct in this city won't tell you that. But I will.

Remarks at campaign fund raiser, *N.Y. Times,* Apr. 28, 1997

And he stuck with those themes right till the end.

I believe that we have made a turnaround. I believe that New York City in a number of areas is now showing remarkable success. That doesn't mean that we have solved all problems. That doesn't mean that we still don't have horrendous and very difficult problems to face. But I think that we face it from success, not trying to destroy the city or to destroy the success that it has, for partisan political reasons.   *N.Y. Times,* Oct. 10, 1997

This is a different kind of city than it used to be. This is now a city in which you can come and do business and the City government will help you against criminals instead of sit back and say, "There is nothing we can do about it." And isn't that really symbolic of so many of the other changes that we have made in the City of New York?   *New York Times,* October 24, 1997

A lot of what we've done is ignored, because it doesn't fit somebody's classical model, but it's quite significant, quite a significant turnaround. I don't know of any city that's had the kind of turnaround that we've had in the last three years. Not just in crime, but in the delivery of services, the mood of the people. We used to be a city where no one wanted to come to, and now you can't get a hotel room. . . . People used to say the city was unmanageable, that it couldn't be run, that it was ungovernable. Now people believe the city can have success.
     New York Times, October 27, 1997

We changed the atmosphere of the city. This city is no longer seen—City government is no longer seen—as being antibusiness. . . . Antibusiness politics was at the core of the way politics was practiced in New York City, from at least the late 1930s, right through 1993. You ran for office against big business. You ran for office running against all the bad, terrible corporations. I even hear a candidate who says that now. I don't hear her right now, but I heard it a lot last night.

Speech to New York City Partnership and Chamber of Commerce, *New York Times*, October 31, 1997

That dig about "a candidate" was reference to the fact that, notwithstanding that Giuliani was so proud of his record in office he could easily have dispensed with the bother of an election, the City Charter mandated that one be held anyway. Elections, of course, mean opposition. And opposition means opposing candidates. As the campaign approached, the Generalissimo put potential rivals on notice.

All of them have some interesting questions to answer. They have all been perennial parts of the City and State governments for over 20 years and did nothing to change any of this. They are much more the insiders of government than I am. I've done more to change City government in a few short years than they ever did. They just sat by and watched all of this happen and did nothing about it. They are among the more partisan politicians in the city. . . .

To the extent my opponents criticize me for these things, they've had many years to correct them. Obviously if I run for re-election, one of the things I'll be asking is, what have they ever done? What kind of record do they ever have? . . . If you wanted a theme, that's part of the theme. . . .

There's no question that in the four years before I was Mayor, the City went through some of the worst things that it went through. During that period of time, the City set records for murder, for example. When we came into office, for four successive years in that administration there were more murders in New York

City than any other years in the history of the City. The City had set a record not matched since the Depression for the loss of jobs. . . . We had to reverse that. And the City was described even by Senator Moynihan as defining deviancy down, and we've turned that around in large part.

Not completely, there's still a lot of work to be done, but now you don't see magazine covers talking about the demise of New York, as they did during that era. You see magazine covers talking about the renaissance of New York. You have them talking about New York City leading America in crime reduction. Magazine covers and national publications and international publications talking about business coming to New York, not the businesses leaving New York.

These are turnarounds that were accomplished against a very, very difficult situation that we inherited, and some, again I emphasize some, not all of the people, that are talking about running for Mayor, were strong supporters of that administration, those policies, and those programs.

So, of course, if they ran, these would be major issues.

New York Times, November 12, 1996

The Mayor made his comments as he stepped up his attacks on the possible Democratic contenders, saying that most were "professional City and State politicians."

New York Times, November 12, 1996

In fact, Giuliani was so caustic about the "very, very difficult situation we inherited" that former Mayor David Dinkins took the bait—and openly speculated that he might come out of retirement for a rubber match against Giuliani. The Generalissimo was delighted by the prospect.

I feel sorry for Mayor Dinkins. I watched him on television last night, and I saw a man who's very angry and very bitter, and I feel sorry for him. . . . I even think what he did in the last day or two is politically advantageous to me, and I question why he did it. I don't understand precisely what he's doing. But I don't have any personal animosity toward him.   *N.Y. Times,* Feb. 1, 1997

Dinkins did not enter the race, but his mere flirtation with running served only to highlight the weak candidates the Democrats had to run against Giuliani. The field included City Councilman Sal Albanese, a little-known populist maverick whom Giuliani ignored. It included Fernando Ferrer, borough president of The Bronx, hope of the Latino community and a thorn in Giuliani's side over the Generalissimo's hopes to move the New York Yankees out of Ferrer's borough.

Last week, a day after telling an interviewer that "I've never called names," he [Giuliani] referred to Fernando Ferrer . . . as "pathetic" and "hysterical."

New York Times, February 28, 1997

Though when Ferrer's candidacy failed to take off and he withdrew . . .

Freddy Ferrer represented the moderate wing of the Democratic Party and the only person left now in that category is Sal Albanese. That means you're going to see a lot of Democrats move over to support me.

New York Times, May 14, 1997

It included Ruth Messinger, the left-leaning borough president of Manhattan, who had been priming to run for mayor against Giuliani since the day he was elected. The Generalissimo was not unaware of her intentions. When, a month into

his term, she insisted on her right to hold hearings on the Generalissimo's proposed budget plans, he was ready for her.
The whole thing is silly. *New York Times,* February 9, 1994

He accused her of "selectively quoting" the paragraph-long section of the City Charter that requires Borough Presidents to hold hearings on a Mayor's budget plan. "It may be the advantage of being a lawyer. . . . You tend to read the whole paragraph instead of just half of it." . . . Mr. Giuliani said Ms. Messinger's request was "not reasonable." *New York Times,* February 9, 1994

When, with the election still a year away, Messinger used money to air a radio ad opposing Giuliani's plan to allow superstores to open in residential neighborhoods, he roared:
Before she's even started running, she's cheating. She shouldn't be allowed to get away with it. . . . After a while, we get tired of all the kind of lying that's going on about this, so we're putting on an ad that lays out the absolute truth about this proposal.
New York Times, November 20, 1996

The Mayor condemned Ms. Messinger's commercial yesterday as a tactic typical of "old-fashioned politicians" and said she was improperly using public money to pay for a political ad. . . . The Mayor said Ms. Messinger's radio ads were the latest in a history of abusing the City's campaign finance law, accusing her specifically of cheating in her 1989 and 1993 campaigns for Borough President. But when asked to substantiate the allegations, the Mayor's aides were unable to document any particular improprieties.

Administration officials, though, cited a complaint filed by the Giuliani campaign in 1993—one of many filed

by various candidates against each other—that Ms. Messinger had improperly contributed to the campaign of Mayor David N. Dinkins. The complaint was withdrawn by the Giuliani campaign after the election, and no determination was ever made by the Campaign Finance Board that Ms. Messinger had acted improperly.

New York Times, November 20, 1996

And finally, to the Generalissimo's great good fortune, the field included the Reverend Al Sharpton, seeking to become the black community's candidate—and seeking respectability after years as an over-the-top street militant. Unfortunately, in the eyes of key elements of the Democratic coalition, Sharpton was, and always would be, lugging far too much baggage around to ever become respectable. Baggage such as: his role in what an upstate grand jury labeled a hoax rape charge made by a troubled teenager named Tawana Brawley, for which he was ultimately (and successfully) sued for slander by a Dutchess County prosecutor; his denial that the Reverend Louis Farrakhan was anti-Semitic; and his incendiary speech denouncing "white interlopers" during a 1995 boycott of a white-owned business on 125th Street that ended with a deranged individual firebombing the store, killing himself and everyone inside.

Particularly since Sharpton was far funnier and more charismatic than any of the other Democrats, he stole the show at their debates—and he roiled the others by presenting them with a Hobson's choice: denounce Sharpton and potentially lose the African American vote; or accept him as a legitimate contender and lose the white ethnic, and especially the Jewish, vote. It was a dilemma Giuliani was only too happy to exploit.

I think Ruth, Freddie and Sal have to face up to the fact that a lot of New Yorkers will find it rather incredible

that they would say that they would support Al Sharpton over me, should that be the choice. You have to take a stand on it. You can't say things like, "I disagree with his comments, but if he wins the Democratic primary, I'll support him against the incumbent Mayor." When they say they would support Al Sharpton over me in this election, they're showing that they put party partisanship ahead of the good of the city.　　*N.Y. Times,* Apr. 6, 1997

And it was a dilemma that grew worse for Messinger when the initial tally in her party's primary had her falling short of the 40 percent needed to clinch the nomination—and trapped into a runoff against Sharpton. Who needed to link the Democratic opponent to David Dinkins, when that opponent could be linked to the Reverend Al?

It does pose for the people of this city a choice, which is Messinger-Sharpton, Sharpton-Messinger—they're virtually one—or the present Mayor. Do you want the $33 billion budget of the largest city in the United States in the hands of Al Sharpton or Ruth Messinger? Do you want the largest police department in the United States and the quality-of-life program we've put into effect in the hands of Ruth Messinger or Al Sharpton? That's the question that will be posed in the next two weeks. They're virtually identical.　　*N.Y. Times* Sept. 11, 1997

I think he's [Sharpton] unqualified to be Mayor. I'm not afraid to say that. I think Ruth Messinger is afraid to say that. There has to be a background of having worked, having had a job, having distinguished yourself at things before you come to the position of being Mayor. [Otherwise] politics becomes a joke rather than a reality. Ruth Messinger doesn't have the independence, I imagine, to say what she really thinks.　　*N.Y. Times,* Sept. 19, 1997

A recount put Messinger barely over the 40 percent mark. Her victory over Sharpton came when the courts rebuffed his lawsuits. Messinger had the nomination she had wanted for so long—without any kind of a mandate. Already far out in front, the Generalissimo was allowing her no quarter.

Mayor Rudolph W. Giuliani described Ruth W. Messinger's plan for a $1.1 billion reduction in City spending yesterday as a "really jerky set of proposals."

New York Times, July 24, 1997

To take out $290 million in police reductions is a joke. I'm sure she will run away from it when you confront her with this. This is what the City did during the fiscal crisis, which I'm a student of. Crime rates went up around that time. And for just about six years, the city was defenseless against criminals.

New York Times, July 24, 1997

. . . The Mayor himself took time last week to call a reporter to offer a line-by-line tutorial dismantling Ms. Messinger's budget plan. When asked if this betrayed some political concern on her part, the Mayor demurred. "I'm not going to let her play some kind of shell game."

New York Times, July 28, 1997

Ruth Messinger prefers the policies of the Dinkins Administration, of the four years before I came into office, wants to go back to most of them. I prefer the progress that we've made together as a city, that now is having us written about as a national model rather than the rotting apple. . . .

You have a right to have that view, people do. She's running away from it. And to say that your record is not up for examination on what you have done in the past

when you run for Mayor is really entirely unrealistic. . . . If you want to turn back, fine. But don't pretend you want to move to the future.

Statements at candidates' debate, *New York Times*, Oct. 10, 1997

He and his minions also enjoyed putting psychological pressure on the beleaguered Messinger—sending squads of campaign workers to her events to give instant rebuttals to her proposals, recording all her public appearances in the hope of rattling her into a gaffe, even sending a cameraman unannounced into her borough president offices to start filming. And he bashed his hapless opponent with fierce personal attacks that gave "overkill" a bad name.

For instance, Messinger had once expressed her opinion that gay sex shops "invigorated" Greenwich Village. Giuliani, who had won passage of a bill that put severe zoning restrictions on sex-oriented businesses throughout the city, saw an opening.

Sex shops in our neighborhoods? Messinger thinks they add character. What do you think?

TV/radio ad by Giuliani campaign, September 1997
New York Times, September 23, 1997

Ruth Messinger says sex shops are an important part of our city's economic and tourism base. . . . give character to our city . . . fabric to a neighborhood.

TV/radio ad by Giuliani campaign, September 1997
New York Times, September 23, 1997

You think it lends character to the city. There are people who think that, and they are entitled to think it. I think it destroys the character of the city, and there are people who are entitled to think that. And let's see who thinks that more people are on your side or people on

my side. That's what an election is about, right? It [the constitutionality of the pornography zoning restrictions] was decided not by Ruth Messinger, but by a judge, which is the way we do it in America.

> Speech in Times Square hotel ("producing raucous laughter and applause from the audience")
> *New York Times,* September 19, 1997

The truth?

The new Giuliani commercial . . . gives prominent position to what appears to be a direct quote from Ms. Messinger. "Sex shops give New York City character." The quote actually came from a television news anchor, who was characterizing Ms. Messinger's position in an informal conversation. Mr. Giuliani, who has very strong feelings about being quoted accurately himself, contends that any criticism [of the commercial] is the work of "people who like to create phony issues."

> *New York Times,* September 26, 1997

And what would young Rudy Giuliani have had to say about the kind of cheap shot that grown-up Rudy Giuliani engaged in over Messinger's stance on sex shops?

Personal attacks have no place in an election unless they can be documented. Any candidate using such a base tactic only proves his own inadequacy to serve in the position he desires.

> Manhattan College *Quadrangle,* October 1964
> Requoted in *New York Observer,* July 12, 1999

Then there was an ill-advised party (certainly for a politician trying to reinvent herself as a centrist in middle age!) that a younger Ruth Messinger had held in her apartment eighteen years earlier, a night she claimed she couldn't remember, a night the Generalissimo was determined not to let her forget.

Mr. Giuliani said that Ms. Messinger . . . held a party in her Upper West Side brownstone in 1979 for John B. Hill, who had been the last prisoner held in connection with a bloody 1971 uprising at Attica Prison.

New York Times, September 23, 1997

Ms. Messinger and her aides also criticized a flier that the Giuliani campaign distributed that refers to her as "anti-police–pro-criminal." The flier accused Ms. Messinger of helping to "incite two days of riots" in Washington Heights in 1992 by joining a march to protest the slaying of a suspect by the police. . . .

The Giuliani campaign stood by it.

New York Times, October 25, 1997

No response to it. I think the negativity of the other campaign is getting so great that I wonder when they're going to recognize that may be one of the reasons why these polls are demonstrating what they're demonstrating. I've never seen a campaign in which there's been more name calling, more charges. Every day, you ask me, my opponent charges, my opponent charges. At some point, you've got to get around to talking about what you plan to do for the City of New York.

New York Times, October 25, 1997

Yes, that's right. Generalissimo Giuliani was claiming to be the *injured* party!

It gives me a sense of how her campaign is sagging.

New York Times, September 27, 1997

This is an important decision on the future of New York City. And I'm going to try to keep it on issues, and I am

going to try to keep it on the things that are really important to people, rather than personal negative attacks. Statement about upcoming first candidates'debate
New York Times, October 10, 1997

I was somewhat surprised at the harshness and the personal invective from my opponent. I didn't think it would be at that level. But, you know, everybody makes the choice as to how they're going to present themselves, and people can decide if that was the right or the wrong choice, to be quite as personal, quite as harsh in the rhetoric and the approach. . . .

People change their styles, and I would imagine in the next debate that my opponent will not be as personal, won't call names as often, because I think what people find is if you do that, it hurts you.
New York Times, October 11, 1997

She's sort of like one negative thing after another after another after another. After a while, the best thing to do is ignore her and maybe she'll stop this kind of negative campaign. *New York Times,* October 23, 1997

Rudy Giuliani had not yet won the election—but he had already won the award for chutzpah. However, with the Columbus Day Parade, he surely pushed the envelope of divide-and-rule ethnic politics when he accused the Jewish Messinger of being anti-Catholic because she did not march the entire forty-four-block length of the parade and did not attend mass in St. Patrick's Cathedral beforehand.

This is a community she doesn't care very much about. It's never been a community that she cares about, ever extended herself to. She wasn't at the Mass today at St.

Patrick's Cathedral. She drops out of the parade at 70th Street. You basically have a campaign that is truly falling apart—she dropped out of the parade on 70th Street. You know, this is a great parade. I'm going to march it twice. *New York Times*, October 14, 1997

(The *Times* account noted that, in fact, Giuliani "marched again only over two blocks of the route.")

Mr. Giuliani repeatedly said that Ms. Messinger had shown disrespect for "the community." Asked which community he was referring to, the Mayor declined to specify, saying: "Meaning the community that celebrates the parade. This is a big, big celebration. This is one that you should revel in and enjoy. I think she basically see very little regard for it. And it was kind of returned in terms of the cold response she got here."
New York Times, October 14, 1997

She was noticeable in her absence from the Columbus Day Parade on Staten Island. She was noticeable by her absence from the Columbus Day Parade in The Bronx. I exclude from that the Columbus Day Parade in Queens because that happened on the Sabbath, but the Columbus Day Parade on Staten Island was on a Sunday. The Columbus Day Parade in The Bronx was on a Sunday. It seemed to me that this is an important community, and you would want to show involvement with them.
New York Times, October 15, 1997

When Messinger did show up at a Columbus Day Parade in Brooklyn, he positively oozed with contempt and condescension for her.

I'm glad that she took my advice and came to the boroughs and finally got out of Manhattan. I think it's interesting that this is the only one that she is participating in in the boroughs. . . .

If anybody doesn't think that politics is a contact sport, they should march in this parade. It's wonderful. The warmth. The love. The embrace of this community is absolutely tremendous. *N.Y. Times,* Oct. 19, 1997

His brazen attempt to drive a wedge between Jews and Catholics did not hurt him. The *Vanity Fair* article alleging an affair between him and his communications director did not hurt him. The scandal at the NYPD over the brutalization of Abner Louima did not hurt him.

All these people are doing—the [Democratic] candidates last night, and David Dinkins—are seeking to divide for their own narrow political purposes, with illogical and irrational arguments. I think it backfires on them when they do it, because I think people want to see leadership, not negative attacks that divide people. . . . They really should stay out of it.

New York Times, August 15, 19, 21, 1997

The contest became so lopsided that Giuliani could even get away with doing a commercial with New York Yankees manager Joe Torre on behalf of the city's recycling program. But only the year before, Giuliani had been accused in a lawsuit of violating that very program.

The mayor . . . vowed to defy the city's recycling law as "absurd" and "irresponsible." *N.Y. Times,* Aug. 13, 1997

In July of 1996, faced with a lawsuit that accused him of violating the City's recycling law, Mr. Giuliani denounced the goals in the law as "absurd" and "irresponsible" and published an article in the New York

Times Magazine that challenged the practicality of recycling and called it "a waste of time and money."

New York Times, August 13, 1997

On election night, Rudy Giuliani stood before a hotel ball-
room full of supporters, triumphant—topping the over-
matched Messinger easily, 57 to 41 percent.

**I remembered what the City was like four years ago. It
was a city that was defined by fear and doubt. It used to
be called the city that was ungovernable and unmanageable. It was a time when people didn't believe in
their city. Many of them didn't believe in themselves
and they would not permit themselves to dream. So we
said together, during this campaign, and in this room,
that we were going to change that. Many doubted that
we could change it. Cynics made fun of us. But look
where we are today. We molded together—together we
molded a vision. And in pursuance of that vision, we all
came together, all of us. We worked very hard, to
improve the quality of life for our great city. We made
the world realize that change is possible.**

New York Times, November 5, 1997

He had been reelected. More important (to him, certainly), he had been validated.

◆ Payback Time at the Campaign Finance Board

In 1997 Mayor Rudolph Giuliani arrived at a town meeting in
Forest Hills, Queens, where natives were restive about a proposed development combining a multiplex cinema with a
superstore.

**The Mayor, arriving a half-hour late, received a quick
refresher on the development. The plan would overwhelm**

the calm neighborhood, clog traffic and drive small merchants out, a gray-haired gentleman respectfully told the Mayor, adding, "Is it a *quid pro quo*, Mr. Mayor?"

The Mayor looked displeased. The man was referring to the fact that the developer of the multiplex, Bruce C. Ratner, is one of his contributors. "You should be ashamed of yourself," the Mayor said to the elderly man in a schoolmasterish tone. "Contributors do not make my decisions. In fact, I am against the theater. So it will not be built."   *New York Times,* September 14, 1997

Giuliani himself should have understood his questioner's skepticism about how the political process works. He had once possessed such skepticism himself.

When you contribute to a political campaign any significant kind of contribution, you should be required to disclose your interest in that government entity, so that the opponent can attack that . . . and argue the conflicts of interest.
U.S. Attorney Rudolph W. Giuliani on *Eyewitness News Conference,* WABC-TV, 1986
Requoted in *Village Voice,* February 27, 1996

To curb such abuses, or the appearance thereof, in the wake of the scandals that rocked Mayor Edward Koch's administration beginning in early 1986 (scandals that U.S. Attorney Giuliani had a prominent role in exposing and prosecuting), the City of New York passed the most far-reaching campaign finance reform law in the country (with U.S. Attorney Giuliani supporting its enactment). The law set ceilings on personal contributions with strict disclosure requirements, provided for public matching funds to lessen candidates' need for fund raising, and—most important—created a nonpartisan Campaign Finance Board (CFB) to enforce the rules.

In 1993 Mayor David Dinkins' campaign committee was fined some $320,000 by the board for various fund-raising transgressions. The fines did not sit well. On the afternoon of Dinkins' last day in office, the Reverend Joseph O'Hare, president of Fordham University and chairman of the CFB, was sent a fax from City Hall, informing him that he was fired and naming his replacement.

The biggest event of Rudy Giuliani's first week in office was his flinty, gutsy insistence that the midnight-appointment Dinkins CFB chairman must go and that the Reverend O'Hare be reinstated—and winning the confrontation. The whole episode reflected badly on the outgoing administration and enabled Giuliani to pose—rightly—as a "good government" white knight.

Mayor Rudolph W. Giuliani demanded the resignation of the new Chairman of the New York City Campaign Finance Board and threatened to cut off the Board's funds or to seek legislation to revamp it if he doesn't get his way. . . .

The Mayor said that the Board members needed to be free from the fear of retribution to be effective and that the Board's independence "has been seriously jeopardized by the 11th-hour appointment" of Mr. Schwartz. The last-minute appointment, Mr. Giuliani said, "unfortunately was made under circumstances that clearly taint his position as Chairman." . . .

Mr. Giuliani immediately rejected Mr. Schwartz's compromise [that he stay on temporarily]. "It's an attempt to put strings on the appointment of the Chairman of an independent body." *N.Y. Times,* Jan. 7, 1994

There are good things about politics and there are bad things about politics. Part of the process of reform is to

try to straighten out the bad things so the good things can really serve people.

Statement on resignation of CFB chairman and reinstatement of the Reverend Joseph O'Hare
New York Times, January 8, 1994

What a difference four years in office makes.

Mayor Rudolph W. Giuliani conceded yesterday that his re-election campaign had made a mistake in accepting $290,000 in illegal contributions that it has now promised to return. He said the error occurred because officials of his campaign had misunderstood an obscure campaign finance regulation.

. . . In several instances, the campaign accepted donations that were obviously over the limit of $7,700 per contributor, according to an audit conducted by the New York City Campaign Finance Board. . . .

The Mayor's explanation for the illegal contributions came after the Campaign Finance Board suspended the Giuliani campaign from receiving any public matching funds until it returned the money to the donors or convinced the Board that the contributions were legal. The Board accused the campaign of receiving more than $300,000 in contributions that were over the limit. The charge jeopardizes more than $1 million in matching funds that the campaign had hoped to get by the end of this month.

. . . Mr. Giuliani said, "We have the obligation of looking at those regulations, and we didn't, and we should have. So it's my responsibility."

New York Times, September 13, 1997

The New York City Campaign Finance Board fined Mayor Rudolph W. Giuliani's re-election campaign

$220,000 yesterday for accepting more than $300,000 in illegal contributions, most of which were given by developers and others doing business with the City government.

. . . The fine was a blow to the reputation of Mr. Giuliani, a former Federal prosecutor who has often contended that he has gone out of his way to run the most scrupulous election campaigns in the City's history. . . .

The Mayor's aides assailed the Campaign Finance Board, saying that the penalty was illegal because the Board had not allowed a new mayoral appointee to be seated at the last minute.   *N.Y. Times,* Sept. 19, 1997

Actually, Giuliani had not only tried to make his own "last-minute appointment" to the board whose independence he had once championed, but his appointee was playing an active role in his campaign, in open violation of the board's patently obvious requirement that its members have no involvement in the campaigns whose fund-raising practices it monitors.

Five weeks later, the board caught the mayor's campaign committee in more violations and levied more fines, bringing the total to $240,000—almost as high as the fines imposed on Dinkins's reelection four years before.

Generalissimo Giuliani was beginning to get really pissed off at this whole good-government thing.

We have returned the money that we felt would create the wrong questions. And we didn't return the money in situations where people would be unfairly accused. The way in which people are playing with reputations is kind of McCarthyite.   *New York Times,* October 24, 1997

The next year the board incurred Giuliani's wrath again. As part of a tug-of-war with the City Council over the mayor's attempt to give Yankees owner George Steinbrenner an unpopular new stadium with a price tag of more than $1 billion, the council tried to put a referendum on the November ballot registering public opinion on the stadium issue. Because by law a City Charter Revision proposal blocks any other referendum question from being considered at the same time, Giuliani quickly convened a revision panel that offered a modest change in the city's campaign-finance law and thus successfully staved off the embarrassment of losing a stadium referendum. The council, however, had already legislated a more significant reform to the original campaign reform law—hiking the original formula of two public dollars in matching funds for every private dollar raised up to a 4-to-1 ratio. After the dust had settled, the Campaign Finance Board announced that both the law and the charter revision were legal—and therefore it would enforce the council's more extensive law.

By now the Generalissimo was the one engaging in the very kind of actions he had once denounced.

Bringing a long-simmering feud to a boil, Mayor Rudolph W. Giuliani threatened yesterday to cut off funds to New York City's Campaign Finance Board, hoping to block its planned fourfold match of private donations to candidates in next month's special elections for City Council.

"We'll probably hold up their money, hold back their money, because it's illegal," the Mayor warned. He accused the Board of "stubbornness and arrogance" and "the height of intellectual dishonesty."

New York Times, January 6, 1999

And then—banishment to the Land of Nod.

Mayor Rudolph W. Giuliani has proposed moving the City's Campaign Finance Board to Brooklyn, a plan that

Board officials say will thwart their efforts to implement new campaign contribution rules that the Mayor has attacked. . . .

Board officials said the move will be disruptive, especially the task of moving and rewiring the Board's computer system. And the move would be an inconvenience to candidates who are required to make periodic filings to both the Campaign Finance Board and the City's Board of Elections, which are now only a few blocks apart. . . .

The proposal to move the office came a few weeks after the Mayor threatened to cut off funds to the Board, saying the increase in matching funds was a "terrible mistake."   *New York Times*, February 4, 1999

20

The Second Term:
Toward a Higher
Quality of Life—or Else

New Year's Day, 1998. Rudy Giuliani is sworn in for a second term. He basked in his accomplishments.

Four years ago when I stood here and I said that New York City was the capital of the world, there was doubt; there was fear; there was the feeling that New York City's best days were behind us. . . . I didn't accept that, I know many of you didn't accept that and over the last four years, in an exercise of human will and determination, in an exercise that showed that human beings can make a difference, you and I together have

**changed the direction of the city more than at any time
in its history. . . .**

Second Inaugural Address, Official Mayor's Office
transcript, http://www.ci.nyc.ny.us/html/om/home.html

But he also had an agenda in mind for the four years that
lay ahead.

**Basically, it is to try to continue and make permanent
the changes we've been able to bring about in safety, in
quality of life, in the kind of things you see happening in
Times Square. To make that permanent, so that this is
not just cyclical for the city, but it represents what the
city will be in throughout the 21st Century.**

Comment in preinauguration interview, *N.Y. Times,* Jan. 2, 1998

His new crusade: improving New York City's quality of life.
It would not be easy, he warned.

**Quality of life is not so much a destination to be reached
as a direction in which to strive. Quality of life is a con-
tinuous process. It demands an ongoing effort. We will
never reach the perfect ideal, but we will fight the battle anew each day.** Second Inaugural Address,
Official Mayor's Office transcript,
http://www.ci.nyc.ny.us/html/om/home.html

And, even as he exhorted them, the Generalissimo notified
his constituents that of those on whom he had bestowed so
much, he would expect much in return:

**All that we have done, all that we must continue to do
together, is based on continuing to liberate the human
spirit, understanding that liberty is a balance of freedom and responsibility, of rights and obligations.**

Second Inaugural Address, Official Mayor's Office
transcript, http://www.ci.nyc.ny.us/html/om/home.html

Translation: having saved the city in his first term, Rudy Giuliani had now decided to save New Yorkers—from themselves. He was about to impose a level of regimentation of their daily lives that many of them had never experienced before. And no matter how petty his intrusion or micromanagement might seem, they had better get used to it. The Generalissimo wanted "civility"—as he defined it. He wanted everything nice and neat—his way. He wanted order. He wanted obedience.

Even before the inaugural ceremonies, the police had erected unsightly barriers in midtown to corral foot traffic into certain intersections, inconveniencing Christmas shoppers, tourists, and other pedestrians, some of whom now had to wait for three light changes just to cross one street. Crackdowns followed on jaywalkers. On drivers who went too fast, or blocked intersections at red lights, or didn't shut off their car alarms. On cabbies. On outdoor food vendors. On struggling artists trying to sell their works on the sidewalk outside the Metropolitan Museum. On bicycle messengers. On anybody in need of attitude adjustment time, all across New York City. And the man in charge of this Behavior Modification Project—Generalissimo Rudy Giuliani.

It's a rule of reason. That's part of living in a civilized city as opposed to a place that's chaotic.

> Announcing plan to ban food carts from much of midtown Manhattan and financial district—plan withdrawn under fire from largely pro-Giuliani business community, whose workforce depends on such vendors
> *New York Times,* May 24, 1998

Motorists who cause gridlock are simply uncivil, Giuliani said. "When you block the intersection, you're basically saying, 'I don't care about anybody else, I just care about myself.'" *N.Y. Daily News,* Nov. 13, 1998

I have to leave here to give out some jaywalking tickets.
Joke to business group, Associated Press, May 10, 1998

People should not feel that they can just have immunity in walking right out into traffic. They should have a sense that there is a consequence to that. They shouldn't feel that they can go through red lights. They shouldn't feel as if they can just make illegal turns. So you try and enforce it as often as you can, knowing that you are never going to be able to enforce it all the time. That's really how I've changed the philosophy of the city, and how we've restored the quality of life in the city. Response to question from British reporter
New York Times, February 15, 1998

Building on his vision of New York as an urban Eden, Mayor Rudolph W. Giuliani announced a string of new initiatives yesterday that he predicted would further transform the traditionally gritty city into a friendly, tranquil place where drivers don't speed and residents treat each other politely.

Unbowed by the chiding he endured in his recent campaign against jaywalkers, the Mayor said he was preparing to move on other standard fare of city life, like littering and blaring car alarms. And saying he was determined to stop annoying behavior before it started, he proposed classes in school to teach youngsters ethics and civility. *New York Times*, February 26, 1998

Some people romanticize the way things were five or 10 years ago. They have nostalgia for the old Times Square, for example. They think it was somehow charming to have graffiti on every wall and sex shops on every

block. But remember what it was really like. Remember that fear, and the disrespect for people's rights that went unchecked in that climate. . . . People who insist on romanticizing the disorder of the past should realize that the reason they have the luxury of nostalgia is that today things have improved. We didn't become the city people most want to live in and visit by encouraging an atmosphere of disorder.   *N.Y. Times*, Feb. 26, 1998

Does everybody remember Plato? Plato developed the notion of the ideal. You never reached it. But in striving to get there, you kept making improvements in society. The ideal republic, the ideal state of honesty, the ideal state of integrity, the ideal state of cleanliness or safety.   *New York Times*, February 26, 1998

(The Generalissimo had the ancient Greeks on the brain during this period. He had closed his inaugural address by reciting the "Oath of Fealty" taken by the ancient Athenians.) Asked whether his latest measures would further drain the city of its vitality and free-spirited nature as some critics have said, Mr. Giuliani responded: "Flippancy, humor, argument and debate, it's all terrific. Anarchy is another matter. It's a question of balance. It's a question of moderation, balance, common sense. I think New York will always be a somewhat more sarcastic and humorous city.   *New York Times*, February 26, 1998

Mayor Rudolph W. Giuliani warned an audience of New York City officials and supporters yesterday that "the cynics and pessimists" would ridicule his new quality-of-life initiatives. . . .   *New York Times*, February 26, 1998

He was right about that.

His proposals for establishing civility in the public schools boiled down to uniforms and a suggestion that "students learn the importance of civility in their history classes." *New York Times,* February 26, 1998

Let me talk about the one that may be in many ways the most metaphysical, esoteric, philosophical, whatever— that may be the most important of all: treating each other in a civil and decent way. *N.Y. Times,* Feb. 26, 1998

. . . When Mr. Giuliani was asked whether the new civility would apply to himself, the famously hot-tempered Mayor—who has used words like "jerky," "stupid," "silly" and "idiocy" in describing reporters' questions— said his was "an honest response." He added, "It's not disrespectful if, in fact, it is a silly question." *New York Times,* February 26, 1998

Mr. Giuliani said that police officers would start enforcing the City speed limit of 30 miles an hour and that they would crack down on drivers during a surprise day of "zero tolerance." *New York Times,* February 26, 1998

There is no right to drive in the way in which you endanger the life of another. In fact, if you think of what freedom is all about, freedom includes mutual responsibilities like this. In a city in which people have to be afraid of crossing the street, that's not a city that has much freedom. *New York Times,* February 26, 1998

No, it isn't. Especially when the public official leading the crackdown on such drivers is transported around town in a vehicle that itself rampantly violates the speed limit—*Daily*

News columnist Michael Daly, trailing the mayor's car one day, clocked him at speeds up to 72 mph.

We challenge your credibility. . . . That's it.

> Statement by mayor's press secretary responding to
> Michael Daly column, "No Speed Limits for Rudy,"
> *New York Daily News,* March 1, 1998

This is an outrageously false story. . . . The reporter couldn't possibly have observed what he observed.

> *New York Daily News,* March 2, 1998

Cutting off a *News* reporter at midquestion, an apparent violation of his no-more-rude-civil servants civility crackdown, Giuliani chastised the *News* as a "paparazzi journal."

The Mayor said his Suburban could not be driven "at 60 to 70 miles an hour without the passengers inside being under a tremendous amount of stress, namely bouncing around, bouncing against the walls. . . . [But] I don't know the precise rate of speed. . . . When I sit in the automobile I don't look at the speedometer."

> *New York Daily News,* March 2, 1998

His observations are totally faulty to start with, even about the lower speeds, because he would not know how fast a car, two in front, is driving. In order to make that estimate, you have to be behind a car for 30 seconds and you have to maintain an equal distance. If there's a car in between you and that car, then you can be mistaking the distance between the first car and the second car, and the second car and the third car. So it would be thrown out of court. A highway patrol officer would not even be able to give a ticket under a set of circumstances like that.

> *New York Times,* March 2, 1998

In veiled references to the death of Diana, Princess of Wales, Mr. Giuliani said Mr. Daly had illegally crossed a solid line in the Brooklyn Battery Tunnel and had acted like a "paparazzi" journalist. "He illegally crossed lanes, speeded toward us, acted in an irresponsible way."

New York Times, March 2, 1998

From the day that I became Mayor, I had a rule, because it followed on the irresponsible activity of my predecessor, David Dinkins, who used to drive through the streets of the city with sirens on, blaring, whether it was an emergency or not. I use lights and sirens only on emergencies.

New York Times, March 2, 1998

"I need a rest," Mr. Giuliani said after spending 11 minutes on the subject. . . . [But] just as an aide was calling an end to the news conference, Mr. Giuliani chimed in that he had "just one other thing."

"I have this romantic wish that the *Daily News* would apologize for this."

New York Times, March 2, 1998

Twenty-four hours later the Generalissimo was still seething.

. . . At a news conference in City Hall, he attacked the story again for seven minutes. . . .

When asked about the incident again yesterday, Giuliani said much of the story was "entirely made up," and he lambasted the press corps for repeating it. "You all tend to band together when a big mistake is made by a reporter or a newspaper," he said.

Boston Globe, March 3, 1998

Giuliani also accused journalists yesterday of erecting a "blue wall of silence" around unethical reporting.

New York Daily News, March 3, 1998

The fact is, the van couldn't possibly have been going 72 mph. If you've ever ridden in my van you would know that, because my van is a very uncomfortable ride. . . . It's much heavier than it should be, for obvious reasons. And whenever it goes above 60 mph people are bouncing up and down, flying all over the van.

New York Daily News, March 3, 1998

The tirade did include one interesting confession, however. **"I've jaywalked since the time that I've raised the issue,"** said Giuliani, who nevertheless insisted that it was dangerous and wrong. **"I've said to myself that you'll eventually catch me jaywalking because I do it as a matter of habit and instinct."**

Associated Press, March 3, 1998

To the great fun of the press corps, the story refused to die. General Motors officially rebutted Giuliani's contentions about his Chevy Suburban.
General Motors is not telling the truth. . . . This is the usual corporate defense of their product. . . . Ask people who have ridden that truck whether you can ride even 50 mph without bouncing around rather uncomfortably. . . . I've had people who have ridden in that truck, people who know the car business, who sell cars, who say it's one of the most uncomfortable rides they've ever had. *New York Daily News,* March 5, 1998

And, nine months later, a TV news team caught Giuliani's car not only speeding but running red lights and logging seven traffic violations in all. Asked about it at a press conference. . .
Report that to the Police Department, and we'll have it adjudicated in court. Thank you.

New York Daily News, December 18, 1998

Daly, however, fared much better than a disabled Bronx man who found himself caught in a curious ticket trap—NYPD officers were lying in wait near the Bronx Zoo, triggering a device to suddenly turn the light red so that they could nail helpless passing motorists with $125 fines. The man went back, videotaped the rogue officers working their scam, the story wound up on the front page of the *Daily News*—and within hours cops came to his home to arrest him for a thirteen-year-old unpaid ticket. A judge immediately dismissed the charge, but the Police Department unearthed and released the man's long-ago police record—including the assertion that he had once been convicted of sodomy. This assertion turned out to be wrong, but Generalissimo Giuliani was unapologetic about that, or anything else.

He was accusing the police officers of giving out improper tickets. He gained the romantic attachment of several of the writers on the *Daily News*, and they failed to report the full nature of the falsification of his information about the police. . . . If he was dishonest enough to steal someone's credit card, then maybe he's dishonest enough to lie about police officers, and they shouldn't be ripped apart in a newspaper without those facts being known to the public. *N.Y. Daily News*, Aug. 7, 1998

♦ Attack of the "Taxi Terrorists"

One group that actively disliked like the new quality-of-life campaign were New York's taxi drivers—who found themselves under a crackdown for such offenses as picking up passengers on the "wrong" side of the street (an "offense" most would-be passengers did not even know existed—and in any case one they desperately wanted to occur whenever they needed a cab!). In mid-May 1998 cabbies, feeling beleaguered, staged a one-day strike.

Mr. Giuliani has denounced the strike as "a demonstration in favor of reckless driving."

New York Times, May 14, 1998

We've gotten a surprisingly large number of calls saying this was one of the most pleasant days in a long time. If they would like to stay home forever, they can stay home forever. The city will function very well without them. It functioned very well today without them.

New York Times, May 14, 1998

Then the cabbies threatened to tie up traffic. To some, this was a time-honored New York protest tradition. To the Generalissimo, it meant war. He threatened to retaliate by letting others cut in on medallion cabs' business—permanently.

They are presenting us with opportunities that I'm more than happy to take advantage of, which the City has not been able to take advantage of for the last 20 to 30 years, to introduce a lot more competition into their industry.

We are going to authorize them [livery drivers] to do it [pick up passengers] until this state of emergency ends. If they [cabbies], for example, announce they're not going to do anything on Thursday, then we won't have to go forward with this. But right now, they are saying that on Thursday they're going to try to close down the city. . . .

You can't let anybody have a stranglehold on your city. I think the people of this city are fed up with the way they've been driving. I've heard these complaints for years, and we're finally doing something about it. . . .

I don't know the value of saying that only a certain number of people can pick up people on the street. I don't know that that doesn't create a monopoly. That

creates a lot of the problems we've had for years. If we really believe that competition brings better services, then what we're doing with yellow cabs means we're creating worse service, right?   *N.Y. Times,* May 15, 1998

The cabbies asked for a meeting with the mayor. Nothing doing.

I don't really care what they're saying. I don't negotiate with people who want to close the city down—never have, never will. . . .

There is not a great deal of public sympathy for the taxi drivers. So as a political issue, this is what you call a no-brainer.   *New York Times,* May 15, 1998

Amid boasts by a cabbie leader that they would turn Manhattan into "a parking lot," the Generalissimo broke the cabbies' job action with military precision—barricades, blockades and all. The press spokesman at the Police Department crowed of victory over the "taxi terrorists."

They can jerk around with all this stuff if they want to. I know what they were doing; they know what they were doing. They know that we broke their strike—destroyed it, really. Nobody showed up today. And that didn't just happen because we allowed business to go on as usual. That happened because we had a plan to stop them from doing it.   *New York Times,* May 22, 1998
Requoted May 23, 1999

I was sending them a message. The message is: You don't get to close down the City of New York. You don't get to do it. Get that out of your mind. Don't think about it.
New York Times, May 22, 1998

The cabbies saved a little face when a judge subsequently ruled that the mayor had violated their First Amendment rights in denying them the right to stage a demonstration. But they were thoroughly licked—and, eighteen months later, when actor Danny Glover held a press conference to vent his anger at being passed over by several taxis, apparently because of his race, the Generalissimo stepped in and kicked them when they were down. Though African American New Yorkers had complained of similar insults through the years (including on his watch) to no avail, Giuliani overnight announced a drastic new scalp-taking policy.

We will take your cab away from you. [This] has been going on for a very, very long time, and maybe this is an opportunity to change that.

New York Daily News, November 11, 1999

We're perfectly entitled to do this. I know we're going to get the same howls and screams and yells that we got when we did this with drunk drivers. . . .

Just think of the practical reality of it. We're suspending the license of the driver on the spot. So, who's going to drive the cab away? If the taxi driver drove the cab away, he would get another summons for driving without a license. . . .

Yeah, sure, we should have done this earlier. Probably we should have done it three years ago, five years ago, but also it would have been done seven years ago, and eight years ago, and 10 years ago, and 12 years ago, and 15 years ago. So you can keep using that excuse forever. This is a good time to do it. It [what happened to Danny Glover] got a great deal of attention because it involved a person of great notoriety.

New York Times, November 11, 1999

There's a good way to avoid all of this, and that's for the owners of the cabs and the cab drivers to come to the reality that life is going to be different now.

New York Post, November 11, 1999

♦ Rudy on Waste Management:
"Yes, Virginia, It's Our Garbage,
But It's *Your* Responsibility"

Staten Island has by far the fewest people of New York City's five boroughs, but on election day 1993 it had provided Rudy Giuliani with his narrow margin of victory over David Dinkins. On that same day, Staten Islanders had also voted by an overwhelming margin to secede from the city—a referendum placebo wish that was not about to be granted but that gave them a chance to vent. And they had legitimate grievances to vent about—in particular, the existence of Fresh Kills, the literal dumping ground for all the city's refuse, which had become not only a blight on the landscape of New York's least-citified borough but also one of the highest points on the Eastern Seaboard, visible by satellites from outer space.

As mayor, Rudy Giuliani needed Staten Island, and he knew it. Accordingly, he felt their pain, and promised to close Fresh Kills—someday.

And don't try to put me on the spot and say when. . . . I'm going to tell you, you should trust me to solve this problem, and I will solve it. And it isn't right for you to look at me like that, like I'm giving—no, listen to me!—like I'm trying to fool you. Because I don't do that with people.

Response to questioner at town hall meeting on
Staten Island, *New York Times,* May 17, 1996

Feeling the pressure from his favorite constituents, and from their irascible borough president, Guy Molinari, at the end of that year Giuliani suddenly announced the permanent closure of Fresh Kills, effective the last day of 2001. Just one little problem: There was nowhere to put all the garbage—some 2 million tons of it a year—that was being buried at Fresh Kills. Neighborhood opposition and concern from environmentalists about dioxin levels had blocked plans to locate incinerators on a share-the-pain basis across the five boroughs. The federal government had banned the city's dumping of sludge at sea. The only option: Sell New York's garbage to out-of-staters. How about New Jersey?

Mayor Rudolph W. Giuliani triumphantly unveiled a proposal yesterday to ship most of the City's residential garbage to transfer stations in New Jersey, but the Administration's glee was quickly muted by an embarrassing lapse in political tact: It did not tell New Jersey of the plan until yesterday morning, and then only in sketchy detail. *New York Times,* December 3, 1998

New Jersey's governor, Christie Whitman, may have been a fellow Republican, but she was not amused, as indicated by a press release she issued, headlined "Whitman to New York's Garbage Plan: Drop Dead." The Generalissimo momentarily found himself at a loss for words.

On reflection, it certainly should have meant that Governor Whitman was briefed, Mr. Giuliani said in a rare show of contrition. "That was a mistake, but it wasn't a bad faith mistake. It was a good mistake."

New York Times, December 4, 1998

He sought to leaven the atmosphere with a little cross-Hudson levity.

"Does any [garbage] go to the Meadowlands?" the Mayor asked. When told no, he said: "Too bad. Well, we ought to get even, right? I mean for the Giants and the Jets."

New York Times, December 4, 1998

But seriously, folks. . .

You've got to understand, the politics of garbage is different from the business of garbage. . . .

This plan is a very fair and equitable one. . . . There are numerous backup plans, but this is the one we're proposing today. There are other places that are interested in getting our trash.
N.Y. Times, Dec. 4, 1998

Oh, yeah, who? Well, impoverished Charles City County, Virginia, that's who. The only catch here: The county had not notified the commonwealth's governor, James Gilmore, of its intent. And the garbage barges would have to be floated straight up the picturesque, historic James River, linchpin of Virginia's tourism industry. Gilmore balked. But the Generalissimo put the situation into perspective for him.

New York City has a specialized problem. It comes from the fact that we're so crowded and our land mass is very small, and that brings great benefits to the rest of the country, like Virginia. People in Virginia like to utilize New York because we're a cultural center, because we're a business center. What goes along with being a cultural and a business center is you're very crowded.

We don't have the room here to handle the garbage that's produced not just by New Yorkers, but by the three million more people that come here that utilize the place every day. So this is a reciprocal relationship.
New York Times, January 14, 1999

As a result of that relationship, the Mayor continued, the rest of the country should help the city with waste disposal. "We don't do it because we're profligate, we don't do it because we're wasteful. . . . We do it because there are a lot of people in the city and that brings great benefits to the American economy. . . . When people move beyond just a sort of knee-jerk political issue here," he said, "there's a whole industry out there, and this will continue and it will be part of waste disposal for the next 50 or 100 years."

The Mayor raised the possibility of litigation to force other states to accept the City's waste. "They can be challenged," he said of proposed restrictions on waste export. *New York Times*, January 14, 1999

Gilmore called that "really an outrageous statement." His fellow Virginia public officials rallied like latter-day Stonewall Jacksons to repel the invasion of Yankee trash, with Gilmore introducing legislation to ban the shipments.

The Mayor's Office has dismissed such comments, which resounded here in the State Capitol during last week's opening of the General Assembly, as mere carping from "pandering politicians trying to achieve their own agenda." *New York Times*, January 18, 1999

Responding to politicians in Virginia who continue to rail against Mayor Rudolph W. Giuliani's plan to export more of New York City's trash, the Mayor said yesterday that he never said other states were obligated to take the City's garbage.

"This isn't a question of obligation. This is a very big business and it supplies lots of jobs for people. There's a business here that goes on, irrespective of statements that the politicians make."

Saying that the City pays "a huge amount of money" to send its trash out of state, Mr. Giuliani said, "There are more places that want to do business with us than you could possibly imagine." *N.Y. Times,* Jan. 19, 1999

There is no reason for you to be offended. No one is obligated to accept New York City's garbage. It is a relationship of mutual benefit entered into freely and voluntarily. Letter to Virginia Governor James S. Gilmore III, January 19, 1999, *New York Times,* January 20, 1999

Who was to blame, ultimately, for (no pun intended) the stink? Why, the press, of course.
The Mayor used the word "spin" and its grammatical cousins nine times in saying that the news media had misrepresented his discussion of a private company's contract to ship the City's garbage to Virginia. . . .

"I didn't say that they were obligated to take the garbage," he said. "Somebody put that spin on it, so now they're spinning based on the spin, and then everything is spun around." . . .

The Mayor said that he felt no need to apologize "for an unfair spin, or an erroneous spin, that somebody else puts on the comments that I actually make. I learned a long time ago in this business not to get spun into being offended by the media when somebody didn't say or intend what it is you're being spun around by." . . .

"If you want the money that goes with it, you take the garbage," he said. "If you don't want the money that goes with it, we can move on and find lots of other opportunities and places." *New York Times,* January 20, 1999

◆ Homelessness: An Arresting Solution

One quality-of-life problem that did not get solved on Rudy Giuliani's watch: the presence on New York's streets of thousands of homeless people, dazed, panhandling, sleeping in boxes or on sewer grates, summer or winter.

Mass homelessness had become a noticeable phenomenon in America's cities by the mid-1980s. In New York, advocates for the homeless won a court decree requiring the city to provide shelter to anyone who requested it and blamed Mayor Ed Koch for not providing enough low-income housing. Koch loudly answered his critics, saying that most homeless people were suffering from mental illness and/or addiction to drugs or alcohol and were there as a result of "deinstitutionalizing" psychiatric hospitals. In 1989, preparing to take Koch on, mayoral candidate Rudy Giuliani left little doubt where he stood. **He also accused the Mayor of "beating up on homeless people" by calling them drug addicted and mentally ill. He said Mr. Koch was "trying to make political points by using harsh words."** *New York Times*, March 29, 1989

Ten years later, in a speech in Phoenix, Arizona, Giuliani—now mayor himself—had a very different take on things. **He disparaged the "romanticism" of homelessness and warned that while food stamps were vital for some people, they created the chance for "more fraud than welfare."** *New York Times*, January 3, 1999

Back home, he expanded on that idea. **There are several subterranean plots that are going on here. No. 1 is, you've got some advocates that don't want to solve the homeless problem. Because now they wouldn't be advocates anymore. . . . There's something** to that, that I know is hard for people who are in a total unrealistic 1960's, 70's and 80's do-gooder mentality, in which they did more harm than good. But there is a reality to that. And it may even be a little bit unconscious, that they don't want this problem to go away because they want people dependent on them.

Comments on WABC Radio, *N.Y. Times,* Aug.13, 1999

To me, it's a psychological problem that some people in the City have had in the past in dealing with their own guilt.   *New York Times,* November 30, 1999

In December 1998, dissatisfied with the city's efforts in dealing with homelessness and responding to complaints by some communities of huge shelters in their neighborhoods, city councilmember Stephen DiBrienza spearheaded a bill that, among other things, limited the size of future shelters opened by the City to two hundred beds. In vetoing the bill, the Generalissimo went ballistic. Claiming—falsely—that the bill was retroactive, he announced that it meant the city would have to open new shelters, and he openly targeted his nemesis, Councilmember DiBrienza, with a threat to flood his district with shelters in retaliation.

"If they overturn the veto, then this will have to happen," Mr. Giuliani said at a news conference, adding that the city would place new shelters "in the communities of those members who were most strongly in favor of this, on the theory that those are the communities that most want it."   *New York Times,* December 17, 1998

At a news conference after the vote [to override his veto], the Mayor said of the Council, "They're just wrong." . . . Mr. Giuliani insisted that even if the bill were amended, it would still require the City to add as many as 400 beds, which he said would mean opening

"two or three or four more shelters that would have to be relocated." Later, he said there might be five shelters.

"They will be put in the districts primarily of those who are most in support of this because that reflects, we assume, the thinking of their community," the Mayor said. "And I can't think of any better way to do it."

New York Times, December 18, 1998

People who believe it is necessary to limit shelters to less than two hundred [beds], I assume, are reflecting the views of their communities. It should be in those communities that the effect of this is felt, not the entire city.

Statement in aftermath of council override, December 1998
Quoted in column by former mayor Ed Koch,
New York Daily News, January 8, 1999

What we will do is, we will re-site in the communities of those members who are most strongly in favor of this, on the theory that those are the communities that most want it. *New York Daily News,* December 21, 1998

The Generalissimo carried out his threat—serving a Christmastime eviction notice on a psychiatric outpatient facility in a city-owned building in South Brooklyn, so he could begin moving homeless people there as punishment for DiBrienza (and, presumably, his constituents for electing him).

The City Council member there is the City Council member who sponsored the limitation on the number of people in homeless shelters. So the assumption is that he's speaking for his community—that his community in essence supports what he did. Otherwise, he wouldn't be their City Council member. *N.Y. Times,* Dec. 30, 1998

Then he backed off—sort of. The psychiatric facility (which was supported by the liberal-minded neighborhood) could stay, and so could the day care and senior services located in the building, but other agencies would have to go to make room for the homeless.

. . . It's a test of whether they're in good faith or they're hypocrites. . . . The mental health program will be preserved. That's the program that, at least, out front, the protestations—the pious protestations—were about. . . . If people object to this, then what they're really objecting to is doing anything for the homeless, which really would be very hypocritical, since the Council member from that district is the person who sponsored the legislation. *New York Times,* January 13, 1999

The Mayor added one more thing. "We're not negotiating this." *New York Times,* January 13, 1999

The Generalissimo, faced with lawsuits and a crescendo of opposition in a neighborhood that had supported him in his past races, wound up backing down entirely. But several months later he hit on a strategy that would advance his aims on two fronts—reducing the homeless shelter population and abolishing welfare—simultaneously. He announced a new policy: Homeless people with children would be told to report to a "jobs center" as a condition of being offered shelter. If they refused, they would have to leave the shelter—and the city would put their children in foster care. New Yorkers, across the board, spoke up against the policy as something out of Charles Dickens.

Scare tactics. . . . If somebody is on welfare and they can't work because they are sick or ill, the City will take care of them and their children. If you are physically unable to care for your children—you're disabled—you are taken care of. It doesn't apply to someone like that.

This applies to people who are able-bodied, able to work, who aren't working. . . .

The apostles of dependency love to want to bring us back to when we had 1.1 million people on welfare. I think this is the highest form of compassion and love, to help people to help themselves, to get them to the point where they can take care of themselves, to ask them to do something in return for the help that they are being given by the City, State and the Federal Government.

New York Times, October 27, 1999

A judge issued an injunction blocking the imposition of the policy during the Christmas and New Year's holidays.

There is no question the decision is wrong. . . . This policy will go into effect. And it's a good policy. And it's a humane policy and it's a decent one. And it's one that flies in the face of years and years of ideological opposition to it, that ended up in people being poorer, more dependent and made into victims as opposed to people who can actually help themselves.

New York Times, December 10, 1999

Andrew Cuomo, Secretary of the U.S. Department of Housing and Urban Development (HUD), questioned what he was doing.

If Andrew Cuomo took the time to understand the policy rather than mischaracterize it, he would undoubtedly reconsider his position.   *N.Y. Times*, Dec. 15, 1999

When a group offering services to the homeless announced it would not evict people from shelters it operated, and a Catholic nun who ran it said of the mayor, "I can't believe that a person of his education and religious training" would pursue this policy, Giuliani was unmoved:

If they don't follow the law, then they lose their contract. The law says that you have to put people in a work situation if they're on welfare, for their good, for their benefit. If they're so ideologically opposed to that they can't carry out the law, then of course they'll lose the contract. *New York Times,* December 18, 1999

He called his policies "compassionate," "loving" and "caring" and said that he had "great confidence, despite the ability of the media to mischaracterize things in the direction of their sort of emotional, ideological bent" that "the wisdom of our homeless policy will eventually emerge." *New York Times,* December 18, 1999

But in the meantime, when a young woman was struck in the head with a brick on a midtown street one day, the *New York Daily News*—in what proved to be a journalistic rush to judgment—published a front-page editorial demanding the city clear the streets. Though he had been mayor for nearly six full years and not done much to address this problem, Giuliani suddenly rushed to seize the issue as his own.

You do not have the right to sleep on the streets of New York City. It doesn't exist anywhere. The Founding Fathers never put that in the Constitution.

Statement on WABC Radio, *New York Post,* November 20, 1999; *New York Times,* November 23, 1999

I know this is going to get some of the ACLU types and others all upset and angry and jumping up and down. However, streets do not exist in civilized societies for the purpose of sleeping there. Bedrooms are for sleeping. *New York Times,* November 20, November 23, December 9, 1999

There are some people . . . who have been released in the deinstitutionalization policies that have gone on the last 20 to 30 years that never should have been released. Statement on WABC Radio
New York Post, November 20, 1999

The presumption is that this was done by a mentally ill person. . . . You're going to have a lot of fear, you're going to have a lot of reaction, you're going to have a lot of over-reaction. *New York Times,* November 20, 1999;
New York Post, December 1, 1999

There were times in which we romanticized this [home-lessness] to such an extent that we invited people to do it. *New York Times,* November 20, 1999

And so the order was given. Police were to roust homeless people, tell them to move on, offer to take them to a shelter—and, if they refused to move on or accept the offer, arrest them. The first night the new policy was put into practice, some twenty-three homeless people were arrested.
A society moves as a progressive society as it convinces more and more people that they shouldn't be sleeping on its streets. *New York Times,* November 22, 1999

The vast majority of people go into programs that deal with their underlying problem. This is far better than what it used to be in New York—which was basically to ignore people living on the streets. *N.Y. Post,* Dec. 1, 1999

If someone decides to live on the street of an American city, or any place else in America, there is obviously something that needs to be addressed. It can't be

addressed with ignoring it. And it can't be addressed by saying if a person doesn't want to help themselves then let them remain on the street. There is nothing gained in ignoring people living on the street and romanticizing homelessness into some issue that it really isn't. *New York Times,* December 2, 1999

His policies, the Generalissimo said, were a **much more humane, more decent and more caring philosophy than just ignoring the problem.**

Speech to Republican Washington Coalition
New York Daily News, December 2, 1999

What's more, they were **enormously successful. . . . I can't help it if the people who helped to create the chaos in the first place are opposing it.** *New York Post,* December 2, 1999

Some noted that, following the mayor's logic to its conclusion, the head of a homeless family who refused workfare could lose his or her children, be evicted from the shelter—and then, because they were homeless again, be arrested. Talk show host Rosie O'Donnell rapped him on the air. His rival in the upcoming U.S. Senate race, First Lady Hillary Rodham Clinton, scored his policies in a major speech. The Reverend Al Sharpton filled Union Square with a fiery anti-Giuliani rally. The Generalissimo seemed delighted.

I almost think this is a good debate to have. Ultimately, it actually helps me. *New York Post,* December 2, 1999

Great. Who's setting the debate? I am. I've got them all debating my policy. *New York Times,* December 9, 1999

They sort of want to return the city to the way the city used to be. I want to see the city get better, be a better

place. The reality is that if someone is sleeping on the streets, you should not ignore the person and walk away. . . . [People] get the impression that we are arresting people for being homeless. That is not true. We're arresting homeless people when they specifically violate a law, for which you would arrest anybody else.

Dec. 7, 1999. Quoted in *New York Observer,* Dec. 20, 1999

His critics, he said, wanted

a special immunity for homeless people. . . . So far, during the intense effort to try to deal with homelessness, we have approached 1,674 people, as of Friday. Only 160 of these people have been arrested. So this is hardly a policy of arrests. You would have to be dishonest to describe it that way. So most of the people that are approached by the police who are homeless are taken to shelters, they are taken to hospitals, they are asked to move and they move. We are not arresting homeless people for just sleeping on the street.

New York Times, December 6, 1999

As time went on, the Generalissimo became more and more defensive—particularly when the man arrested for the brick attack turned out to be a career criminal who was neither homeless nor mentally ill. Rather than admit that he had overreacted and that his vaunted new initiative on homelessness had been based on a fit of hysteria, Giuliani furiously dug in his heels.

The man didn't have an address. He was living at the Port Authority Bus Depot and panhandling. He fits every description of homelessness. In fact, he was homeless. *New York Times,* December 5, 1999

The Mayor insisted he was a roaming panhandler.

New York Times, December 18, 1999

By this week, the Mayor had changed his tone, saying his policies were designed to help people help themselves, and describing his campaign to clear the homeless from sidewalks as "compassionate" and "loving." . . .

Asked this week at a news briefing whether a recent series of abrupt and seemingly contradictory decisions on the homeless formed a coherent policy, Mr. Giuliani briskly replied: "Yes." But he added: "I mean, they're coherent to people who have an open mind about it. They're not coherent to people who are ideologically befuddled and overwhelmed." . . .

Mr. Giuliani regularly mentions the $40 million increase (in the Fiscal 2000 budget) in his speeches around the city and country, saying his administration has done more for the homeless than any other. In fact, this is the first year Mr. Giuliani's spending for the homeless has reached the levels seen under Mayor David N. Dinkins. . . .

Yesterday he linked the two [new policies] as part of a broad policy on homelessness, saying that "they both move homeless people toward accountability."

New York Times, December 9, 1999

Mr. Giuliani dismissed concerns that the timing of his announcement made his policy seem punitive. "I don't care," he said. "It was an excellent time to do it. That is when you very often can get people to understand even better why you're doing it."   *N.Y. Times*, Dec. 9, 1999

We could have gone with it a week, 10 days before. Or we could have gone with it a week later.

Comment in wake of brick attack on Nicole Barrett, Nov. 19, 1999. Requoted in *New York Times*, Dec. 9, 1999

Anything I do is going to be tied to my Senate race. I'd have to stop being Mayor.   *N.Y. Times,* Dec. 9, 1999

He said that newspapers in the city "dishonestly state our position." As for critics on the homeless? They're afflicted with "intellectual dishonesty."

New York Daily News, December 9, 1999

At his daily news conference, the Mayor ... accused his critics of deliberately misreading the numbers to further disparage his policies. "They are misreading the statistics. If you just use your ability of any kind of critical analysis without falling all over for them, then what you will realize is that the number of people that the police have taken to the drop-in centers are an infinitesimal number of people that would not show up in the increase. It's about 25 people a day. We have 6,500 people in the shelters. That's less than one person per shelter." Mr. Giuliani said the presentation of the statistics offers "a way in which people want to misunderstand the policy, and get you to misrepresent it, to take advantage of it."

New York Times, December 21, 1999

◆ On Mosquitoes as a Health Threat

I haven't seen a mosquito around since the summertime, but I will go check. In fact, I'll go home now and check.

> Statement at press conference responding to complaints by people living near Gracie Mansion of mosquito infestations, December 1998 (statement made, article reported, with mayor "pointedly looking at his watch as if he had something urgent on his mind")
> *New York Times,* September 20, 1999

The more dead mosquitoes, the better.
Statement as city suddenly launches massive program
of airborne spraying against mosquito infestation after
several deaths are reported across city,
New York Times, September 10, 1999

**I don't think the media should try to push this out of
proportion.** *New York Post,* September 10, 1999

◆ Kiss Your Grammy Good-bye

Since their inception, the Grammy Awards—music's equivalent to the Oscars, the Emmys, and the Tonys—had been
held either in New York or Los Angeles (except for one time
in Nashville). Mayor David Dinkins, in particular, had assiduously courted the gala ceremony, and landed it three times
in four years—but did not survive as Mayor long enough to
preside over the 1994 ceremony. Rudy Giuliani did that
instead.

There was some question as to whether the successor who
much criticized Dinkins's priorities as mayor would try as hard
to host the glittery but lucrative Grammys in the future, but
those qualms seemed put to rest three years later when the
National Academy of Recording Arts and Sciences (NARAS)
announced that its award ceremony was Grammys were coming back to the Big Apple.

**He [the Mayor] said he hopes the February 26 ceremony
would become "a signature event for the Grammys,
Madison Square Garden and New York City." He said
the last time the Grammys were held here, in 1994, the
City took in $12 million from direct spending and about
$25 million altogether.** *N.Y. Daily News,* Jan. 8, 1997

This is the difference between a city that's real, and a city that's on tape.
> Statement at press conference, January 7, 1997
> *New York Post*, June 16, 1998

A year later New York beat out L.A. again.

I am thrilled to welcome the Grammys back to New York City. The Grammys are staying where they belong.
> Statement at City Hall press conference with NARAS
> president Michael Greene, September 1997
> *New York Daily News*, February 10, 1998

But at the press conference to announce the nominees for awards, Giuliani was under the impression he had been invited to read off the names of nominated entertainers—and a woman on his advance staff conveyed that message to NARAS president Mike Greene. Greene was definitely not under that impression, and heated words ensued.

Mayor Giuliani dared the hosts of the Grammy Awards yesterday to pack their bags and get out of town.

Enraged at Grammy chief Michael Greene for allegedly shouting obscenities at a mayoral aide, Giuliani vowed to boycott the February 25 awards ceremony at Radio City Music Hall.
> *New York Daily News*, February 10, 1998

If you want to abuse a member of my staff, abuse me and see if you get away with it. . . .

I think what he [Greene] did was disgusting and reprehensible. . . . He used language with her that you shouldn't use, and not only hasn't promptly apologized for it, but is lying about it.   *N.Y. Daily News*, Feb. 10, 1998

Actually, Greene had tried to apologize, but it wasn't good enough.

The staff member sent the flowers back, because [Greene] refused to acknowledge what he did.

New York Daily News, February 10, 1998

Not only that, but the Grammys could leave, as far as the Generalissimo was concerned.

If they want to go back to L.A., they can. We could replace the Grammys in about a day.

New York Daily News, February 10, 1998

You say we're going to lose $40 million? We'll replace that with three other things in a day.

Statement at City Hall press conference,
February 9, 1998, *New York Post,* June 16, 1998

We'll replace the prestige.

New York Daily News, February 10, 1998

Hopefully, we would get organizations that would treat us in the same respectful way in which we treat them. It's just like the normal rules of conduct that civilized people have with each other.   *N.Y. Times,* Feb. 15, 1998

If Mike Greene stops abusing people, he will create a much better atmosphere for the Grammys, whether in New York or elsewhere.

Statement at City Hall press conference,
February 9, 1998, *New York Post,* June 16, 1998

As the day of the event came closer, there was no budging in the Generalissimo's position.

Mayor Giuliani said yesterday he is not taking any calls from Grammy boss Michael Greene, and vowed not to attend the awards even if he gets a full apology.

"I think he has probably tried to reach me, but . . . I know the comments he's making—which are that the members of my staff aren't telling the truth." . . .

Giuliani laid out his terms, which require Greene to say, "It was wrong of me to yell and scream at a member of your staff. . . . It was wrong of me to threaten to kill her . . . and it's not going to happen again."

Giuliani said, "That apology, I accept in a second." . . .

Giuliani said he doesn't want to go to the Grammys and can't anyway—because he has a town hall meeting on Staten Island at 8 P.M.   N.Y. Post, Feb. 24, 1998

Somehow, the show managed to go on without him. And on June 16, 1998, the National Academy of Recording Arts and Sciences announced that the Grammys were returning to Los Angeles. The Generalissimo had already prepared New Yorkers for the move.

You may be able to attend the Grammy Awards in Los Angeles, but there's a 26 percent greater chance you'll be victimized while you're there.

> Discussing relative crime statistics among U.S. cities
> while presenting mayor's Management Report
> *New York Post*, February 11, 1998

Next to Michael Greene at the announcement was smiling L.A. Mayor Richard Riordan. Riordan—a self-effacing, smooth, low-key, behind-the-scenes operator—had been elected the same year as Giuliani (also as a Republican), was the virtual opposite of him on the temperamental scale, and had presided over a comeback of his city every bit as impressive as the one Giuliani boasted of in New York. And why should Riordan not have been smiling? He knew that whatever the Grammys were worth, $25 million or $40 million, it was all L.A.'s as long as Rudolph Giuliani was Mayor of New York.

21

Rudy and the Yankees, or The Generalissimo Decides to Buy a Billion-Dollar Stadium for His Friend George and the Hell with Everybody Else

[Giuliani's] father, a Manhattanite exiled to his wife's Brooklyn neighborhood, was a Yankee fan. The son had no particular allegiance until the day his father dressed him in a Yankee uniform and sent him out to play in the heart of Dodger territory. "The first thing they did was throw me in the mud," Giuliani recounted during a campaign commercial in 1993 that briefly described his travails as the only Yankee fan in Brooklyn. But the full story is much better.

New York Times Magazine, December 3, 1995

One day a group of four or five children put a noose around my neck and tried to hang me from a tree. My grandmother saw this and started yelling, and they stopped. But my proudest moment was when I didn't renounce the Yankees. I kept telling them: "I am a Yankee fan. I am a Yankee fan. I'm gonna stay a Yankee fan." All of our family in that four-block area were Dodger fans, so this was a constant fight for me—go out and acquire statistics to prove that the Yankees were better than the Dodgers. The most wonderful thing was that the last time they played in the World Series, in 1956, the Yankees won—which I used for 10 years to totally destroy all my Dodger relatives. To my father, it was a joke. Put a Yankee uniform on the kid and it'll irritate all my friends and relatives and it'll be fun. But to me it was like being a martyr: I'm not gonna give up my religion. You're not gonna change me.

New York Times Magazine, December 3, 1995

And thus began the lifelong allegiance of Rudolph William Giuliani to his beloved New York Yankees.

He watched Roger Maris hit his record 61st home run at Yankee Stadium, he said, and was there when Reggie Jackson set a World Series record by hitting three consecutive home runs. *New York Times*, October 6, 1997

Years later, as mayor, he became a familiar sight in field-level box seats, right behind the team's dugout.

I like to be as close to the action as I can.

Providence (R.I.) *Journal-Bulletin*, October 22, 1998

Those were seats in high demand, to be sure, but Giuliani had a special friend: Yankee owner George Steinbrenner.

Now, it came to pass that Mr. Steinbrenner—a man who in his tumultuous time had gone through eleven different managers of the club (hiring and firing Billy Martin no less than five times each) and had twice been suspended from baseball for illegal activity—decided that he wanted what other owners had gotten from their cities: a brand-new stadium. This despite the fact that Yankee Stadium was a shrine of baseball history, that the team was drawing more than 2 million fans there, and that the City of New York, during its fiscal crisis in the 1970s, had halted every public works project except one. Forgoing even construction of the Second Avenue subway (a vital mass transit link still desperately needed two decades later), the city had finished, on time (and with mammoth cost overruns), a top-to-bottom reconstruction of Yankee Stadium for Mr. Steinbrenner.

Another argument in favor of the Yankees staying where they were: The stadium was vital to the prestige, and all hopes for economic renewal, of the borough of The Bronx. Not that this mattered much to George Steinbrenner, who routinely (and inaccurately) denigrated the area around the stadium as unsafe, and actively sought to discourage people from attending games there (then complaining when the Yankees did not lead the American League in attendance!). Steinbrenner wanted out of The Bronx. He wanted a new ballpark built for him on the West Side of Manhattan, near midtown (regardless of the nightmarish traffic congestion a stadium would cause in that location). Or he would take the team across the river to New Jersey, where New York's two football teams had gone. And he was not afraid to resort to crude gestures to get what he wanted—such as demeaning Mayor David Dinkins by making Dinkins sit next to the director of the New Jersey Sports Authority at a preseason Yankee boosters' luncheon after Steinbrenner's second suspension (which originally was supposed to have been a lifetime ban) was lifted in 1993.

Steinbrenner was, simply, a bully. But the City of New York was not without leverage in the matter. The city owned the land on which the stadium sat—and with it, the right of eminent domain. The city would also, if push came to shove, have an excellent legal case that the Yankees had for years deliberately falsified their spending figures for maintenance of the ballpark in order to avoid paying their full lease fees. Manhattanites did not want a new stadium, and opponents had already served notice they would tie up any such move in court for years. The administration of Governor George Pataki had staked out that West Side site for a badly needed expansion of the city's Convention Center. Baseball had a stated policy that gambling revenue could not be used to support a major-league franchise, and New Jersey had no plausible way of financing a new stadium except through money generated by its share of Atlantic City casino profits. And the Garden State's new governor, Christie Whitman, was a tax-cutter who showed no interest in spending or borrowing any money to lure another New York sports team.

Steinbrenner was, in other words, a bully whose bluff was ripe for being called. And who better to call it than rough, tough, fearless Rudy Giuliani, the man who had stockbrokers handcuffed in their offices, who broke taxi strikes and drove schools chancellors out of town?

Yet, strangely, the one time when all New Yorkers would have *welcomed* Giuliani acting in a high-handed manner, when his city *needed* him to behave in his usual dictatorial way, he did not. In dealing with George Steinbrenner, owner of his favorite baseball team, Rudy Giuliani was suddenly mysteriously transformed from a mayor into a messenger boy.

. . . Mr. Giuliani accused Mr. [Bronx Borough President Fernando] Ferrer of making it "much more difficult" to persuade the Yankees to stay by criticizing the team's owner, George M. Steinbrenner 3rd. And he even suggested the blame would fall on Mr. Ferrer if the Yankees moved away.

The attack on Mr. Ferrer, a Democrat who, it just so happens, has started raising money for a possible challenge to the Republican Mayor in 1997, came as Mr.

Giuliani offered perhaps the clearest indication yet that the Yankees are intent on finding a new home after 72 years in Yankee Stadium.

"I can't guarantee, although I would like it, that I can keep them in The Bronx," he said. "One of the main reasons I can't guarantee it is because of the attitude of the Borough President." . . .

He also pointed out that New York had lost the Brooklyn Dodgers to California in 1957 because the City refused the request by the late Walter O'Malley, the team's owner, to build a stadium. "I guarantee you," he said, "we learn from the mistakes of the past." . . .

"Despite what you think of George Steinbrenner and the Yankees, they're a business organization," he said. "And if they think they're going to be in a place where the political leadership of that place is going to attack them, this is a very, very valuable franchise that a lot of places would like to have."   *N.Y. Times,* Dec. 14, 1995

The Mayor who likes to say "no" has whispered a tentative but unmistakable "yes" to the idea of moving Yankee Stadium to the West Side of Manhattan. . . . The Mayor, for his part, said he would "love to have that debate" with his opponents, accusing them of the same anti-business mentality he said forced four sports franchises from the city, beginning with the Dodgers in 1957. . . . "I think it's a terrible issue for them," Mr. Giuliani said. "It's their philosophy that's run this city into the ground, this virulently anti-business attitude."
New York Times, April 11, 1996

The price tag of the new stadium Giuliani proposed to build: a mere $1 billion, by far the most expensive such project in history. With a dome, yet. (Not counting the land. Or the $600,000 consultant's fee to prepare the proposal.) But not to worry, said the mayor. New Yorkers wouldn't feel a thing.

Purely from a financial analysis point of view, the place where the city could build a new stadium at virtually no cost to the taxpayer, or very little cost to the taxpayer, would be in Manhattan. Because the value of property in Manhattan is so great, you can finance it at very little cost. There might even be ways to finance it at no cost or a profit. . . . When you look at those numbers, the amounts don't mean as much as the ability to finance it and therefore not have to cost the taxpayers any money, or a minimal amount of money.

New York Times, April 6, 1996, and April 23, 1998

Asked yesterday if he would allow a company to pay for the right to change the hallowed name of Yankee Stadium, the Mayor replied with a laugh, "It depends on the amount of money." *New York Times*, April 6, 1996

The "no-cost" billion-dollar-stadium ruse could not be maintained with a straight face for very long.

Backing off claims that a new Manhattan stadium would pay for itself, Mayor Giuliani said yesterday that taxpayers would have to cover part of the cost of any effort to keep the Yankees in New York.

New York Daily News, April 13, 1996

The taxpayers would pay whatever could not be financed and maybe that would be nothing. And the taxpayers might have to pay out of the capital budget some of the capital improvements that occur around the stadium. *New York Daily News*, April 13, 1996

People should have confidence that we'll put a responsible plan for the people of the City of New York there, one that would cost the taxpayers the least amount of money.   Statement on WABC Radio
New York Daily News, April 14, 1996

But look beyond the price tag, Giuliani urged New Yorkers. **We do not have a large indoor arena for mega-events. . . . We are out of consideration for a Superbowl, a Final Four in the future, for any convention that needs to seat 20,000 people or more.**
                      Associated Press, April 12, 1996

They weren't buying it. And two years later, with the Yankees in the midst of a record-breaking 125-win season, they still weren't. New Yorkers loved their Yankees—and wanted them to stay right where they were.
Eager to play down the possible $1 billion cost for a new Yankee Stadium, Mayor Rudolph W. Giuliani is reiterating the idea of naming a new stadium for a corporation that would help pick up the tab. . . .

"Naming rights of baseball parks have gone as high as $100 million, and it's estimated that naming rights for a Shea or a Yankee Stadium would exceed that amount by a considerable amount," the Mayor said Friday on his radio call-in program on WABC-AM. . . .

Although the estimated cost of $1 billion for a new home for the Yankees came from a report commissioned in part by the city, the Mayor dismissed it throughout the week as the unsubstantiated exaggeration of opponents.

On his radio program, he said he would use the coming days to educate New Yorkers about the costs and benefits of retaining both baseball teams by "explaining

how it can be done, without nearly the difficulties that many who just oppose any kind of development, or any change, really, will suggest." *N.Y. Times,* Apr. 19, 1998

I really doubt that there is in this room a bigger Yankee fan than I am, a person who started going to Yankee Stadium earlier than I did. Romantically and emotionally, I would love to keep the Yankees in The Bronx. At the same time, I have to focus on the fact that we could lose the team. I have to look at the practicalities of that.

New York Times, April 21, 1998

This spending will result in, bare minimum, at least $1 billion more for our economy and thousands and thousands of jobs. We need these jobs. And politically those who are worried about unemployment and the change from welfare to work, we need a city that has a constantly expanding set of jobs. And I would think that these people who are trying to block this—all of whom come out of this political philosophy that drives jobs out of the city—would only have some deference to the plans that we have. *New York Times,* April 22, 1998

But when he proposed keeping alive the city's commercial rent tax—an irritant to the business community whose gradual elimination had long been a pet goal of City Council Speaker Peter Vallone—in order to pay for the new stadium Steinbrenner wanted, Giuliani crossed a line into uncharted territory. And he wound up taking the entire city along with him.

A moderate Democrat who shared many of the mayor's priorities, Vallone had not looked for fights with Giuliani in their five years serving together, and—mostly thanks to Vallone's gentlemanly streak—their personal relationship had generally been good.

Speaker Peter Vallone, I congratulate you on having developed the City Council into such a respected and effective legislative body. And I look forward to our partnership and friendship with you and the other members of the City Council in working together for our city.

First Inaugural Address, New York Times, January 3, 1994

But very quickly, whenever he stood up for what he saw as council prerogatives, the speaker had been served notice that—in a moment—the relationship could turn otherwise. When he raised questions about conditions at the Rikers Island prison (which was in his district). . .

Mr. Giuliani fired back with a written statement accusing Mr. Vallone of acting "irresponsibly" and spreading "misinformation." *New York Times,* March 29, 1994

When the council passed a bill requiring public hearings before any city agency could be privatized . . .

[Council members are] being used as an intermediary for unions that would like to stop even the thought of privatization even before it gets to surface. They are also trying to get involved in the negotiating process on behalf of the unions. That is clearly what they are doing. That's just patently obvious. *N.Y. Times,* Apr. 29, 1994

And when the council tried to push an alternative plan to close a budget gap near the end of Giuliani's first year in office, the Generalissimo said the council did not even have the right to pass a plan of its own.

If they override the veto, we would take the viewpoint that their action is null and void. They don't have the power to modify the budget. If they wanted to force me to take account of that, they'd have to go to court.

New York Times, November 29, 1994

Other such standoffs followed—over a Vallone proposal for added money for schools construction that Giuliani agreed to only after months of stonewalling, over an abortive Giuliani zoning plan to allow superstores in residential neighborhoods that the council blocked—but, aside from a call by the speaker for revision of the City Charter to give the council more power, relations between the two branches remained on an even keel. Now, however, Giuliani was talking about wrecking what Vallone hoped would be one of his signature achievements in public office. And Vallone was running a long-shot race for governor against George Pataki. Needing an issue—and belatedly realizing that Giuliani had given him one—he announced that the council would put a referendum on the November ballot: Should city funds be spent on a new stadium in Manhattan?

Referendums on baseball stadiums lead to baseball teams leaving. *New York Times,* May 24, 1998

That's sort of the absence of leadership. In the places that have done that, they've driven their baseball teams away. I mean, you can play that game and it'd be easy to say that, and most people in a public opinion poll probably agree with it. But I got elected to be a leader, not a panderer. And the fact is that I'm not going to see the two teams driven out of New York. *New York Times,* April 21, 1998

Speaking as though a plan to build a stadium for the Yankees in Manhattan were a *fait accompli*, Mr. Giuliani said: "I think you've got to be a leader. I know most of the public disagrees with me. I think 10 years from now they'll say, 'Mayor Giuliani made the right decision.'" *New York Times,* April 21, 1998

The result of such a referendum was a forgone conclusion. Steinbrenner knew it—and immediately came out from behind his Oz-like curtain to hurl thunderbolts (and empty threats to move the team) at Vallone. Giuliani knew it too. He offered a carrot to the council—withdraw the referendum, and he would empanel a Charter Revision Commission that would repeal term limits for council members. (A two-term limit on all city officeholders had been enacted in a 1993 referendum drive that was bankrolled by Ronald Lauder, the Republican millionaire who had helped sabotage Giuliani's first race for mayor and that took the city's political establishment by surprise. A subsequent council-backed effort to extend the limits—which will force two-thirds out of the body's members out on a single day, December 31, 2001—had failed.) When that didn't work, Giuliani resorted to the stick: an ultimatum to Vallone and the council either to take the referendum off the ballot now, or he would break off all negotiations on the city budget. Vallone didn't blink. And the council did something that had not happened since the new City Charter had been adopted. It passed the municipal budget on its own.

. . . The Mayor accused the Council of "illusory calculations" and of spending "make believe money."

New York Times, June 7, 1998

Even as Council members were casting their votes on the second floor of City Hall, Mayor Rudolph W. Giuliani was holding forth on the first floor, letting loose a string of adjectives—"damaging," "illusory," and "make believe"—to describe the Council's budget.

"This is the most irresponsible budget I have seen as the Mayor of New York City," he said. . . . He said he would do everything he could, including freezing City

financing, to stop the Council plan from bloating the City's deficit. *New York Times,* June 6, 1998

There are lots of versions of what this person said to that person, people yelling at each other, jumping up and down and negotiating. The reality is that irrespective of any issue with the Stadium, this budget is way out of the realm of reason. . . . This is the kind of thing that happens when people do election-year budgets.

New York Times, June 6, 1998

One thing galled him, the Generalissimo admitted—the council had cut $1 million in funds for the Office of the Mayor. "I would imagine that's in order to create some kind of irritation for me; thank you," he said. Noting that "I can play that game," the Mayor said that he would use his impoundment powers to cut $1 million from the Council's budget. . . .

. . . "This isn't over yet," the Mayor said.

New York Times, June 6, 1998

And indeed it was just beginning. Within twenty-four hours, Giuliani notified the council that city revenues had somehow, inscrutably, dropped $251 million below his original forecasts—this despite an all-time-record boom on Wall Street. The Mayor, a Republican, said that unless the Democratic-controlled Council cuts the spending it had added to his proposed budget, the Council will have to raise property-tax rates to balance the books.

"I think this is a very good exercise for them in leadership, or the possibility of leadership. If you want to lower taxes, you have to lower expenses. . . .

"With regard to any remaining gap, I am hopeful that we can work together so that it will not be easy for you to raise the tax rates. . . .

. . . "They would like the best of both worlds—'Let's reduce taxes and be heroes, but also reduce spending,'" the Mayor said. He said the Council had created its own bind by passing the budget against his wishes, unlike each budget in his first term. "Often I took the burden away," he said. "I would make the tough choices for them, and then get blamed for it. Now they're going to have to make the tough choices." . . .

Asked about the budget dust-up as he left his news conference yesterday, the Mayor said with a laugh, "I enjoy it." *New York Times,* June 7, 1998

But of course, the Generalissimo being the Generalissimo, he couldn't resist making those "tough choices" himself.
In the letter [to the Council], the Mayor said that over the next five days he planned to veto most of the items that would be needed to bring spending into line with the new revenue estimates. . . . Mr. Giuliani said he had settled on about three-quarters of his vetoes, which he called "a road map as to how to straighten their budget out." *New York Times,* June 7, 1998

He zeroed in on the council's "member items."
You know what member items are—"My favorite program. The little community group that supports me." A couple of relatives here, a couple of friends there.
New York Times, June 8, 1998

Taking direct aim at his adversaries in the Council budget battle, Mayor Rudolph W. Giuliani used his line-item veto power for the first time yesterday to eliminate

nearly $5 million that the City Council had allocated for itself.   *New York Times*, June 9, 1998

The Executive Budget maintains adequate funding for this type of service. The City Council's addition is an unwarranted increase which does not include sufficient justification. . . .

This appears to be a member item for which insufficient justification is provided.

Veto message of Mayor Rudolph W. Giuliani
to City Council, *New York Times*, June 11, 1998

Among the vetoed items: programs to help fight breast cancer and asthma among inner-city residents (where the disease is rampant), and improvements in library services.

That's probably the biggest theme that runs through the budget. We've vetoed all the member items. There are many things in this budget that are disguised as programmatic expenses that are really member items for a particular member to have something for himself or herself for a political reason.   *New York Times*, June 11, 1998

The Generalissimo issued a threat of nuclear brinkmanship to back up his vetoes.

I'm realistic enough to understand that whatever I do with the vetoes, they're going to override. It's largely symbolic.

[But the City Charter] gives the Mayor the power of impoundment. And it gives the Mayor the power to set up accounts in each one of the agencies and to hold back the spending of money until we're sure that we're not going to have a shortfall in some part of the budget, or the entire budget. And you'll know I'll use those powers aggressively.   *New York Times*, June 10, 1998

Again, the council did not blink. It overrode Giuliani's vetoes. The City of New York was now facing a full-scale constitutional crisis that had one root cause—the determination of Rudolph Giuliani to use his powers as mayor to build a billion-dollar stadium for the owner of the New York Yankees that, it seemed, only the two of them wanted.

It's too late for negotiations. We will carry out the powers that the City Charter gives the Mayor to hold spending back, which I'm allowed to do, and there are several different ways in which I can do it. . . .

This is a gubernatorial election-year budget on behalf of the Speaker. That's the whole way it's played out today. It's almost like a convention, not a City Council hearing.   *New York Times,* June 17, 1998

With annual appropriations for dozens of service providers who depended on city funds left in limbo, the issue went to court. In the meantime, the Generalissimo played an ace in the hole—he quickly put in place a Charter Revision panel, whose recommendations may not be accompanied by any other referendum on the ballot in that same election year. Meaning: The Charter Revision may be a sham, it may have been formed purely to prevent the people from expressing their will, but so what? It would prevent Peter Vallone's referendum from being voted on—and spare Rudy Giuliani and George Steinbrenner the embarrassment of a floodtide of public condemnation. That issue went to court too. Not that the Generalissimo was all that confident of the outcome going in.

I'm not a fool. This is a city in which the judges are largely members of the Democratic Party, and on the State Supreme Court they're selected by the Democratic Party chairmen. They're not selected by the Mayor, the Governor or some merit-appointment process.
                                            New York Times, June 12, 1998

And indeed, Vallone and the council won the first round—with a Bronx Supreme Court judge ruling the stadium referendum should stay on the ballot.

To reduce the City's negotiating position at a critical time with the Yankees in order to get a couple of votes in a gubernatorial election—I really think you should be ashamed of yourself. *N.Y. Times,* Oct. 10, 1998

In the end, Giuliani won on appeal. The Yankee Stadium referendum did not appear on the ballot, and George Pataki easily beat Peter Vallone in the governor's race. On the other hand, Giuliani eventually accepted the council's budget. The Generalissimo continued to huff and puff on the Stadium issue from time to time. . . .

The idea of not spending money on a team is very, very popular among people until you lose the team, and then when you lose the team all the public officials who didn't do the right thing they want to throw out of office. *Providence* (R.I.) *Journal-Bulletin,* October 22, 1998

When the NFL's New England Patriots announced that, for lack of a suitable new stadium in the Boston area, they were moving to Hartford, Connecticut, Giuliani thought he had a perfect object lesson:

"Take a look at what happened in Boston. That could happen here. Not only could it happen here, it has happened here."

Referring to efforts to keep the Yankees in The Bronx, Mr. Giuliani said that "the silly political pandering that's been going on by the politicians in the city" could force the teams [the Mets as well as the Yankees] out of New York.

"You're going to lose the teams the way Boston and Massachusetts have now lost the original Boston Patriots,

now the New England Patriots—the way my predecessors lost the Brooklyn Dodgers, for which this city should be ashamed, and the way they lost the football Giants and the Jets." . . .

"It happens because politicians are unwilling to stand up to people that are just knee-jerking about this. . . . They're unwilling to, like, take a look at the future and say, yes, it's worth spending some public money if we can keep this economic engine in our city. If you don't do that, somebody else takes them away from you. That's what happened in Boston. And now you have precisely the day-after reaction, all the people that were, like, criticizing all of these politicians for the possibility of using public money, they're going to come down on them big time."   Statement on WABC Radio
New York Times, November 21, 1998

Weeks later, when the Patriots—having extracted the concessions they wanted in Massachusetts—reneged on their commitment, leaving Hartford and Connecticut officials with proverbial egg on their faces, the episode stood as testament to something else: the perils that befall public officials who want a sports team too much.

But, in the meantime, amid much good feeling all around, the Yankees capped their 1998 season with a four-game sweep in the World Series. The Generalissimo's apropos suggestion for the youth of New York: become truants from school.

Die-hard Yankee fan Mayor Giuliani said yesterday he would let his son, Andrew, skip school to attend today's ticker-tape parade and suggested other children should do the same because they could learn something from baseball.   *New York Daily News,* October 23, 1998

. . . In the run-up to the Yankees victory parade, the Mayor said that he learned more about life on the base-

**ball diamond than he did in the classroom, and atten-
dance dropped 13 percent at City schools on parade
day.** *New York Times,* October 29, 1999

And Giuliani found another outlet to express his loyalty to
his favorite team—especially when First Lady Hillary Rodham Clinton donned a Yankee cap at a White House ceremony for the defending world champions even as she was
mounting a "listening tour" to prepare for a run at the same
U.S. Senate seat he had his eye on.

**I would be more than happy to teach anybody in the
White House about the history of the Yankees, or go
over statistics with them. Show them where Yankee Stadium is located, where Shea Stadium is located. I could
take them through things. Or we could discuss "Where
were you when Reggie Jackson hit three home runs to
win the 1977 World Series?" I was at Yankee Stadium.
Or "Where were you when the Yankees won the 1996
World Series at home?" Gee, I was there. Or, um, "Who
do you think was a better center fielder—Joe DiMaggio,
Mickey Mantle, Bernie Williams?" Things like that.
Under the right set of circumstances, we could even
have a debate about this.** *New York Times,* June 11, 1999

**Where was she when Roger Maris hit his 61st home
run? Probably in Illinois somewhere.**
Washington Post, June 30, 1999

**All I would say is that I've been to Yankee Stadium prob-
ably a thousand times in my life, and I've never seen her
there.** *New York Times Magazine,* August 1, 1999

Behind their cancer-survivor manager Joe Torre, the 1999
Yankees epitomized the class so lacking in either their owner
or the city's mayor—and won the World Series again. And

again, defining the ticker-tape parade as "alternative educa-tion," Giuliani urged city school kids to play hookey.

[Social services teachers should] relate it to the ongoing social situation in the city. . . . It seems to me that this would be an excellent school trip. Maybe the kids could write an essay about it for the school newspaper, have an essay contest—there are lots of things that can be done.

New York Times, October 29, 1999

And New Yorkers trooped out to dangerous, old Yankee Stadium, 3 million strong—the highest attendance in the team's storied history, the mark George Steinbrenner had said the people of New York would have to reach if he was to con-sider staying in The Bronx. He thought they would never reach it; they had. The bully owner was now left with no rationale for his new billion-dollar dome on Manhattan's cramped West Side—and began talking about extending his lease after all. And Mayor Rudy Giuliani was left with no excuses for the spec-tacle of government gridlock he had put New Yorkers through.

Listen closely now.

I generally take baseball very seriously. Baseball to me is not political. . . . I love it. It's a source of relaxation and enjoyment. I really understand it. . . . This is real for me. This is not a political exercise.

New York Post, October 21, 1999

MAYOR RUDY GIULIANI SALUTES
THE NEW YORK YANKEES
Banner hung in front of City Hall for pre–World Series rally, October 21, 1999

I will never, ever politicize baseball.

New York Daily News, August 6, 1999

22

Mayor Under Siege!
Mayor Under Siege!

◆ The Rudybunker

One morning in June 1998, New Yorkers awoke to read the following:

Having tamed squeegee men and cabbies, murderers and muggers, Mayor Rudolph W. Giuliani is now bracing for a whole new order of urban treachery and cataclysm by building a $15.1 million emergency control center for his administration—bulletproofed, hardened to withstand bombs and hurricanes and equipped with food and beds for at least 30 members of his inner circle.

The ambitious project, which will sprawl over 46,000 square feet of one of the smaller buildings of the World Trade Center complex, will be big enough to accommodate at least 50 different City, State and Federal agencies and will allow them to coordinate responses to disasters from the smallest sewer explosion to the largest nerve gas attack.

Among its amenities will be back-up generators in case of power failures, a storage tank with enough water to last at least a week and technology that will include a secure "red" phone for the Mayor and video-conferencing capabilities so that he can talk to and see the President of the United States if necessary. . . .

Speaking on condition of anonymity, law enforcement officials said that the new center would be bulletproof, able to withstand the shock of some bomb blasts

and have a ventilation system that could be closed in the event of a biological or gas attack. They said telecommunications would also be able to withstand the blow of a nuclear assault. . . .

The Mayor would have a bit of privacy as well because the center will be built with a separate area where he can meet with select commissioners, a room with a pullout couch for him to sleep and a shower separate from the others. *New York Times,* June 13, 1998

Now, New Yorkers naturally assumed they were on the "A" list of any Armageddon-minded enemy of America and had seen enough disaster movies in which Manhattan gets wiped off the map by aliens, typhoons, meteors, killer apes, what have you. What shocked them—and had them scratching their heads, at least until they burst out laughing—was how their mayor seemed to have it down on his calendar for next Tuesday already. And he wasn't exactly making similar provisions for them!

The White House pointed out, politely, that if the mayor really needed to speak to the president during a crisis, its phone number was listed. The Generalissimo's critics had a field day, with "Rudy's Nuclear Winter Palace" winning the contest as funniest parody name for the Rudybunker. Even security experts questioned the wisdom of putting the city's entire law enforcement and civil defense high command in one place next to the World Trade Center (which had already been bombed once) . . . on the twenty-third floor (where the elevators could be put out of commission, as they had been at the World Trade Center) . . . right along the East River (where one terrorist with one speedboat and one Stinger missile could wipe out them all out in two seconds flat) . . . in a building the city didn't even own (but in which a loyal real-estate supporter of the mayor turned out to have an interest) . . . when the city already *had* an emergency command center in conveniently situated, easily protected, perfectly secure One Police Plaza.

Rudy defended his bunker—and acted amazed that he was even being questioned.

This is really an attempt to put the City for the next 20 years in a position where it can deal with the kinds of emergencies that might be unique to America's biggest city, its most densely populated city, and the best-known city in the world. And I would think that even City Council members would refrain from playing politics with this. *New York Times,* June 14, 1998

This was around the same time, you see, as the brouhaha over the council's unilaterally passing the city budget rather than surrender to the Generalissimo's ultimatums over a Yankee Stadium referendum. Ah, but the Generalissimo had pulled a fast one on his legislative branch—and guess what "member items" in the budget were *not* going to be vetoed?

Mayor's Office of Emergency Management. Design, $1.5 million. Construction, $15.1 million. This is in the capital budget for this year. I know that there are some Council members that don't read the budget, but that's their problem. This money has already been obligated in terms of contract. *New York Times,* June 14, 1998

The Mayor refused to provide details about the center, saying such information could help those who "who want to take advantage of victimizing the City." . . .

Currently, operations during all large-scale City emergencies are directed from an eighth-floor room of police headquarters that is lined with maps, television monitors and banks of phones for City agencies. The

Mayor said yesterday that there "were things lacking" at the center.   *New York Times,* June 14, 1998

Mr. Giuliani, at a news conference on Saturday, defended the bunker with characteristic vigor, accusing critics of playing politics with the safety of millions of New Yorkers. And he made a special point of correcting the notion that in planning for disaster, he was thinking about himself.

"It's not for the benefit of the Mayor," he said. "It's for the benefit of New York."   *N.Y. Times,* June 15, 1998

With only 30 beds, who stays and who goes? Mayor Rudolph Giuliani, who one day could face such a decision, said he had not made up his mind. "People admitted would depend on the nature of the emergency," he said. "It has nothing to do with my family."

Newsday, June 14, 1998

The City is working to meet any potential terrorist threat of germ warfare. It's the reason why I established a new agency in the City, quietly, because I didn't want to frighten people or alarm them.

New York Daily News, November 9, 1998

September 1999. The bunker is built. And it gets its first "under-fire" test—a hurricane scare that turned out to be simply high winds and heavy rain. The Generalissimo went on the airwaves to declare victory.

. . . The day after Tropical Storm Floyd blew through town, Mr. Giuliani talked on the radio about how splendidly the crisis center had performed during the storm. Then he recalled the earlier newspaper criticism, which he described as "kind of a blow to the morale of the people who envisioned this, who were all professionals."

New York Times, September 28, 1999

I don't want to hold my breath, but I really would like to see now the people who editorialized against it—actually I'll tell you who it was—to see if they do what they would like to see public officials do, which is, if you make a mistake, say you did and say, "We were wrong."

Statement on WABC Radio
New York Times, September 28, 1999

Then the big test: New Year's Eve, 1999. Dawn of a new millennium. Would there be terrorism in Times Square as 2 million gathered to watch the ball drop? No, there wouldn't be. And the crowds were so good-natured that the large numbers of cops on duty proved not to be necessary—so the mayor's "crisis command center" was all dressed up with no place to go. Which, after all those laughs at his expense and all the money spent to build the damn thing, was not something that Giuliani was eager for the assembled media to see.

With no emergencies to manage, officials in the Office of Emergency Management's celebrated bunker—including representatives of local utilities and dozens of City, State, regional and Federal agencies—infuriated the 75 or so journalists watching them work through a glass wall yesterday by repeatedly lowering a screen specially installed to block the view. Only when television reporters went live, and when the Mayor appeared, was the screen raised.

Asked five times why the view could not be kept clear, a Mayoral spokesman, Matt Higgins, said only, "Because it's not being done."

But in his briefing, the Mayor suggested a simple explanation. "It's easier for people to do their work if people aren't staring at them," he said. "Who knows what they may want to scratch or do or whatever."

New York Times, January 1, 2000

◆ Fort City Hall

In August 1998 the United States launched cruise missile strikes at targets in Afghanistan and the Sudan that it alleged to be part of the terrorist ring of Osama bin Laden, whom it accused of masterminding the bombings of two U.S. Embassies in Africa two weeks earlier. The Clinton administration warned Americans to brace for possible retaliation. And so—initially, especially after what had happened at the World Trade Center five years earlier—New Yorkers were not unduly alarmed at the security measures they saw being taken at City Hall in Lower Manhattan.

What we're doing is the normal thing that we would do when there is an international incident, which unfortunately we face more often now than maybe we did in the past. . . .

We have no intelligence that suggests there would be any target here. It is a precautionary measure that is taken and, unfortunately, we have had to take those measures before when there have been bombings, terrorist attacks or other things that have taken place in different parts of the world.   *New York Times,* August 21, 1998

So familiar are situations like this that Mr. [Police Commissioner Howard] Safir said City officials have given this security level a name: Condition Bravo.

Mr. Giuliani quickly added: "This sounds a lot worse than it actually is. That sounds like something out of Dr. Strangelove."   *New York Times,* August 21, 1998

A week later, with suspects in the embassy bombings in custody and incarcerated (in the same federal jail where Giuliani had locked up many of his prosecution targets as U.S.

Attorney; indeed, easily overlooked by many downtown visitors, it was right next to his old office in historic Foley Square), the government announced it would try the case in New York. So a little stepped-up security did not seem out of the ordinary.

. . . City officials announced immediate plans to increase security in a section of Lower Manhattan dominated by court and municipal buildings.

Mayor Rudolph W. Giuliani said most of the measures would be modest.

But he acknowledged that a few of them—including the erection of barricades and the closing of a portion of Pearl Street—would cause some complications for traffic and pedestrians, annoyances that he sought to place in some context. . . .

"We were informed of the decision as they were bringing the people back," Mr. Giuliani said. "The City has to react to it. And we will. We will react to it. We're part of America, and the United States should prosecute these people." . . .

"There is no reason for anyone to be alarmed," the Mayor said. He added that the City was "just taking reasonable precautions, reasonable steps, to protect against the possible problems that could occur."

New York Times, August 28, 1998

But a funny thing happened with Operation Bravo and the restricted movements in and around City Hall. The measures turned out not to be temporary. And they turned out to be far in excess of what the United States Government itself felt necessary in the nearby federal courthouse—by far the likeliest target for a terrorist attack, under the circumstances. A building that had once been a bazaar of ideas and free speech in the marketplace of urban democracy—politicos crowding the front steps for press conferences and interviews were a common sight, and it did not even get its first metal detector until 1984—was locked down tight. Concrete blocks. Metal barriers. Wire fences. Rooftop sentries. Police cruisers blocking the entrance, with cops challenging every visitor and rebuffing any who could not demonstrate they were on official business. Even those who *were* on official business were subjected to still more security challenges inside and, frequently, arbitrarily forced to go far out of their way. The building once commonly thought of as New York's answer to Hyde Park Corner had suddenly been turned into Sing Sing Prison on visiting day. There were two possible logical explanations: Either Mayor Rudy Giuliani, after he had seen the measures in place, decided he liked what he saw. Or he had been looking for an excuse to impose such measures all along, and the trial— which was months if not years away—was just a fig leaf. Either way, it quickly became apparent that the object of the exercise was not to protect City Hall from violence. It was to protect Generalissimo Rudy Giuliani from being forced to confront, and to acknowledge, the existence of political dissent.

The Generalissimo even used the state-of-emergency excuse to ban all public gatherings (except those he approved of, like World Series celebrations for the New York Yankees) and all press conferences from the City Hall steps—an intention he had tipped off months earlier, before any terrorism scare, when City Council Speaker Peter Vallone's announcement for governor had offended him. In its aftermath, he announced the discovery of a long-standing police rule—a rule mysteriously unknown to most City Hall veterans until that moment—strictly limiting all such gatherings.

"For some reason that I have to check into, the police did not uniformly enforce the rule" that limits gatherings on the steps to about 30 people, Mr. Giuliani said. He added that when he was running for office, he con-

scientiously held his news conferences in City Hall Park.

"It's understanding that, just chaotically doing what you want, sometimes can interfere with the ability of people to walk in the building, walk out of the building," the Mayor said. "City Hall should be open for public access. This is a police rule that they've had for some time. It's not a big deal. I don't know exactly what happened yesterday, but we'll find out why, and we'll go back to everyone respecting it."

New York Times, March 12, 1998

Civic groups and state and city legislators filed suit against the press conference ban. Housing Works, a radical AIDS-services organization despised by Giuliani, won a federal court order allowing it to hold a press conference on the steps, with the judge questioning how Giuliani could allow massive Yankee rallies and a ticker-tape parade for astronaut John Glenn while denying the leftist outfit's request.

The Federal Government has decided to try these terrorists in New York. At the same time, it's a Federal judge now who's trying to decide what the security arrangements should be. And he wants the security arrangements to be less than the security arrangements that he has for Federal buildings in Washington and other places.　　　　New York Times, November 28, 1998

. . . Mayor Giuliani said this week that the Police Department—and few others—have the expertise to make decisions about security. . . . But critics say that even now, the general public has more access to other public buildings than they do to City Hall. Judge Baer noted—and a spokesman for the United States Marshal's office confirmed—that news conferences are still

permitted in front of the courthouse where the terrorism suspects are to be tried. *N.Y. Times,* Nov. 28, 1998

On appeal, Housing Works got to hold its press conference—but in the parking lot in front of City Hall rather than on the steps themselves. Then, on appeal from Vallone (whose gubernatorial run and clash with Giuliani over the budget vetoes and the Yankee Stadium referendum were now over), the Generalissimo opened the door to City Hall, just a crack—literally.

Three months into a controversial security crackdown that has blocked almost all access to City Hall, Mayor Rudolph W. Giuliani said yesterday that he would allow the public to take guided tours of the building. . . . Mr. Giuliani, in a news conference of his own, said he would open City Hall at least three days a week, for two hours a day. But he said people would be allowed in only for organized tours, because the police had advised him to maintain tight security measures. "Ultimately, if something happens to this building," he said to reporters, "the person who will be blamed for it is not you or Peter Vallone, it will be me." *New York Times,* December 3, 1998

With tempers boiling over, some City Council members decided to take matters into their own hands—and defied the ban.

I think Council members who try to provoke the police into arresting them should be embarrassed of themselves. *New York Times,* December 10, 1998

But he backed off from what he knew would be the disastrous publicity of arresting them. And, again after a plea from Vallone, the ban was modified: Groups of fifty or less would be allowed to hold rallies or press conferences in the parking lot.

And, if accompanied by council members (and, presumably, if they were good), they could even set foot on the steps.

A year later the restrictions on free speech and personal movement at City Hall were *still* in effect, and the Generalissimo was getting increasingly annoyed that the peasants had not accepted the situation. But they hadn't. More suits were filed. And the rationale for the lockdown was wearing increasingly thin—the claim, for instance, that the FBI had told him to do it.

The Mayor was asked about the concrete barriers he has placed around City Hall ("This is what I've been advised to do by the Police Department and the Federal Bureau of Investigation"). *N.Y. Times,* Dec. 31, 1998

Only problem: Ten months after Giuliani made that statement, a Bureau spokesman—and the head of its New York office—both explicitly stated that the FBI had never made any such recommendation. Confronted with this, the Generalissimo insisted:

The security of the building is a matter for the police and the FBI, and the reality is I don't make these things up. They have made recommendations through the Joint Terrorism Task Force to us about what we should do, specifically with regard to building security and security in this area because of the presence of the terrorists in the prison nearby.

New York Daily News, October 14, 1999

There are thousands of people in the park. The park is not closed. The park is open. People are walking around the park, and they are enjoying it. . . . We live in a world in which there are dangers. There are dangers of terrorism. I have to be responsible about that. Others can choose not to be. *New York Times,* October 14, 1999

At year's end, an impatient Vallone—himself now a contender to succeed Giuliani as mayor—announced his intention to have the Council pass a municipal statute that would regulate access, and free speech rights, in and around New York's closed-off seat of government. The Generalissimo's response had a we've-been-here-before ring to it.

Mr. Giuliani said at his daily news conference that he needed to read the legislation before commenting on it. But he vowed to take the Council to court to fight any effort that he perceived as an effort to limit his authority over security at City Hall.   *N.Y. Times,* Nov. 24, 1999

23

Rudy and the First Amendment

You don't have to be too polite about somebody who's taking advantage and trampling on the rights of other people.   Comment on WCBS Radio, November 5, 1998
Requoted on WCBS-TV, November 6, 1998 and
New York Post, November 7, 1998

When Rudolph Giuliani made that statement, in the wake of the police action to shut down the Harlem rally of Khalid Muhammad, it had been almost a decade since he had resigned as United States Attorney in New York. But even as he was putting an iron clamp on City Hall itself, it was clear that he had never given up the prosecutorial mentality. To most Americans, the Bill of Rights is the bedrock of their precious liberties. To Rudy Giuliani, prosecutor, it was clear on more than one occasion that he viewed it as an obstacle course.

And, as mayor, Giuliani zeroed in, again and again, on the constitutional guarantee that seemed to irk him the most—the First Amendment, with its rights to freedom of speech, freedom of the press, and freedom of assembly.

Long before the lockdown on press conferences on City Hall's steps, the pattern had begun—with Giuliani and his administration stiff-arming the news media and forcing journalists to file Freedom of Information suits just to obtain routine information. From there it had spread.

- A rule barring city employees from speaking to reporters.
- Street musicians charged $45 for a one-day permit.
- Artists banned from selling their work on city streets unless they had a license—for which they had to win a lottery.
- A similar ban on "unlicensed" artists selling their work on the sidewalks in front of the Metropolitan Museum, per order of the City Parks Department—even though visitors had long viewed that as part of the museum-going experience and the museum itself had not pressed for such a ban.
- New licensing fees for newsstand vendors—and a claim, announced by the city, that it had the right to revoke any newsstand operator's license without a hearing.
- Refusal to allow more than twenty taxi drivers to assemble in protest against new city regulations, followed by blanket refusals to allow other groups to stage demonstrations near City Hall—long a New York custom.

By the end of 1999, in fact, over these and other actions, Generalissimo Giuliani had provoked nearly thirty First Amendment–related lawsuits—and, in whole or in part, eventually he had lost every one of them.

. . . The Mayor, a former Federal prosecutor, is clearly riled at the frequently-voiced suggestions that both his

**style and his substantive programs lack proper respect
for the First Amendment. At a recent news conference,
for example, a reporter asked the Mayor how he would
respond to those who say he wants to squash dissent.**

"They're wrong," the Mayor curtly replied.

New York Times, July 6, 1998

**An exhibition of paintings is not as communicative as
speech, literature or live entertainment, and the artists'
constitutional interest is thus minimal.**

Appeal by Giuliani administration against street artists'
claim of First Amendment protection
Giuliani v. Lederman and *Giuliani v. Bery et al.,* filed
with U.S. Supreme Court, February 24, 1997

But occasionally Giuliani's rationalizations for the suppres-
sion of criticism tripped even him up—as when he tried to
limit the size of an Independence Day press conference by the
New York Civil Liberties Union protesting his free-speech
policies, shortly after he had thrown open the front of City
Hall for a celebration of Yankee pitcher David Wells after
Wells pitched a perfect game. Or when he presided over no
less than three Broadway ticker-tape parades in one month
(there had been only eleven in the previous twenty-eight
years) while simultaneously telling the radical organization
Housing Works that—for security reasons—it could not possibly have a parade permit.

**This is wonderful. I think the more ticker-tape parades I
can have during the time I am Mayor, the more great
memories I'm going to have later on.**

Announcing city parade to honor astronaut-Senator
John Glenn, *New York Times,* November 13, 1998

**The Mayor defended rejecting applications for parade
permits by other groups, including the activist group**

Housing Works to mark World AIDS Day. "Obviously, you can't grant everyone's request," he said. "If the City were to grant permits to everyone who wanted to have a parade, all the City would do is have parades," Giuliani said. "We wouldn't have gridlock. We'd be totally frozen."   *New York Post,* November 13, 1998

It was such blatant inconsistencies—actually, in legal parlance, the words are "arbitrary and capricious"—that persuaded a federal judge to order a permit be granted for a Housing Works rally, over the Giuliani administration's objections. Not that the Generalissimo, he who once practiced law, had much regard for judges anymore—if he ever did . . .

Idiotic. . . . not honest. . . . products of the Democratic machine.

> Reaction by Mayor Rudolph W. Giuliani to losses in court
> over First Amendment issues, *New York Times,* May 23, 1999

The imperial Federal court. . . . [The judges] think they're put there by God.

> Reaction to court order that he allow a march against
> police brutality near City Hall, October 1998
> Requoted in *New York Times,* May 23, 1999

. . . unless the judges gave him what he wanted, as happened when a court upheld as constitutional his new policy of confiscating the cars of drivers pulled over and charged with drunken driving.

I'd like to remind everyone that the New York Civil Liberties Union and other advocates do not determine the Constitution.   *New York Times,* May 20, 1999

❖ *New York* Magazine

The tag line seemed simple enough—"Possibly the only good thing in New York Rudy hasn't taken credit for"—and a clever way for *New York* magazine to advertise itself on local buses. The Metropolitan Transportation Authority initially thought so too—until Giuliani objected, conjuring up a complaint that somehow his name was being exploited for commercial reasons without his consent. So the MTA accommodated the mayor and rejected the ads, even sending one of its lawyers into a federal courtroom to make an argument that a first-year law student could have swatted down like a fly.

Do we, as a matter of policy, really want politicians to be at the mercy of the advertising community in the United States? . . . "Bill Clinton, our President, doesn't eat low-calorie health foods, and he really should." The advertisers of America will go on and on, and there will be ads like that appearing every day of the week.

Argument by lawyer Kenneth A. Plevan, *N.Y. Times*, Nov. 29, 1997

The magazine won—as any constitutional scholar could have predicted, with the city and the MTA found to have violated its First Amendment rights. Then, at Giuliani's behest, the MTA appealed, only to compound its embarrassment by losing again. *New York* finally got to run its ad—months later, after spending thousands of dollars in legal fees to make its point. But Rudy Giuliani did not spend a penny in legal fees for doing that. Despite the fact that his complaint was of a purely personal nature—and in no way involved the legal interests of the City of New York—he used government lawyers, from both the City Corporation Counsel's office and the MTA, to press his case for him.

When a Federal judge upheld the magazine's right to place the ads, ruling that the Mayor "cannot avoid the limelight of publicity—good and bad," Mr. Giuliani grumped that he might sue the magazine, but eventually decided against it.   *New York Times,* August 17, 1998

No public servant shall use or attempt to use his or her position as a public servant to obtain any financial gain, contract, license, *privilege or other private or personal advantage, direct or indirect,* for the public servant or any person or firm associated with the public servant.
Chapter 68, Section 2604, sub-section 6(c)(4) of the ethics provisions of the New York City Charter (Emphasis added)

Several months later Kiwi Airlines began running an ad that said "Great job, Rudy! But some people still wanna leave New York!" Whether he had suddenly found a sense of humor about such things or because this ad stroked his ego, Giuliani did not lift a finger to block it.

On the other hand, two years after the controversy, *New York* magazine was still quite profitable, and Kiwi Airlines was bankrupt.

◆ Khalid

In 1998, when the racial demagogue Khalid Muhammad first tried to stage a Million Youth March in Harlem, the Generalissimo said:
They have a right to demonstrate, but the Corporation Counsel and the Police Department have the right to put reasonable bounds on where, when, how and to what extent.   *New York Post,* August 7, 1998

Even when you are filled with hate rhetoric, you do have a right to demonstrate and protest to a certain extent. But you don't have a right to do it any place you want, anywhere you want, anytime you want.

New York Times, August 7, 1998

Giuliani said City officials would "handle ourselves in a reasonable way and constitutional way" in negotiating where the march could be held.

"But, then again, we're not going to allow a hate-monger to take over our city in any substantial respect. That just will not be permitted." *N.Y. Post,* Aug. 8, 1998

But a federal court overruled Giuliani's attempt to keep the march from being held in Harlem. And when it was, and ended with police storming the stage to (literally) shut Khalid up. . .
Mr. Giuliani gave several explanations for the police action. Early yesterday, he said at a news conference that organizers of the event had flouted a "sacred" court order by going past a 4 P.M. deadline. "If you want to know why the police came in at 4:01, go read the court order," he said. "This is all about creating a respectful society. The court said that they had between 12 and 4; it meant exactly that."

But that explanation seemed at odds with the comments that the Mayor made shortly before the rally, in which he said that the police would allow "some reasonable flexibility" in ending it at 4 P.M.

Finally, in a call to a reporter last night, Mr. Giuliani sought to reconcile his previous comments. He said that the police would have indeed allowed the rally to run late if the chief organizer, Khalid Abdul Muhammad, had not begun inveighing against the officers in a speech laced with obscenity and anti-Semitic slurs.

"They were quite prepared to be more flexible, but when the speech turned to incitement to riot and murder, they closed down the event," the Mayor said. "I had given them the discretion to make that determination."

New York Times, September 7, 1998

The police acted commendably. They listened to four hours of people, including women, who got up and talked about killing Jews and taking off their scalps and cutting off their heads. *N.Y. Daily News,* Sept. 7, 1998

◆ Khalid II

A year later Giuliani didn't attempt to move Khalid's march elsewhere. He refused at allow it at all.

[Khalid and his followers are] reprehensible. They had an opportunity to properly apply. They haven't. So, as far as we're concerned, it's over. *N.Y. Times,* Aug. 27, 1999

And, again, a federal court intervened to order a parade permit. The Generalissimo's reaction reflected his deep devotion to the constitutional principle of judicial review.

[A] distortion of reasoning . . . totally unwarranted. This is an example of a judge putting his head in the sand and somehow being so overwhelmed with the inability to make a distinction between a proper First Amendment demonstration and an excuse for violence that he really just can't see the difference.

New York Times, September 1, 1999

The appeals court affirmed the lower court's order.

Boy, I tell you, judges have the luxury of keping their heads in the sand. Judges, these judges, have their head

**in the sand. Thank goodness they don't have to govern a
city, because things would be really dangerous. . . . I
think their decision is irresponsible. I think their decision puts the City in a very difficult situation and the
Police Department in a very difficult situation. And I
think it's one of the more irresponsible decisions that I
have seen a court render.** *N.Y. Times,* Sept. 2, 1999

◆ The Klan

In the wake of the second Khalid march, his opposite number
on the racial extremist scale—the Ku Klux Klan—also applied
for a rally permit. Though Giuliani's denunciation of the Klan
met with virtually universal approval among New Yorkers, his
methods—once again, denying the Klan the right to assemble—again did not meet with sympathy from the federal
courts. So the Generalissimo tried a novel argument.

**They all have the right to make their statements and we
have the right to disagree with the ones that we think
are wrong, but I also understand how many cops that's
going to cost us, and how there may be a robbery someplace that we don't interrupt or a person dying of a
heart attack that we don't get to, or a shooting that goes
on that we have one less cop there. It's all appropriate,
it's all correct, but at the same time, we have got to run a
city.** *New York Times,* October 20, 1999

The court didn't buy it. Though the city was vindicated on
one point—the Klan members could not wear their notorious
masks—the march was on. The Generalissimo knew exactly
where to place the blame: the 1960s.

**This is another example of the ideology extended from
the 60s. This ruling says people don't have to take responsibility for what they say or what they do, even as they**

support organizations that encourage anti-Semitism, anti-Catholicism, racism and hatred.

New York Times, October 22, 1999

(In the end, the Klan got its wish—and with it the right for about two dozen of its members to stand in Foley Square, surrounded by hundreds of hostile counterdemonstrators whose decibel level easily drowned out anything they might have had to say.)

◆ The Sex Industry

The one First Amendment case that Giuliani seemed to have won was his local law that rezoned many of the city's sex shops, topless bars, and other adult businesses out of Times Square and residential neighborhoods.

They're not only going to have to get around things, they're going to have to reform themselves and change the essential nature of operation that they are.

New York Post, July 20, 1998

Giuliani said yesterday that the crackdown would be even more aggressive. "A club may be violating this new zoning law . . . but it may also be violating health codes, building codes, fire codes and other things," he said. "So this is our opportunity to look at the whole group of laws to make sure that they're in compliance." Penalties for violations could be severe. "In some cases, it's fines," Giuliani said. "In some cases, it's putting them out of business." *New York Daily News*, July 22, 1998

Of course, the Generalissimo advised his radio listeners, they could always take matters into their own hands.

One of the things you might want to do, which is perfectly legal, you can take pictures of people going in there. It really does cut down on business.

Advising neighborhood residents to take photographs of
visitors to adult sex shops, WABC Radio
New York Daily News, May 22, 1998

He declared victory.

Former Mayor Edward I. Koch once bet us that we would never win. He hasn't paid his bet yet.

Statement, July 1998. Requoted in column by former mayor
Edward I. Koch, *New York Daily News,* February 5, 1999

But not so fast. Rudy's law said that any establishment which devoted 40 percent or more of its space to the sex trade could be shut down or rezoned. But, at the end of 1999, New York State's highest court ruled that, because of a loophole in the law's language, some sex shops had managed to (one will pardon the expression) turn the trick. They were able to meet the 60 percent test—and they stayed in business. Curses! Foiled again!

People are engaging in shams to get around the law.

New York Daily News, December 21, 1999

[The court ruling] did not strike down the zoning change, thank goodness. The bad news is that we have to go back and rewrite the regulation.

New York Times, December 22, 1999

24

"The Brooklyn Museum Had Lost Its Charm"

The most successful cities have always been those in which the arts have flourished.
Second Inaugural Address, *N.Y. Times,* Jan. 2, 1998

Down in Baltimore, museum curator Arnold Lehman would well have agreed with that sentiment—and he saw a chance to make his mark by moving up to New York to become director of the Brooklyn Museum, a cultural institution that featured some of the finest art and artifacts collections that nobody ever saw, overshadowed as it was by its world-renowned Manhattan counterparts. Mr. Lehman resolved to change that by importing a show of works collected by British advertising executive Charles Saatchi. Called "Sensation," it had caused exactly that in London, owing to the fact that several of the avant-garde works on display had been certifiably out there: an almost-beatific portrait of a convicted child murderer. A decomposing shark carcass, and dissected cross-sections of pigs and cows, soaking in formaldehyde. Sculptures of little girls with penis shapes bursting out of their faces. And a portrait by an African émigré artist, entitled "Virgin Mary," showing a black Madonna-like figure on a canvas that was daubed with clumps of elephant dung and adorned with clippings from porno magazines.

The museum and its new director anticipated controversy—in fact, they looked forward to it. After all, this was New York, self-styled capital of cultural sophistication. And so what if some did not like the show? Hadn't the ancient

Romans said it best: *De gustibus non disputandum est*? "There's just no arguing about taste?"

Ah, but the ancient Romans never encountered Mayor Rudolph W. Giuliani.

Anything that I can do isn't art. If I can do it, it's not art, because I'm not much of an artist. And I could figure out how to put this together. You know, if you want to throw dung at something, I could figure out how to do that. *New York Times,* September 24, 1999

Well, OK, fair enough so far. But Generalissimo Giuliani did more than express his distaste for the show. He demanded the exhibit be shut down—bluntly reminding the museum that the city owned the land on which it stood and contributed more than $7 million to its annual budget.

Well, it offends me. The idea of, in the name of art, having a City-subsidized building have so-called works of art in which people are throwing elephant dung at a picture of the Virgin Mary is sick. If somebody wants to do that privately and pay for that privately, well, that's what the First Amendment is all about. I mean, you can be offended by it and upset by it, and you don't have to go see it, if somebody is paying for it. But to have government subsidize something like that is outrageous. . . . The City shouldn't have to pay for sick stuff.

Statement at press conference, September 22, 1999
New York Times, September 23, 1999; requoted in
New York Times, October 6, 1999

My objection to this is the fact that public money is being used to subsidize it.

Statement on WABC Radio, September 24, 1999
New York Times, September 25, 1999

But his objection quickly expanded—as he accused the museum of anti-Catholic bigotry for displaying "Virgin Mary" (even though the artist was himself Catholic).

Public taxpayer dollars should not go for aggressive desecration of national or religious symbols of great significance and sensitivity to people. . . .

When it comes to Catholic bashing, this kind of thing is never treated as sensitively as it sometimes is in other areas. If this were a desecration of a symbol in another area, I think there would be more sensitivity about this than a desecration of a symbol that involves Catholics. . . . [The exhibit] cannot and should not be suppressed, but you should not have to pay for it. And as the Mayor of the City, who's going to stand up for that if it isn't going to be me?

Statements on WABC Radio, September 24, 1999
New York Times, September 25, 1999

You don't have a right to government subsidy for desecrating somebody else's religion. And therefore we will do everything that we can to remove funding for the Brooklyn Museum until the director comes to his senses and realizes that if you are a government-subsidized enterprise, then you can't do things that desecrate the most personal and deeply held views of people in society. I mean, this is an outrageous thing to do. . . . Last time I checked, I'm the Mayor.

New York Daily News, September 23, 1999;
New York Times, September 24, 1999

Throwing gunk on important religious symbols, I'm not going to have any compunction about trying to put them out of business—meaning the Board [of the

Brooklyn Museum]. Maybe that's the best way to preserve the museum and the good parts of the museum
for everyone else.   *New York Times,* September 25, 1999

Sick and disgusting. . . . You can't have the right to have
a government subsidy to desecrate someone else's
religion.   *Newsday,* September 27, 1999

There's nothing in the Constitution that says the First
Amendment requires that taxpayers fund aggressive,
vicious, disgusting attacks on religion.
                    New York Daily News, September 28, 1999

I think it is a disgusting show.   *N.Y. Times,* Sept. 30, 1999

I am baffled by what they have done. I do not understand why you would take a venerable institution like
this and reduce it to the worst kind of disgusting commercial sensationalism. I understand they want to make
money, but this is what you do, like, on then 42nd Street
of about 20 years ago, not what you do at a venerable
and great museum. . . .
     The people running this exhibit should not be allowed
to put their hands in the taxpayer pockets, take money
out to pay for this. If they feel it is necessary to cut up
animals, put them in formaldehyde and show their inner
parts to people, if they think that it's necessary to throw
feces on important national and religious symbols, then
they should pay for it themselves.
                    New York Times, September 27, 1999

Without having seen them, the Generalissimo dismissed
the artistic validity of the works on display.
A biology experiment at best.
Statement made in Washington, D.C., *N.Y. Times,* Oct. 1, 1999

He publicly questioned the sanity of all involved in the show. . .

Belongs in a psychiatric ward.

> Statement made in Stockdale, CA, September 30, 1999
> *New York Times*, October 1, 1999

I am adult enough, sensible enough and educated enough to look at this and say, "These are displays of significant psychological problems that should take place someplace else other than in a museum designed for children." Statement on WABC Radio, October 1, 1999

> *New York Times*, October 2, 1999

. . . and their real motives.

There's no question that the motivation is commercial motivation; you'd have to be a fool not to see that.

> Statement in Bakersfield, CA, September 30, 1999
> *New York Times*, October 1, 1999

This is not art. . . . It's the worst kind of commercialism. This exhibit, if it wants to go on, should go on funded privately. *New York Daily News*, October 2, 1999

The Generalissimo's stand was rejected by a 2-to-1 margin among New Yorkers, according to the polls, with even Catholics in opposition—but it was not without its benefits. Such as being invited to appear on three national news shows on the same Sunday morning.

So maybe—this is hard, I know, to really deal with— maybe this is a matter of principle and it isn't something that has to do with political calculation.

> Defending his action in light of negative public reaction reflected in polls, *Meet the Press*, NBC, October 3, 1999

First Amendment hysterics.
> Characterizing his opponents on Brooklyn Museum controversy, *Meet the Press,* NBC, October 3, 1999

Taxpayer dollars shouldn't be on either side of this dispute. We can't support religion. We shouldn't support vicious attacks on religion, either.
> Comment on *This Week,* ABC, October 3, 1999

Disgusting. . . . Pigs that are cut up and their insides are shown, cows whose heads are torn off. . . . Pedophiles on parade. . . . Dung being thrown at the Virgin Mary. . . . I couldn't possibly approve this as a use of taxpayer dollars.
> Comment on *Fox News Sunday,* October 3, 1999
> *New York Daily News,* October 4, 1999

The museum rejected Giuliani's ultimatum. The show went on. And he cut off the city's funding.
We'll see them in court. *N.Y. Post,* Sept. 30, 1999

In the meantime, the Generalissimo's fulminations had served as free advertising for the exhibition—and helped it to draw record crowds.
Sure, it gives more attention. But the other thing would be to ignore it, and allow this kind of disgusting display to go on, to allow taxpayer dollars to be used and wasted in this way. So you really have no choice. I mean, that's a facile, knee-jerk argument that's used all the time. Now, if I ignored it, then the argument would be on the other side: "How can you ignore something as disgusting, as horrible as this?" *New York Times,* October 3, 1999

Whenever you do this kind of sensational, shock kind of thing it produces large numbers of people. I was a little

· 370 ·

disappointed by the comments by someone that this was considerably larger than the Monet exhibit that they had. *New York Times,* October 5, 1999

But he had no regrets.

If another museum does the same thing that this museum does, if it aggressively attacks, let's say, a different religion, I'll have the same reaction to it. The question is: What can I do about it? Let's change the facts. Let's say another museum does some kind of vicious attack on the Protestant religion, or on the Jewish religion, taking symbols of either, and desecrating them, or using pornographic material around the Star of David, or whatever. Or human excrement thrown at Martin Luther, or Martin Luther King. [I] would take the same view that this is wrong, highly inappropriate. And then the City, if it were connected to it, would seek to dissociate itself from it. If you're asking me, would I in the same way seek to not have the City put up funds in order to support an attack on other religions? Yes, I would do the same thing. *N.Y. Times,* Oct. 5, 1999

He was doing it, he said, for the sake of morality, of civilization—and of hygiene.

I think what's going on at the museum is perverted and disgusting, and may be a sign of how people who believe they're intellectuals can't make sensible distinctions of taste and morals any longer, which is really kind of a shame. *New York Daily News,* October 12, 1999

I would ask people to step back and think about civilization. Civilization has been about trying to find the right place to put excrement, not on the walls of museums. The advance that we had in our civilization was that we figured out how to deal with human excrement without putting it on walls. So I wonder who are the barbarians, and who aren't?

It took thousands of years of human development to figure out a sanitary, sensible and civilized way to deal with human excrement. It seems to me that people who are saying you shouldn't use public funds to support putting excrement on walls is actually quite a civilized position, and an intelligent one.   *N.Y. Times,* Oct. 13, 1999

[The] intellectual dishonesty . . . [and] intellectual pretension . . . [of] people who say, "Oh, well, you know, in the name of art, people can put excrement on walls."
    New York Times, October 16, 1999

The issue went to court. The Generalissimo's lawyers tried to claim that the show's "no-one-under-17" admission policy (later amended) violated a lease clause establishing the Brooklyn Museum as an institution for the artistic education of children. While that argument got nowhere, Giuliani did succeed in embarrassing the museum by forcing the revelation of just how much it had compromised itself—financially, if not artistically—by acceding to the demands of the works' owner in order to stage the show. On the other hand, the museum embarrassed Giuliani right back—with the revelation that it had given the city ample notice of what was to be in the "Sensations" exhibit, and the administration's representatives (when they bothered to attend board meetings) had never expressed any objection.

They sent a letter to the Commissioner [of Cultural Affairs] in which they left out—deliberately, I imagine, or they certainly left out the whole attack on religion that's at the core of what's going on. The letter was very, very deceptive. There is nothing that mentions feces and the private parts of women taken from porno-graphic magazines placed around the Virgin Mary. They [his representatives] cannot read into people's minds. *New York Times,* October 5, 1999

The City of New York has a right to know about how this museum sold out for money. This is supposed to be a public museum for the public good. . . .

Some of the facts [about the financing of the exhibit, and the Museum's relationship with owner Charles Saatchi—Ed.] we knew, some we didn't know. We didn't know that there virtually had been a total sellout of the museum to millionaires and multimillionaires trying to make money off this exhibit. You might recall that we objected some time ago—I did, publicly—to their con-cealing documents. Well, it turned out they concealed a lot more than a few documents. They concealed a lot of documents. And we asked the judge to reopen dis-covery. And then it appeared as if she rushed the deci-sion and cut that off to protect the people of the museum. The judge almost seemed to rush to a decision to cut off any discovery of those facts. She had originally not allowed us very much discovery, which is why we didn't find out about it on our own. And now, as soon, as these facts were revealed, within a day she releases her decision. *New York Times,* November 3, 1999

That decision—yet another First Amendment defeat for Rudolph Giuliani. His attempt to remove the board and to evict the museum from the premises—leaving its entire collection on the sidewalk, presumably—was rejected. He was ordered to release the museum funding he had illegally with-held—and was barred from withholding funds in the future.

The judge is totally out of control. She's lost all reason. . . . [She is] abandoning all reason under the guise of the First Amendment. It's bad enough that they're desecrating the Virgin Mary with excrement and pornographic literature.   *N.Y. Post,* Nov. 2, 1999

The judge is trying to gloss over and not deal with the fact that the purveyors of this trash are making millions and millions of dollars. You've got to be putting your head in the sand to think this is about the First Amendment. This is about making millions and millions of dollars by aggressively and viciously attacking the religion that many people in New York City hold dear.

New York Daily News, November 2, 1999

Precipitous . . . the usual knee-jerk reaction of some judges. This is all about dollar signs. It isn't about free speech. It's actually a desecration of the First Amendment as much as it is a desecration of religion, to use the First Amendment as a shield in order to take money out of the taxpayers' pockets in order to put that money into the pockets of multimillionaires.

New York Times, November 2, 1999

Intellectually dishonest. . . . We hope that we can get before a more objective group of judges [at the Appeals Court] who do not let their own ideology blind them to the facts, which is what the judge has done here. If you got before a group that were not part of the politically correct, left-wing ideology of New York City, [they] would look at this very, very differently.

New York Post, November 5, 1999

By the time an openly skeptical panel of federal appellate judges heard the case in January, "Sensations" had closed—

though not before an enraged, elderly, devoutly Catholic man attacked and defaced "Virgin Mary." Asked whether he thought his own rhetoric might have inspired the incident, Giuliani demurred:

I haven't said anything for about a month or a month and a half. So that would be a real stretch.

New York Times, December 18, 1999

In the aftermath of the episode, the Brooklyn Museum's reputation for good judgment and integrity had suffered a bit. (Ironically, Giuliani's thug tactics foreclosed what might have been a more open discussion as to whether the works on display in "Sensation" constituted genuinely good art.) But New York City's reputation as a cultural capital, tolerant of new ideas and receptive to daring artistic approaches, had been damaged far more. At the height of the Generalissimo's threats, many of the Brooklyn Museum's fellow cultural institutions were afraid even to sign a public letter to the mayor defending the museum's right to make its own unfettered artistic choices—such was Giuliani's reputation for inspiring fear that they thought, if they did so, they could be next.

And almost forgotten were words Rudy Giuliani had once uttered, now carrying a faint but very ironic echo.

I wouldn't express my personal views in a policy action as Mayor.

Statement as first-time mayoral candidate reassuring New Yorkers that he would not form public policy positions on the basis of his Catholic religious beliefs

Village Voice, March 7, 1989

As the Mayor of New York, I would work as hard to protect someone's right to believe in God as he or she sees fit—or not to believe in God—because I realize that my

· 375 ·

right to practice my religion depends completely on my commitment to defend someone's right to practice theirs, or to practice no religion at all.

The condition of diversity—the condition most obvious to anyone looking at New York—mandates that we live in respectful disagreement. It makes that demand because the alternative is that we cannot live at all. We must be allowed to celebrate what we believe in.

New York Times, April 21, 1994

25

The Race for the Senate: Target Hillary

As he took to the campaign trail in October 1994 to help Republican candidates across the nation—even as he was dissing his party's nominee for governor of his own state—Rudy Giuliani attracted attention . . . and questions about his political ambitions beyond City Hall.

I have a simple view about the future—try to do your job the best you can. I do not think that in a job like Mayor you spend a lot of time thinking about the future or you make a big mistake. *N.Y. Times,* Oct. 24, 1994

Near the end of his 1997 reelection campaign, the question came up again—especially because Giuliani would be the first mayor in New York history forced to leave office by term limits. Would he pledge to serve out his full term and not run for another office? He waxed just a tad coy.

I intend to be the Mayor of New York City for the next four years. I resist all of the old games that are played, because I always hate to make the same mistakes that

people have made in the past. So I have, I don't rule options out. I rule them in, and my intention is to be Mayor of New York City for the next four years. . . .

Possibilities make my job as Mayor easier to bargain, leverage and fight for the City of New York. Particularly as the Mayor who is a lame duck Mayor on the day that I get sworn in. It ain't bad for people who are saying, "This guy has possibilities." It makes it a lot easier for me to negotiate with Albany, Washington, for the benefit of the City.   Response to question at candidates' debate
New York Times, November 1, 1997

After the election, he maintained that noncommittal position.
I love this job, and if all things remain the same, I'm going to spend [the next] four years doing it. I don't know what opportunities will present themselves in the next year or the year after. . . . I don't rule out considering any option that might come along. . . . I've always tried, when I'm running for office, to avoid pledges.
National Journal, December 20, 1997

I am not exploring any idea of running for anything right now.   Remarks during visit to give speech in
Washington, D.C., *New York Times,* March 12, 1998

I don't know what my future plans are. I haven't figured them out yet. I probably am not going to figure them out for some time.
Remarks during visit to give speech in Buffalo, NY
New York Times, April 5, 1998

But then, after the 1998 elections, the landscape of New York politics changed with the bombshell announcement by

United States Senator Daniel Patrick Moynihan that he would give up his seat at the end of his fourth term.

Now, Giuliani had been avidly courted by Republican leaders to run for that very seat when he was still U.S. Attorney—and when becoming mayor of such a heavily Democratic city seemed an unattainable goal. But, aside from the fact that Moynihan was unbeatable, Giuliani decided that a life on Capitol Hill was not for him.

. . . Ultimately, the legislative arena proved far less appealing to him than did remaining United States Attorney. In 1989, when he decided to run for Mayor, the choice was easier, Mr. Giuliani has said, "because I like administering and I think I'm good at it."

New York Times, December 30, 1994

Besides, he had had a taste of Washington—and didn't like it. **[The Washington press corps] makes it unpleasant, because they are so damn negative. They're looking for critical things to write about you . . . and that makes you feel a little like you're being hunted. New York is much more balanced.**

Comment in *Barron's* upon leaving Washington to take up duties as U.S. Attorney in New York, 1983
Requoted in *American Lawyer,* March 1989

There's a tremendous isolation that goes on in Washington.
Comment during visit to give speech in Phoenix, AZ
New York Times, January 3, 1999

And besides, he liked Moynihan—indeed, in his first inaugural address he used the senator's line, "defining deviancy down," to describe the social deterioration he saw happening in New York City.

We're very, very fortunate to have him. I wanted to make sure that he knew that, and that all of you knew how much I support him and how much I count on him as the Mayor of the City of New York.

Remarks during surprise drop-in at Moynihan fund raiser,
New York Times, April 22, 1998

But now a job was open. A job he might not really want, a job he might have acknowledged he was not cut out for, a job that would leave his agenda as mayor unfinished and subject to immediate reversal by a liberal Democrat, but a job that would keep him politically alive while he sorted out his next move—instead of being term-limited out of public office and having to fight his way back in against the likely opposition of an unforgiving Al D'Amato and George Pataki.

"In a legislative body, you tend to be in this abstract world." Did that mean, a reporter asked later, that he was perhaps temperamentally unsuited for a legislative body, like the Senate? "Maybe I'd be good for a legislative body," he mused. "Practical reality isn't a bad thing in a legislative body."

Comments on visit to give speech in Phoenix, AZ
New York Times, January 3, 1999

And when First Lady Hillary Rodham Clinton let it be known that she was considering establishing residency in New York so she could run for the open seat—overnight making it the highest-profile congressional race in the nation—the Generalissimo began warming to the idea of becoming the giant-killer of the GOP.

I'd be less than candid if I didn't say that the idea of a race like this is kind of intriguing.

Comments on *Crossfire,* CNN
Requoted in *New York Times,* February 20, 1999

I'm considering very, very carefully whether to run.
> Remarks on visit to Tompkins County in upstate
> New York, *New York Daily News*, March 20, 1999

I am really looking forward to this race. I hope she doesn't disappoint me.
> Speech in Washington, DC, at invitation of *American
> Spectator* magazine. *New York Times*, November 10, 1999

Now, Mrs. Clinton had never lived in New York and would be moving there in order to run for political office. Some might apply the label "carpetbagger" to her. But young Rudy Giuliani would be furious at such a suggestion. As a college-student columnist, favoring Robert Kennedy's move into New York in order to do precisely what Mrs. Clinton was doing, he had been rather forcefully eloquent on this subject:

Senator Keating claims he is running on his record, but his only real issue has been that Robert Kennedy is an intruder in New York state politics. . . .

[Keating supporters] wonder whether or not it is right for a man to run for the Senate from New York when he has only recently established residence here. Then they maintain that Kennedy is a cynical, power-hungry politician moving into New York and using it as a spring-board to higher office. . . .

[The carpetbagger issue] is a truly ridiculous reason for not voting for a man in the year 1964. Without doubt, the Kennedy candidacy in New York is perfectly in accord with the Constitutional stipulation that a Senator must be a resident of the state he represents on the day he is elected. . . .

The main question is whether or not we in New York are going to make a decision on a candidate by the standards of parochialism. . . . Let us hope that

cosmopolitan New Yorkers can rise above the ridiculous, time-worn provincial attitude that has so disunified our nation.

The charge that Robert Kennedy has come to New York to use this state for some kind of sinister, cynical power grab in order to move into higher office is another example of a screen put up by Senator Keating and his friends to avoid discussing the real issue: which man could better serve New York.

Manhattan College *Quadrangle,* October 1964
Wysiwyg://3/http://www.thesmokinggun.com/archive/
rudycolumn1.html. Requoted in *New York Observer,*
July 12, 1999; *San Francisco Chronicle,* July 14, 1999;
Columbus (Ohio) *Dispatch,* July 17, 1999

But the older Rudy Giuliani—the one whose career ambitions were potentially blocked by Mrs. Clinton's interest in the seat—had a very different take on the relevance of resorting to appeals against "carpetbaggers." In fact, he sounded just like the backers of Kenneth Keating he had once mocked.

Born in Illinois and carried to power in Arkansas, with no connection of any kind to New York, Hillary has set her sights on the New York Senate seat and maybe . . . probably set her sights even higher.

Hillaryno.com, website of Friends for Giuliani, March 1999

Is it fair? Ha, ha, ha, ha. Come on, it's politics.

New York Daily News, March 31, 1999

She presents us with an opportunity and we take advantage of it and then that's not fair? I mean, is it fair that she comes to New York and raises lots of money? Her consideration of candidacy has gotten her a great deal of attention. We're taking advantage of her consideration to raise money and to develop volunteers should I decide to run for the Senate. It's smart politics.   *New York Times,* March 31, 1999

We want to take advantage of those people who think that she shouldn't run for the Senate, of which there are many, and who feel very fervently about it. I would be foolish if I didn't take advantage of that.
New York Daily News and *New York Times,* March 31, 1999

Mr. Giuliani expressed amazement at the response [to the website]. "Maybe, if I can continue to do that good, who knows? The sky's the limit." *N.Y. Times,* Mar. 31, 1999

The last WebSite that was as active as this was the Victoria's Secret Web site.   *N.Y. Daily News,* Mar. 31, 1999

The First Lady formed an "exploratory committee" and embarked on a statewide "listening tour."
Maybe she should explore New York a little more. I formed an exploratory committee about six weeks ago.
New York Times, June 4, 1999

When she visited City College and gave a speech critical of his policies on education, the Generalisssimo professed to be pleased—and it gave him an idea:
I'm glad she found her way there. I think it's nice to see that she's finding her way around New York. Maybe I'll travel to Arkansas.   *New York Daily News,* June 3, 1999

There are a number of places I want to visit, but the one that I'm really interested in seeing—if it exists—is the Whitewater River. I've heard a lot about the Whitewater River. . . . I'm hoping that I'll be able to do a press

conference right from—directly, live from the Whitewater River. It'll be fun. *New York Post,* June 16, 1999

There is no Whitewater River in Arkansas (just a scandal by that name involving Hillary Clinton's former law firm in Little Rock, which the Generalissimo was eager to remind the whole world of). But there is a *David Letterman* show in New York. And on it went Giuliani, affecting a bad Southern accent, to taunt Mrs. Clinton:

I've never lived here. I've never worked here. I ain't never been here. But I think it would be cool to be your Senator. *New York Daily News,* June 15, 1999

Six weeks later the Generalissimo made the journey. And, when his hotel flew the New York City flag, he decided that it would be nice if the Arkansas State flag flew—on top of New York's City Hall. To reciprocate a gesture made to an *individual,* on a *political* trip, by a *hotel.* Black members of the City Council expressed outrage that the Arkansas flag includes the Confederate star (though they were well advised to drop the subject, considering that Mrs. Clinton had been First Lady of that state for twelve years and, like her husband, never expressed any reservations about that star). Council Speaker Peter Vallone expressed chagrin—but learned he would have to pass legislation to stop it or prevent a similar stunt in the future. (Hell, the building remained practically under martial law at this point, never mind what flag the Generalissimo was flying from it!) "Goofy," said the White House press secretary.

The Generalissimo played the wide-eyed innocent over his little provocation.

I think we are making a lot out of nothing because it is probably a very slow news day. But I have it in perspective. This is the silliness of partisan politics. . . . What's the White House doing commenting on this

unless they are running somebody's campaign from the White House? Gosh, that couldn't be possible.

New York Times, July 29, 1999

He was "amazed and surprised" by what his hosts had done, he explained, and merely wanted to make a nice "act of reciprocity." And, honest . . .

I really haven't thought about Hillary much.

New York Times, July 29, 1999

I thought that was a beautiful gesture and a very nice thing. *New York Post,* July 28, 1999

We should feel very proud about the rest of the country, that we are very proud to be part of the United States of America. We are very similar, very much the same, in many ways a reflection of American culture and American values of all different kinds. It was a nice reciprocal gesture to know how open we are to people all around the country. Excuse me if I think that some of the reaction to all of this is hypocritical with a capital H. Everyone in Arkansas appreciated it, and maybe a lot of them will come here and spend their money. We want them to think of our city as a warm, inviting and nice place. So excuse me if I think it's hypocritical. Thank you, Jose.

Defending his decision to fly Arkansas State flag from City Hall, WABC Radio, *New York Times,* July 31, 1999

And when a smiling First Lady was photographed wearing a Yankee cap at a White House ceremony to honor *his* favorite baseball team, the Generalissimo was ready to remind one and all of his superior pedigree in that regard:

I would be more than happy to teach anybody in the White House about the history of the Yankees, or go over

statistics with them. Show them where Yankee Stadium is located, where Shea Stadium is located. I could take them though things. Or we could discuss, "Where were you when Reggie Jackson hit three home runs to win the 1977 World Series?" I was at Yankee Stadium. Or "Where were you when the Yankees won the 1996 World Series at home?" Gee, I was there. Or, um, "Who do you think was a better center fielder—Joe DiMaggio, Mickey Mantle, Bernie Williams?" Things like that. Under the right set of circumstances, we could even have a debate about this.

New York Times, June 11, 1999

Where was she when Roger Maris hit his 61st home run? Probably in Illinois somewhere.

Washington Post, June 30, 1999

All I would say is that I've been to Yankee Stadium probably a thousand times in my life, and I've never seen her there.   *New York Times Magazine,* August 1, 1999

Of course, Rudy Giuliani was not all that familiar with New York State—outside of New York City—himself. And it showed, occasionally, embarrassingly.

I was up in Monroe County and the heat was ameliorated by the tremendous beautiful breeze. When you get up in the mountains, you get a tremendous breeze.

New York Post, July 7, 1999

Oops. Monroe *County* consists of Rochester and its environs. The Generalissimo had in fact been in Monroe *Township* in *Orange* County—a good two hundred miles or more away. What do you have to say about that, Mr. Mayor?

I have a great deal of knowledge of the State of New York—far more than you actually think I do. I have a very significant knowledge of the whole state, spent a lot of time in different parts of the state throughout my life. I've always spent a great deal of time upstate. I know Saratoga really well. I've been to Lake George. I worked in Syracuse, and I worked in Utica, and I've worked in Albany, and I've worked in Binghamton, and I've worked in other parts of the state.

New York Post, July 7, 1999

For a *New York Times Magazine* profile, Giuliani was asked what qualities he thought Hillary brought to the Senate race.

I guess the one quality that comes to mind immediately is never having lived here, never having worked here and never having a public record or office in the state. So those are the qualities I think of immediately—you may think of others. *New York Times Magazine,* August 1, 1999

She bought a house in Westchester County—making her an official New Yorker.

I've been paying taxes in New York just about all my life, and she hasn't? If she hasn't paid taxes in all these years, I don't know what good it does to pay them for just a few months. We'll have to see what kind of issue that becomes. *New York Post,* November 2, 1999

The carpetbagger jibes—a campaign tactic the young, idealistic Rudy Giuliani had held in such contempt—continued, with no end in sight.

I spent a day today in Washington. I was on a listening tour.

Joke during speech at invitation of *American Spectator* magazine, Washington, D.C., *New York Times,* November 10, 1999

I am also considering a new requirement in running for the Senate from New York. See if this would work. You

**have to demonstrate that you can get from LaGuardia
Airport to your house, and that you know the way by
yourself. What do you think?**

Remarks during speech to Republican Washington Coalition.
New York Times, December 2, 1999

The premise for this witticism was, supposedly, that Washington–to–New York air traffic the day before had been delayed and disrupted to accommodate a campaign flight by the First Lady's plane. Which was not true.

**It was a joke! Gosh, you've got to lighten up. . . . But Mr.
Giuliani then said his information came from four separate people "who told me the pilots announced" at the
Washington airport "that flights were delayed because
of the First Lady's campaign." Mr. Giuliani added that
"as far as I know, it's true."**   *N.Y. Times,* Dec. 3, 1999

But the First Lady of the United States was not just a carpetbagger, you understand. She was also, to hear Giuliani tell it, the Left-Wing Succubus From Hell, come to defile the Empire State in its sleep.

The demonization strategy started subtly.

**What he will probably raise, again and again, is Mrs.
Clinton's "collectivist" health plan fiasco in 1994, her
support of the teachers' unions and anything else that
would imply captivity to conventional liberalism.**

Description of Giuliani campaign strategy by writer James
Traub, *New York Times Magazine,* August 1, 1999

**Hillary, whatever she is—we don't know what she is,
she really hasn't articulated it—at least the way the
stereotype is, she comes across as much more left-wing.**

New York Times Magazine, August 1, 1999

When I asked Giuliani if he planned to paint Mrs. Clinton as the incarnation of the entrenched ideology that he routed from New York City, he said complacently, "I don't think I'll have to. . . . When I look at the people around her, they tend to be the most left-wing of the left-wing Democrats."   *N.Y. Times Magazine,* Aug. 1, 1999

But by now you know that, with Rudy Giuliani, nothing stays subtle for very long.

The Mayor's Senate exploratory committee recently sent out a letter asking potential contributors to "immediately" send money because Mrs. Clinton's "left-wing elite is pouring everything into this race."

New York Times, November 30, 1999

If you don't want to see Hillary Rodham Clinton in the United States Senate, I need your immediate support. . . . It looks like I'm the only one who stands between Hillary Rodham Clinton and the Senate.

If she gets to the Senate, Hillary Clinton will immediately become the champion of every left-wing cause you can imagine. . . .

This is not just a battle between two people. It's a battle between two very different visions of America. . . .

My guess is that Mrs. Clinton sees this race as just a stepping stone for higher office. . . .

The left-wing elite are also furious that my tough law-and-order, pro-free enterprise policies have succeeded in making New York City great again. . . .

PS. I must raise at least $15,000,000 to $20,000,000 to beat Hillary Rodham Clinton in the Senate race of the decade.

Fund-raising appeal letter from Rudolph W. Giuliani
to potential contributors, Nov. 1999
N.Y. Times, Nov. 30, 1999 and *N.Y. Daily News,* Dec. 1, 1999

This appeal for money underscored another fundamental element of the Generalissimo's strategy: However much he might despise Hillary Rodham Clinton for being from Arkansas and excoriate her as a left-wing Democrat, he also respected (and feared) her ability to raise campaign funds, dollar for dollar, with him.

The use of soft money has been made into an art form by Clinton campaigns. And very often, you know, the finger is pointed at Republicans, but there's nothing like what was done in the last Clinton Presidential campaign—money from China, money from elsewhere, money raised on telephones from the White House. *New York Times,* November 12, 1999

But even as he denounced the practice, the Mayor pointedly declined to say that Republicans would not do the same for him. *New York Times,* November 12, 1999

He ran his first ads, on upstate channels, to rebut ads run on her behalf by the Democratic State Committee.

Rudy—ready to do more, for all of us.
Advertisement aired on upstate New York TV and
radio stations, November 1999

He said the ads were intended "to introduce the things that I have done, who I am, what I stand for, to the people in upstate New York that don't know me as well and don't know the record we have and the things that I would be running on if I run for the Senate." . . .

Mr. Giuliani said that he is eager for the Federal Election Commission to review the Clinton ad. Still, by saying that he "will not be put at a disadvantage," he has left open the possibility that he, too, may use soft money. *New York Times,* November 13, 1999

Tens of thousands of E-mails launched by the Mayor's committee this week urge supporters to make a Yuletide donation to help Giuliani "match Hillary Clinton every step of the way.

"The last five days of 1999 are very important to Mayor Giuliani," the E-mail says. "This will be the first time that Hillary Clinton has filed any sort of financial report, and it will indicate how much money she has raised in preparation for her Senate run. . . . It is therefore very important to show that we can remain competitive with the Clinton money machine."

New York Daily News, December 29, 1999

Moments earlier [in the midst of New York's New Year's Eve celebrations], Mr. Giuliani had excoriated Mrs. Clinton for being part of the "Clinton machine," the "Arkansas kind of approach to things."

New York Times, January 1, 2000

Hi, this is Mayor Rudy Giuliani, and I wanted you to come to New York City this winter and paint the town red.

Advertisement placed on upstate television stations, featuring Mayor Rudolph Giuliani, paid for by NYC & Co., December 1999–January 2000

Funny thing about that. "NYC & Co." was the new name for the old Convention & Visitors Bureau. Which was now run, thanks to Mayor Rudolph Giuliani, by his former *wunderkind* communications director, Cristyne Lategano. And in response to abuses of the same privilege by Giuliani in his 1997 reelection race, public officials were now prohibited from showing their faces on such "public service" ads while they were involved in election campaigns. But that law only applied locally. Exploiting a loophole, were we, now?

Oh, give me a break. I've been doing that for years. I don't intend to stop being the Mayor of New York City and promoting the City of New York.   *N.Y. Times,* Jan. 4, 2000

◆ The Navy Yard: Off-Limits to Hillary Supporters

The Brooklyn Navy Yard, where literally hundreds of ships were launched to help win World War II, had long since sat dormant and under-utilized. On the other hand, New York's film and television industry was growing rapidly. So it seeeemed like a match made in heaven when it was announced that Miramax, the multi-Oscared independent movie company based in Lower Manhattan, and actor Robert DeNiro would become partners with the city in a venture to develop the Navy Yard into a Hollywood-style sound stage. And, as icing on the cake, Miramax's new magazine *Talk*—edited by Tina Brown, lately of *The New Yorker*—would have its launch party at the Navy Yard.

Now, it was known throughout this period that Miramax's impresarios, the brothers Harvey and Bob Weinstein, were major Democratic Party contributors. And that, at the height of the Republican move to impeach her husband, Harvey Weinstein had dramatically introduced Mrs. Clinton at the gala premiere of *Shakespeare in Love* as "First Lady of all our hearts." None of that presented a problem—not until Hillary expressed an interest in the same Senate seat the Generalissimo also wanted, and the buzz got around that *Talk* would have her on the cover of its first issue.

Permission to hold the magazine's launch party at the Navy Yard was suddenly withdrawn.

People have a right to make their own conclusions about how they want their property used, and I think it would have been a very onerous event anyway.

New York Daily News, June 24, 1999

Talk to the Navy Yard. . . . I think the Navy Yard would have treated me the same way, even though I am from Brooklyn, was born in Brooklyn and my father worked at the Navy Yard. I don't think this is an issue of discrimination against somebody from Arkansas. . . . I don't care one way or the other. . . .

I think you have got to have another question. I can't believe this is the only thing that you'd like to ask about. Or have we gotten to the point of ultimate frivolity? . . .

No, no, no, no, no. We have exhausted the subject. If there are no more questions about another subject, then I can go back to work.

New York Times, June 24, 1999, and
Washington Post, June 30, 1999

He got another question—how did he feel about Hillary Clinton being given an award by the Hadassah?
Are they going to have that ceremony at the Navy Yard? Oh, OK, well, as long as it's not at the Navy Yard, I'll have no comment about it. Thank you.

Closing comment at press conference prior to walking out,
New York Times, June 24, 1999

Really irrelevant. . . . I guarantee you most of the people in this city feel that way about celebrity soirees. Who really cares if a party is in the sky, on the earth, or someplace or other, except for Hollywood celebrities and New York celebrities? That's the stuff newspapers like, gossip columns like. *N.Y. Daily News,* July 10, 1999

The party went on—at the Statue of Liberty. But things got much more serious, at least to an angry Harvey Weinstein and Robert DeNiro, when (apparently because of a behind-the-scenes turf war between two of his deputy mayors) the Generalissimo pulled the plug on their sound-stage deal, taking on instead a partner who had earlier been dropped from the project by the city because it considered him undercapitalized.
The press release says "explore" at least three times, so it was explored. That's what the word means. It doesn't mean "agreement." It doesn't mean "deal."
New York Times, October 14, 1999

Weinstein and DeNiro fired back in a public statement that "in getting us to agree to a press conference on May 3rd to announce the plan, the Mayor told us we had a deal. All that remained to do was 'dot the I's and cross the T's.' There is no question that our proposal, from the leading film producers on the East Coast, is better for Brooklyn and the needs of the city."
Well, that's some other world. That's some other world, other than the world of equity, fairness. The word in the press release, repeated three times, is "explore." It was written as explore, it meant explore. Explore means there is no deal to any sensible, fair and honest person.
New York Times, October 15, 1999

MAYOR GIULIANI ANNOUNCES MAJOR FILM AND TELEVISION PRODUCTION FACILITY TO BE BUILT AT THE BROOKLYN NAVY YARD—FACILITY TO SERVE AS PRE-EMINENT EAST COAST FILM AND TELEVISION PRODUCTION STUDIO AND CREATE THOUSANDS OF FILM, TELEVISION AND CONSTRUCTION JOBS
Press release issued by Mayor's Press Office, May 3, 1999
Requoted in *New York Times,* October 20, 1999

◆ On Pardons and Pandering, Mistakes—and Malice

For all her political experience, Hillary Clinton was still a first-time candidate trying to navigate the unfamiliar shoals of New York ethnic politics. That meant she could be counted on to make mistakes. And—if she didn't understand it at first—that also meant she could count on Generalissimo Rudy Giuliani to be there, exploiting every mistake she made, no matter what ends he had to go to in order to do so.

Mistake #1. White House counsel Charles Ruff gets the decidedly dumb idea into his head that President Clinton should offer executive clemency to members of the Puerto Rican terrorist organization known in English by the initials FALN (for Armed Forces of National Liberation), who were accessories to its campaign of bombings and bank robberies supposedly designed to win independence for the island (despite the fact that support for independence, as expressed repeatedly by Puerto Rican voters for decades, continues to register in the low single digits). Citing their long sentences and the fact that they were not direct participants in these acts, Ruff sells Mr. Clinton on the notion—provided, the president stipulates, that they renounce violence first. Meanwhile, two leftist Puerto Rican members of Congress who are backing Mrs. Clinton persuade her to publicly come out in favor of clemency. Only afterward—amid the spectacle of the FALN members initially refusing to forswear future violence or express any regret for those killed and injured by their group, the inevitable massive backlash of public opinion, and charges by Capitol Hill Republicans that the clemency offer was part of a scheme to help her win New York's Hispanic vote—does she realize she has been badly advised and change her position.

He's [President Clinton] taking a very questionable and bizarre situation and making it appear even more questionable and bizarre.

New York Daily News and *New York Post,* Sept. 17, 1999

Every day this becomes more astonishing.

New York Daily News, September 23, 1999

It doesn't make sense to give clemency to people who are not remorseful. . . . I know she originally supported it, but now she strongly opposes it. She'll have to answer questions on why she changed her position.

New York Times, September 7, 1999

When Mrs. Clinton sought to limit the political damage by saying simply that she stood by her last statement on the subject, he jabbed his finger into the still-open wound left by the Monica Lewinsky scandal:

Stands by her husband? Oh, this is on the terrorist thing. OK, all right, you know I get confused. Sometimes it's stand by him, sometimes it's stand against him. It's getting confusing now. *New York Times,* September 9, 1999

Now, you might think, based on this case, that Rudy Giuliani was laying down a principle that he would never pander to ethnic political sentiment when the issue was releasing someone from prison who had conspired against the United States.

But you would be wrong. Jonathan Pollard was caught spying for Israel in 1985. Because of the extent of damage done by his espionage, and his refusal to cooperate in explaining what information he stole and whom he had passed it on to, he was sentenced to life. Fifteen years later he remained unregenerate and unapologetic—and the national intelligence community was so adamant his sentence not be reduced that

President Clinton had rejected even a personal plea from Prime Minister Yitzhak Rabin in the matter.

But Jonathan Pollard was also a Jew, and embracing his cause could split Jewish voters off from Hillary and the Democrats. So, for *him,* Giuliani said, let there be clemency.

Pollard's life sentence is "disproportionate to other people who had served time for precisely the same crime." *New York Times,* October 5, 1999

Mistake #2. The First Lady had once offered her personal opinion in favor of a Palestinian state at a time when that was still a technically taboo topic with the Israeli and U.S. governments (but was taboo no more).

Mayor Rudolph W. Giuliani has stoked the controversy, asserting that Mrs. Clinton's remarks were "a very big mistake." *New York Times,* February 28, 1999

Making a trip to Israel, she hastily adds a visit to the West Bank. Suha Arafat, wife of the Palestinian leader, uses Mrs. Clinton's presence to engage in an off-the-wall diatribe about how Israeli occupation troops are using poison gas. Mrs. Clinton, unsure just what she is hearing and not briefed on how to react to such an event, gives Mrs. Arafat the obligatory diplomatic air-kiss, leaves—and issues a statement rebuking her comments only later.

I would have objected to it. I'd have made my position clear, and I certainly wouldn't have embraced the person who said it, hugged them and kissed them. Maybe Mrs. Clinton will have another explanation of that, some other position on it a few weeks, a few days from now. . . . Her whole position on Israel has changed so many times that I guess we should just wait for her final position. . . .

A lot more pressure should be put on the Palestinian Authority [in peace negotiations with Israel] than the Clinton Administration has been willing to do.... There really is not a moral equivalent between the State of Israel and the Palestinian Authority.

New York Post, November 13, 1999

I would not embrace a person who said that afterward, because I would understand that by embracing someone, you approve. Well, look, you know, it's all hypothetical. I mean, I can't imagine myself in that situation.

New York Times, November 13, 1999

Before the month is out, a television ad—paid for via an "independent expenditure" by a pro-Rudy front group—is repeating the Suha-Hillary embrace across New York State in slow motion like it is the second coming of the Zapruder tape, accompanied by ominous music and narration. Giuliani journeys to Washington to deliver a speech before the group that has spontaneously (wink-wink), independently (yuk-yuk), with its own money (hardy-har-har) put this attack ad on the air.

My views are developed over 20 or 25 years of what I believe is in the best interests of the United States and my understanding of the history, the background and the experience of the State of Israel. They are not developed for the purpose of one political campaign or another political campaign.

Speech to Republican Washington Coalition
New York Times, December 2, 1999

In the wake of the incident, Prime Minister Ehud Barak himself stepped in to declare that he saw Mrs. Clinton, and her husband, as among the best friends Israel had ever had.

The Generalissimo, who had literally played with fire in the days before the assassination of Barak's role model Yitzhak Rabin, chose not to argue that point with him.

◆ The Brooklyn Museum

Asked for her stand on the art exhibit "Sensations" at the Brooklyn Museum and Giuliani's attempts to shut it (and, for that matter, the museum itself) down, the First Lady stuck to a safe position: defense of the right of the museum to make its own choices, right or wrong, without political interference. The Generalissimo's deconstructionist analysis of what she *really* said went like this:

Well, then she agrees with using public funds to attack and bash the Catholic religion. There is no way out of this. These public funds are being use to aggressively bash the religious views of a significant number of people in this city and state and country. And the question is: can taxpayer dollars be used for this kind of disgusting, anti-religious—in some ways aggressively anti-religious—kind of demonstration.

The fact is that any expression of opinion that I have now is going to be interpreted in light of running for the Senate—OK, fine. But I think you can find great consistency in the things that I have said and done. I haven't been shy about engaging in controversies when I held deeply held views before and I am not going to be shy about doing it now. *New York Times,* September 26, 1999

On this issue, we have diametrically opposed views. I don't think public funding should be used to attack religion or do the kind of things that are being done here. Mrs. Clinton believes public funds should be used. I bet

**you are going to find 100 disagreements like that, philo-
sophically.**   Statement on *This Week,* ABC, October 3, 1999
New York Post, October 4, 1999

Tim Russert of NBC News speculated in an on-the-air interview that Giuliani's outrage over the Brooklyn Museum show was
a gambit to win over the state's Conservative Party—which had
not endorsed him in his three tries for mayor and without whose
support no Republican had won statewide office since 1974.
**I didn't calculate it that way. I know a lot of people
interpret this different ways. I have a right to my own
First Amendment views.**
Statement on *Meet the Press,* NBC, October 3, 1999
New York Post, October 4, 1999

(For more on the Brooklyn Museum controversy, see
Chapter 24, "The Brooklyn Museum Had Lost Its Charm.")

✦ The Homeless

As the Generalissimo began his roundup of the homeless—
while trying to force through a new policy of evicting homeless
people who refused workfare and placing their children in foster care—the First Lady came to New York to deliver a major
address scoring his policies.
**It sounds like she and Al Sharpton are on the same posi-
tion on this.**   *New York Daily News,* December 1, 1999

**It sounds like the same misunderstanding Al Sharpton
has. . . . If you're not familiar with New York, you may
not understand the complexity of the approach.**
New York Post, December 1, 1999

The response to homelessness is not some romanticized general response. It's a practical response to problems that have created homelessness in the first place. The City of New York has been doing this for some time now. It's a complex set of responses. If you're not familiar with the city, familiar with New York, you may not understand the complexity of the agenda. So to take one of the few situations in which someone's assisted, and to try to make that into the whole program, could portray a misunderstanding of how the program works.

New York Times, December 1, 1999

Television talk show host Rosie O'Donnell used her opening monologue to rap Giuliani for being "out of control" on the issue—and, the next day, invited actor Tim Robbins on as well to (besides plug his new film) discuss the mayor's failings further.
Mr. Giuliani dismissed Ms. O'Donnell and the actor Tim Robbins, who had criticized the Mayor's homeless policies on Ms. O'Donnell's show earlier in the day, as part of "the Hollywood group that is heavily associated with the Clintons." *New York Times*, December 9, 1999

Mayor Giuliani blasted the "highly ideological Hollywood" friends of the Clintons. "I feel great. Every once in a while, if you could pick the people on the other side—you know, I couldn't have done any better. . . .

"There's no question that [Rosie O'Donnell] is a political operative. . . . It sounds to me like a paid political commercial. . . .

"[Our policies have been] enormously successful. . . . I can't help it if the people who helped to create the chaos in the first place are opposing it. I almost think this is a good debate to have. Ultimately, it actually helps me." *New York Post,* December 9, 1999

I guess it's a carry-over from her campaign fund-raising appearance for Hillary Clinton, so I can understand where she's coming from. December 7, 1999

Quoted in *New York Observer,* December 20, 1999

I think it's a partisan political organization [*The Rosie O'Donnell Show*]. I don't think they'd invite me. She's either some kind of campaign manager—fund-raiser for sure. For some reason, she doesn't like my body. . . . She had problems with my head or something.

New York Daily News, December 17, 1999

But then HUD Secretary Andrew Cuomo announced that because of a court ruling that the Giuliani administration had illegally blocked Housing Works, the radical ACT-UP affiliate, from receiving federal funds (by, among other things, lowering the group's service-rating scores so as to disqualify it from eligibility for AIDS grants), his department would remove New York City officials from the grants process and administer the program from Washington.

By now the Generalissimo was feeling beleaguered—and he saw a conspiracy (Cuomo's former New York regional director had signed on as Mrs. Clinton's campaign manager). So, even though he had violated loyalty to his party in a vain attempt to get Cuomo's father, Mario, one last term as Governor, he lashed out.

There is no question that Andrew Cuomo runs a major league political operation. He wants to take over the handing out of money directly, which is otherwise described as political patronage. . . . Unfortunately, it's quite apparent that he has brought his politicizing of HUD to New York. Now when his representative who was the regional director of HUD has become Hillary Clinton's campaign manager, it appears as if he is trying

to direct patronage to those people who are his political supporters, possibly Al Gore and others.

New York Times, December 22, 1999

By the next day, with twenty-four hours to think about it, he was in a full-fledged rant.

They are all involved in politics. They are all thinking about how they can help Al Gore, Hillary Clinton. I wish they would stop it. It actually is silly. You've got to be living on Mars not to figure out what's going on. This is Clinton politics come to New York. It's what they use to do in Arkansas. . . .

Last night his wife [Kerry Kennedy Cuomo] goes to a fund-raiser, a Democratic fund-raiser, and talks about how Andrew did this. Andrew is well-known in Washington, although you give him a certain amount of protection in the New York media, is well known in Washington for having highly politicized HUD, unlike any other Secretary. . . .

These are people who practice politics this way, who can't understand that it actually can be practiced honestly and decently, and you are going to see more of it. And I basically am not affected by it. And in fact you know what it's going to do, the more Cuomo and [Democratic political consultant James] Carville and this one and that one do this, it's just going to help me.

New York Times, December 23, 1999

(For a fuller treatment of Rudy Giuliani's views on this subject, see Chapter 20, "The Second Term: Toward a Higher Quality of Life—or Else," under the heading "Homelessness: An Arresting Solution.")

• Campaign Flip-Flop #1:
Milk Price Supports

Upstate dairy farmers are perenially seeking higher milk price
supports from Albany in order, they say, to help keep embattled small family farms in business. In New York City, where
the biggest market of consumers is located, it is de rigueur to
oppose any increase. As mayor, Rudy Giuliani sounded and
acted like a typical New Yorker. But as a senatorial hopeful,
mindful that he needed upstate votes to beat Hillary Clinton,
he suddenly switched sides. Or, rather, he chided the press
corps for not being aware that he had *already* changed his
views on the issue. And just when was this announcement
made? he was asked.

**My earlier concerns had been satisfied. I announced
that, actually, about two months ago. It was at night, it
was at a diner, and there were only two or three members of the press around and you never reported it.**

New York Times, August 20, 1999

 • Campaign Flip-Flop #2:
The Minimum Wage

Democrats in Congress pressed during the 1999 session for an
increase in the minimum wage. Republicans, controlling both
houses by narrow margins, tried to hold their members in line
against what they knew was a popular position. Thus did Rudy
Giuliani please his would-be future majority leader, the
archconservative Trent Lott, by weighing in with this opinion:
**At this point, I would not be in favor of it, until I saw
that it had no impact on reducing the number of jobs.**

I'd have to be convinced that it would not deprive entry-level workers of jobs. *N.Y. Daily News,* Sept. 29, 1999

What I'd like to see from Congress is a demonstration of how that [a minimum wage hike] would affect the welfare-to-work program. We have moved 510,000 people off welfare in New York City.

Statement on *Meet the Press,* NBC, October 3, 1999
New York Times, October 4, 1999

So, a few days later, Washington columnist Mark Shields asked Giuliani a very logical question: Why was he opposed to a rise in the minimum wage?

Well, there must have been a focus group or two in the meantime to let the Generalissimo and his campaign staff know that this was not a winning issue for him, because. . . .

No, no, no, no, no, no, wait, wait, wait—I didn't say that. . . .

[It's] a good thing that we have to look at, but you've got to understand that. . . . you could be costing some of those people jobs. October 9, 1999

Quoted in *New York Times,* October 27, 1999

And the backtracking began.

My stand on the minimum wage is that I have asked a study to be conducted to determine the impact it would have on poor people getting jobs. If the impact is minimal, I'll support it. If the impact is substantial, then I'll try to find ways to ameliorate that, which is what I have done in the past. So I think what I am doing is actually much more caring, and much more compassionate and that is not to just look at a poll and be in favor of something. . . . I anticipate that I'll eventually support it, but first I have to see what the study shows.

New York Times, October 25, 1999

Had he flip-flopped?

One of the biggest canards I ever heard. I'm doing exactly what I said I would do. But you've got to pay attention and you've got to be intellectually honest to come to that conclusion. *N.Y. Times,* Oct. 26, 1999

It should have no impact on welfare to work.
New York Times, November 29, 1999

By the time Giuliani said he could support it, a raise in the minimum wage was dead—for at least that session.

• Abortion—Campaign Flip-Flop #3?

Mr. Giuliani, a Roman Catholic, once advocated that the Supreme Court overturn *Roe v. Wade*, the 1973 decision that legalized abortion, [but] he changed his position in his first race for Mayor in 1989. *N.Y Times,* Nov. 26, 1999

I wouldn't express my personal views [on abortion] in a policy action as Mayor. This is a very sensitive issue about which our citizens are deeply divided.
Village Voice, March 7, 1989

He said his actions on the issue would be studiously "neutral." *Village Voice,* March 7, 1989

I would uphold a woman's right to an abortion. It is a Constitutional right, a legal right. Despite my personal views on the subject, I know how to live up to my oath. United Press International, April 8, 1989

But gradually Giuliani shifted from grudging acceptance of abortion's legality to actively advocating the position that abortion *should* be legal.

The simple fact is that whether I am the Mayor or he's [David Dinkins] the Mayor, it's going to be the same for women who want an abortion. I'm going to fund abortion, to make certain that poor women are not deprived of an abortion, and I'm going to oppose making abortion illegal. That's a non-issue.   *N.Y. Times,* Sept. 20, 1989

At a breakfast meeting in Atlanta with Republicans who favor abortion rights, Mr. Giuliani said a political party that favored *laissez-faire* government in fiscal affairs should also allow people to make choices in their personal lives.

"For a party which has such a strong belief in economic choice—which really comes out of the notion of freedom—it would seem to me that it would be entirely consistent that that choice would also extend to the most personal and difficult decisions that people have to make."   *New York Times,* October 24, 1994

That included late-term abortions—"partial-birth abortions," in the words of right-to-lifers who considered the procedure infanticide. At least, as long as he was Mayor of New York it did.

Opponents of abortion saw the "partial-birth" procedure—admittedly grisly—as an issue around which to focus their organizing efforts. The Republican Congress in Washington passed several bans on the procedure—and only President Clinton's veto stopped them from becoming law. Many state legislatures followed suit, with courts striking down the statutes in all but a few cases. The entire matter would inevitably have to be resolved by the U.S. Supreme Court—and where the vote figured to be close. Meanwhile, in New York (which legalized abortion on demand by state law some three years before *Roe v. Wade*), no such bill had made it to the governor's desk—but the Conservative Party served notice that it would not endorse Giuliani in his Senate race without his agreement to support a partial-birth ban, and it was widely believed that the Conservatives held the balance of power; if they ran their own candidate, they could tip the balance in favor of Hillary.

What would Giuliani do? To pro-choice advocates, in the summer of 1999 he seemed to be wavering. Asked specifically about late-term abortions, he demurred:

That's something I think I'll address myself to if and when I announce and I get a chance to think out all of those positions.

Statement during campaign visit to Saratoga, NY
New York Daily News, August 18, 1999

Three months later he seemed resolutely pro-choice again.
My position on abortion is precisely the same today as it was yesterday. I haven't changed overnight. . . . New York should not be ashamed of the [state] law [legalizing abortion]. Statement made to *Albany* (N. Y.) *Times-Union*, November 1999. Requoted in *N.Y. Times*, Nov. 26, 1999

But then his campaign manager went on *Meet the Press* and gave a rambling statement (worthy of Chauncey Gardner, the character Peter Sellers played in the film *Being There*) that left Giuliani's pro-abortion-rights supporters reason to be more concerned than ever.
Right now, the Mayor is pro-choice. **That's his position and that's his position, and it hasn't changed and the Mayor believes what he believes in.**

Statement by Giuliani Senate campaign manager Bruce Teitelbaum, *Meet the Press*, NBC, November 28, 1999 (emphasis added). *New York Times*, November 29, 1999

Again Giuliani had to clarify where he stood.

My position on abortion is exactly the same as it has always been. I don't see my position on that changing.

New York Times, November 30, 1999

◆ Greetings of the Season, Jew-boy

When Hillary Rodham Clinton's press spokesman blamed Giuliani for the sacking of Schools Chancellor Rudy Crew, the mayor shot back:

I say Merry Christmas to everyone, including some press flack who can't figure out how to celebrate Christmas.

December 24, 1999

Requoted in *New York Times,* December 31, 1999

The man's name is Wolfson. *Wolfson.* Did we all get that?

Oh stop it, come on. It sounds to me like everybody is taking themselves too seriously. My goodness. What I was saying was that wasn't a day for negative personal attack by anyone. It was the day before Christmas, and can't you have a holiday? *N.Y. Times,* Dec. 31, 1999

◆ Rudy: Why It Should Be Me

What I would say to the people of the state is, if you like the job I did as Mayor of New York City [and] you want somebody that's going to work as hard for your community and the rest of the state, then vote for me.

New York Times, November 2, 1999

I think the best thing for me to do is to do my job the way I've always done it and then try to point out to people why, if they agree with me, I would be a more effective Senator from their point of view. *N.Y. Times,* Jan. 9, 2000

In fact, he was so busy governing, he might not even have time to announce his candidacy.

Look, I've run in a lot of political races, and real tough ones. You've got to do it on your own time. And you really cannot worry about an opponent or think about an opponent. *New York Times,* November 30, 1999

He even mused aloud about somehow continuing to govern New York City *after* going to Washington. Asked what would happen to the city when he was gone:

Wow, that's a tough question. You know, I think, actually, a lot of people come up to me and say—some are being flattering and some are sincere—they'll say to me, "The city has moved in a very positive direction. We're very worried that after you leave, it'll turn back in the other direction." So here's what I say to them: "If you put me in the Senate, I can make sure that doesn't happen."

Comment at business breakfast held at the 21 Club, December 2, 1999. Quoted in *New York Observer,* December 20, 1999

And what did he think about the campaign being waged so far by Mrs. Clinton?

Extremely negative, extremely personal.

Remarks to Republican Washington Coalition *New York Daily News,* December 2, 1999

26

Rudy: The Making (the Coming-out?) of a Republican

Young Rudy Giuliani had been a bleeding-heart liberal Democrat, as evinced by his student columns for his college newspaper.

He described John Kennedy as "great and brilliant." Barry Goldwater was an "incompetent, confused and sometimes idiotic man." The writings of a John Birch Society extremist were the "disgusting, neurotic fantasy of a mind warped by fear and bigotry."

New York Daily News, May 13, 1997

The young Rudy had little sympathy for the extremists who took over the Republican Party in 1964 with the nomination of Barry Goldwater, whom he considered a right-wing "patsy," [and] a sycophant of the John Birch Society. . . . After the election, the *Quadrangle* analyst continued to roast "the Goldwater people . . . [who] succeeded in inflicting a tremendous defeat on the Republican Party. Now these same people who have come very close to destroying the party founded in 1854 seem to think they have some right to hold onto the leadership of the Republican Party." . . .

. . . In fact, he personally doubted that the American electorate would ever accept the "so-called conservative philosophy of government," with all its "erratic" and potentially "dangerous" prescriptions. . . .

He gave astringent advice to the vanquished Republicans, whom he felt must "adequately address themselves

to the problems of discrimination, of poverty, of education, of public housing and the many more problems that Senator Goldwater and Company throw aside in the name of small *laissez-faire* government. . . .

Strong, large government is necessary to deal with industries that are national and international and with problems that cities and states have ignored."

New York Observer, July 12, 1997

But eight years later, the tables were turned. In a reverse image of the GOP's Goldwater debacle, the left wing of the Democrats captured the party, nominated George McGovern for president—and was similarly buried in a landslide. Rudy Giuliani, registered Democrat, voted for McGovern—but was becoming disillusioned and soon quit the party.

I came to think that McGovern and the Democrats had a dangerous view. By the time I moved to Washington, the Republicans had come to make more sense to me.

New York Times, June 9, 1985

Of course, by then, the Republicans were also in possession of access to the career path that Giuliani had chosen for himself—government prosecutor. So he joined the Justice Department—and the GOP.

The thing that convinces me that I'm a Republican is when I watch a Democratic convention. The collectivist urge of the Democratic Party I think is very destructive. The Republican Party, when it functions correctly, has more confidence in the individual human being, and more willingness to allow the individual human being to emerge. *New York Times Magazine,* August 1, 1999

To win his race for mayor in 1993, Giuliani had to downplay the Republican tag. He was the "Fusion" candidate, he kept repeating—evoking the memory of virtually everyone's favorite mayor, legendary Fiorello LaGuardia, the Republican (and a very liberal one at that) who had formed a party by that name in order to capture City Hall and enact a reform program in the 1930s and '40s. And his margin of victory was provided by New York's Liberal Party (though by this time, as the joke went, it was neither liberal nor even a party anymore.)

But, once in office, he did things and espoused views that—certainly by New York standards—could only be considered conservative.

Government has a role, but a far less expansive one than has been the norm in New York City. . . . The fact is if you look broadly in New York, government has always answered the question of should government do it by answering it yes. What government should have done is occasionally answer it yes and more often answer it no.
New York Times, February 28, 1994

The fact is that we're fooling people if we suggest . . . the solutions to these very, very deep-seated problems are going to be found in government.
New York Times, March 20, 1994

And, though he came into office speaking of "nonpartisan" and "bipartisan" government, and though most of the votes for him on election day had in fact been cast by Democrats, he very quickly began firing Democratic public servants—and replacing them with loyal Republicans. After his bloodbath of city government managers and press aides in February 1995:

"The only thing I would do differently, maybe," he said, "is having done what Governor Pataki did, which is to do a much heavier cleaning out when I first took office than we actually did." . . .

The remark came in sharp contrast to his stance earlier in his term, when he had pointed to the many government holdovers as evidence that he believed in a fusion, nonpartian government. *N.Y. Times,* Feb. 11, 1995

A few months after that, describing his game plan to get things accomplished in City Hall, he frankly described the relationship of the political parties in terms of partisan warfare:

I'm a Republican Mayor in a city that is heavily Democratic, and there is at least one house of the Legislature that's heavily Democratic. The fact is that at times, in order for me to build up public support, I've got to make an issue public. I've got to try to get public opinion to work on the people who oppose a particular kind of change. *New York Times,* June 20, 1995

Yet, if Giuliani was now describing Democrats as the enemy, only eight months *earlier* he had engaged in a love-in with these enemies, endorsing their candidate for governor, Mario Cuomo. Faced with cries of "traitor" from others in his party when he did that, Giuliani had answered:

I'm a Republican. I'm proud to be a Republican, and I support every other Republican candidate for State office other than the one for Governor. And I support Republicans in Massachusetts, in New Jersey, I've gone as far as Michigan to support Republicans. I believe in the Republican Party and I'm going to remain a Republican. *New York Times,* October 29, 1994

But two years later, as Bob Dole was preparing to challenge President Clinton, Giuliani was at it again, exasperating his fellow Republicans and reaffirming his status as a maverick.

Mayor Rudolph W. Giuliani began the week with a sharp attack on the Chairman of New York State's Republican Party, accusing him of party bossism, and ended it with a rebuke of Bob Dole, the presumed Republican Party nominee. The question after all of this is: Does he still consider himself a Republican at all? . . .

With words and actions over the last week, Mr. Giuliani had all but renounced allegiance to his party. At one point, he went so far as to say that his critics were misguided because they had not "moved from beyond being captives of a particular political party."

New York Times, June 8, 1996

Most of Clinton's policies are very similar to most of mine. 1996 statement attributed to Giuliani by columnist Jack Newfield. Quoted in column by Newfield in *New York Daily News,* June 8, 1999

In the run-up to his reelection, Giuliani kept pushing this theme. Why, he even borrowed one of the favorite lines of . . . First Lady Hillary Rodham Clinton.
It takes a family, it takes a village, it takes a city, it takes all of us to help bring up children.
1997 State of the City address
Requoted in *New York Daily News,* June 3, 1999

The Mayor insists that he rarely even thinks about partisan politics and that when he speaks out, he does so only in the interests of the City. In an interview on Wednesday night on New York 1, a local cable news network, Mr. Giuliani . . . claimed to spend "99 percent of my time on the substantive issues of governing," evidently leaving just 1 percent for politics. . . .

The voters, he went on, have soured on partisan politics.
New York Times, June 8, 1996

I think they're tired of the Republican notion that only Republicans have the answers to problems and they condemn all Democrats, and the Democratic notion that only Democrats have the answers to problems and they condemn all Republicans. I think the people of New York City, the people of America, are tired of excessive partisanship. *New York Times,* June 8, 1996

We have taken New York City beyond partisan politics. A lot of the success of New York City is because my Administration has run this city for the good of this city, not as a Democratic city, not as a Republican city.
1997 statement. Quoted in *New York Daily News,* June 3, 1999

I find that the people you would describe as a moderate Republican or a moderate Democrat, roughly, I agree with nine out of 10 times. September 1997 statement
Quoted in *New York Daily News,* June 3, 1999

But, with his reelection safely won, Rudy Giuliani knew that he need never face the still relatively liberal, largely Democratic electorate of New York City again. If he ran for office in the future, it would be on a broader canvas, where the demographics and the parties would be more balanced. And thus, from that moment forward, the mixed messages and the zigzagging stopped. Rudy Giuliani came to assert himself, and to define himself, more and more as an ardent, partisan Republican whom the right wing of his party should feel perfectly at home with.

The changes that have occurred in New York City have a lot to do with policies and programs, ideas and thoughts that have been at the core of the Republican Party for a generation.

> Speech to Republican audience, Washington, D.C.
> *New York Times,* March 13, 1998

I think Republican principles, both at the City and State level, are responsible for the turn-around of the City and State. *New York Times,* October 13, 1998

The changes in New York City, although the press has a hard time accepting me, happen because largely the things that we are doing are quintessential Republican programs. Associated Press, January 3, 1999

> Requoted in *New York Daily News,* June 3, 1999

What I tried to emphasize with both of them was how I organize my thinking around giving people more freedom and discretion in their own lives.

> Describing his visits with new GOP House Speaker
> Dennis Hastert and British Conservative Party leader
> William Hague, *New York Times,* February 20, 1999

Unlike 1996, this time he declared his willingness—early—to do battle on behalf of his party in the 2000 presidential election.

I don't want to see a continuation of this Administration. . . . We have to unite as Republicans. . . . There are right now 10 candidates for President, maybe 15, and every single one of them is better than Al Gore, right?

> Speech at GOP Prescott Bush dinner, Milford, CT,
> May 1999, *New York Daily News,* June 3, 1999

We have 412 expressionless statues in Central Park. You have Al Gore.

Remarks to speech at invitation of *American Spectator* magazine, Washington, D.C. *New York Times*, November 10, 1999

We darn well better have a Republican President . . . who can give focus to our foreign policy, who can decide in advance what we're going to do . . . and not be sitting there confused and befuddled when an original policy doesn't work. May 1999

New York Daily News, June 3, 1999

I think that this President will be the first President in a long time that hands America over weaker than he found it. . . . The next President—and the Congress—is going to have to rebuild that.

Speech to Holy Cross College business alumni
New York Post, June 23, 1999

Giuliani lined up behind the GOP front-runner, Governor George W. Bush—even allowing Bush to speak at the city's annual ceremony honoring firefighters killed in the line of duty and to have Bush's media consultants record the scene for use in the presidential campaign. And, the *Times* reported, "wearing a pair of cowboy boots in deference to the Texas Governor," he declared:

Here tonight, we're united with Governor Pataki and Governor Bush because we Republicans put people first, don't we? We put children first. Government comes someplace else. *New York Times*, October 6, 1999

◆ The Reagan Library Speech

A week before the Bush visit, Giuliani had visited the Ronald Reagan Presidential Library in California to give a major address before former First Lady Nancy Reagan and a specially invited audience. Preparing to run for office for the first time ten years earlier, Giuliani had fiercely disavowed being tied to Reagan by his Democratic opponent David Dinkins.

What kind of Republican? Is he, for instance, a Reagan Republican? He pauses before answering: "I'm a Republican." *Village Voice,* January 24, 1989

But on this evening, he praised the fortieth president as **a leader who gave people a reason to believe again.**
New York Daily News, November 4, 1999

[He was] a force for good in the world. Let us be thankful that he was born, and that the human family can reap the countless benefits that his life has brought us.
Speech delivered at Ronald Reagan Presidential Library
New York Times, October 9, 1999

[Without him] maybe there'd be no Republican Mayor of New York City.
Speech delivered at Ronald Reagan Presidential Library
New York Times, October 1, 1999

He even singled out what was widely regarded as Reagan's most reckless (and most ridiculed) move in defense policy— his proposal for a "Star Wars" antimissile system in outer space—for praise.

A missile defense system is as vital now as it was when President Reagan first proposed it more than 15 years ago, maybe more so given the proliferation of nuclear weapons under President Clinton.

Speech delivered at Ronald Reagan Presidential Library
New York Daily News, October 1, 1999

I spent a good deal of the day yesterday at the Reagan Library and Museum and it focused me on just how much this country is in need of the kind of leadership that we had during the Reagan-Bush Administration, the kind of focus in our foreign policy, the kind of support for our military that we had then, the kind of unified purpose that Americans had.

New York Times, Oct. 1, 1999

Giuliani even had this to say about the notorious (and ultimately disastrous) economic strategy America pursued during the Reagan years:

Who says that supply-side economics doesn't work? Of course it works.

Speech delivered at Ronald Reagan Presidential Library
New York Times and *New York Daily News*, October 1, 1999

Supply-side economics—a completely untested theory sketched out on a cocktail napkin for then-presidential candidate Ronald Reagan—had been adopted as doctrine by him and passed into law by Congress in 1981 at his administration's behest as the centerpiece of his fiscal policies. It proceeded, over the next twelve years, to more than *quadruple* the national debt of the United States—and then triggered one of the worst recessions in American history, one that cost New York City alone (in the statistics so often cited by Rudy Giuliani himself) *400,000* jobs.

The Generalissimo was on such a high, coming back from his speech at the presidential library, that he did not want to be reminded of such things. Besides, he was already gushing over the GOP congressional leadership's push to revive supply-side economics in the form of a $792 billion tax cut that would wipe out the nation's current hard-earned surplus and with it any chance of making necessary reforms to Social Security and Medicare. In a word, he pronounced their proposal: **Great.**   *New York Times,* October 22, 1999

◆ The Test Ban Treaty

In 1995 Rudy Giuliani had gone to the United Nations and spoken bravely against the
potent strain of isolationism that once again is infecting our political discourse.   *N.Y. Times,* Sept. 20, 1995

But in 1999, when Senate Republicans engaged in perhaps the single most destructive act of American isolationism since the Treaty of Versailles was rejected after World War I, Rudy Giuliani beefed up his credentials as a party regular—and went along with them.

The issue was a treaty that had long languished in the Senate in which the United States (and many other signatories) would agree to stop *all* testing of nuclear weapons (including underground). For the United States, such tests were no longer militarily necessary; for emerging nations thinking about acquiring the bomb, they were essential. Resentful nuclear "wannabe" nations frequently cited continued, occasional testing by the American superpower as a prime impetus for them to refuse to give up attempts to join the nuclear club; a total halt by America remained the nation's best diplomatic leverage to prevent disastrous nuclear proliferation.

But, when Democrats pressed for a vote, Senate Republicans saw a chance to embarrass Bill Clinton—the commander-in-chief they had tried and failed to force out of office in an impeachment trial. And Rudy Giuliani, who aspired to join their ranks, signaled that he would help them do so if he could. **[The treaty was a] dangerous precedent [that] could cause "lasting damage."** *New York Times*, October 9, 1999

Right now, I would vote no if it were put to a vote, but what I prefer to see is that it be put off and the Administration have to answer for the fact that we now have nuclear weapons in Pakistan, in India. Nuclear weapons under Clinton have expanded dramatically in China and nothing's been done about it. And this treaty would not address any of that.

Comments on CNN, Oct. 9, 1999, *N.Y. Times*, Oct. 16, 1999

The Senate Republicans voted the treaty down, duly humiliating Clinton—and in the process dealing a potentially fatal blow to U.S. international leadership on this issue. From his forward command post in New York, Generalissimo Giuliani blamed the whole thing on Hillary's husband and the Democrats.

[It is] one of the big defeats of the Clinton Administration. In essence, the Clinton Administration and the Senate Democrats required a vote and they required a vote now. I think, as all the newspapers said, they made a very big mistake.   October 14, 1999

Quoted in *New York Times*, October 16, 1999

◆ The Patients' Bill of Rights

Perhaps the single most important item of domestic legislation that has been pending in Congress for the last several years, the patients' bill of rights (in various forms) would regulate and reform the power of health maintenance organizations, which have grown to become predominant in American medicine, and would give patients a crucial new right to sue their HMOs for malpractice—including the refusal to authorize needed care.

As befits someone who presumably has thought deeply about the responsibilities involved in becoming a United States Senator, Rudy Giuliani has the following detailed position on this subject:

It's not before the Senate right now, so if I was a Senator, I'd wait until it was before the Senate and then try to figure out something that works.   *N.Y. Post,* Oct. 8, 1999

♦ Attention, Republicans: I'm Your Man

There is no reason for a Republican in this state not to support me. I do the things Republicans want done. Not only do I do them, I have done them.
New York Times Magazine, August 1, 1999

Quite true. But for more than six years, Rudolph Giuliani had done his best to keep his constituency from learning that truth about him.

27

Alex Trebek Calls It "Potpourri"

♦ On New York—and Being Mayor of It

. . . I have had a tremendous love affair with the city of New York since I was a little boy. When I was a young

lawyer, for fun I would go around photographing the city. One of my pictures is on Amtrak. I've tried very hard to get a perfect picture of the Brooklyn Bridge.

Interview with columnist Maureen Dowd
New York Times, July 12, 1997

I remember being in London with Denny Young [counsel to the mayor] in 1990. And the first question was, "Do you actually live in New York City?" And I said, "I do." And the guy looked at me like I had survived one of the worst perils of modern life.

Remarks at business breakfast at the 21 Club, December 2, 1999. Quoted in *New York Observer,* December 20, 1999

Being Mayor of New York is like a roller-coaster: up, down, up, down, up, down.

Statement after transit workers' strike is narrowly averted
New York Times, December 16, 1999

One of the things I enjoy most about being Mayor is visiting school children, reading with them, and hearing about what they want to be when they grow up.

Press Release 476-98, "Mayor Giuliani Helps Announce Debut of the Children's Book 'Day in the Life of a Mayor,'" Mayor's Press Office, October 13, 1998

This could be my last State of the City speech. I'm never going to have a better job. I've loved it tremendously.

State of the City address, *New York Times,* Jan. 14, 2000

We can't let our citizens live in fear. . . . Our only hope is Spiderman.

Statement made by "Mayor Giuliani," appearing in syndicated comic strip *The Amazing Spiderman* by Larry Lieber, *New York Daily News,* May 7, 1997

Stuffing. More stuffing.

> Cry joined in by Giuliani as he works preparing Thanksgiving Day dinner plates in kitchen of social-service organiation. (Article reports, "Overall, the Mayor received a gracious reception. . . . [But] when he left the building, one worker shouted, 'Giuliani's out of the building,' and a round of applause went up. 'Yeah, get out!' another worker shouted.")
>
> *New York Times,* November 26, 1999

◆ On Sleep

I like to get four to six hours. If I get seven hours' sleep, then for two nights I'll only sleep two or three hours, because I'll be very, very wide awake.

> *New York Times Magazine,* December 3, 1995

◆ On the Cost of Neckties

Shaking hands as he walks along, Giuliani leads his entourage down Park Avenue, pausing to look at a tie in a store window. "It's ridiculous to pay $80 for a tie. I could find the same thing for $20."

> *New York Times Magazine,* December 3, 1995

◆ On Opera, Part I

When *Tosca* opened this fall at the Amato Opera Theater, New York City's First Opera Buff was in an aisle seat looking much happier than he ever does on television. It was his first look at this amateur troupe in the basement of a small town house on the Bowery. The lights dimmed and a couple of rickety light fixtures hanging from the ceiling began moving upward, paro-

dying that signature moment at the Metropolitan Opera when its great crystal chandeliers ascend to the gilded ceiling. Giuliani watched the old brass fixtures with the wide-eyed joy of a 6-year-old following his first kite.

"That's adorable!" he said. "I love it! That's great!"
New York Times Magazine, December 3, 1995

♦ On Opera, Part II (and Being Told at a Town Meeting, "You've Sold Your Soul for Votes" on the Abortion Issue)

"Bah!" Mr. Giuliani cut [the woman] off. "How do you know the state of my soul? I don't know the state of your soul! How do you know the state of my soul?"

"Let me finish, let me finish. I didn't mean to offend you," she protested.

"You didn't offend me!" he crowed. "It's very presumptuous of you to think that you know my soul! It's presumptuous of me to think that I know yours."

"I was using an expression that's very . . ."

"Well, it's an insulting expression. That's the way Gounod's Faust opens—with the selling of a soul. Great French opera, you should watch it. Based on a German legend." *New York Observer,* December 20, 1999

♦ On His Private Life (and His Marriage) and His Political Future

I think as long as your private life is not impinging on your job performance, it's nobody's business. That's the way I look at things in politics as a citizen. My concern with the people that are in politics representing me is what kind of job are they doing, not what's going on in

their private lives. That's the concern of gossip colum-
nists and of voyeurs, not of serious people.

Providence (R. I.) *Journal-Bulletin*, October 22, 1998

◆ On Why He Hates Campaign Fund Raising

You've got to sit in a room for like a half-hour or an hour
and call like 50 people who are on a big list. It's like a
make-believe conversation. It isn't a real conversation.
It's, you know, "Hi there, I'm . . ." (The Mayor at this
point made gibberish noises)." *N.Y. Times,* Oct. 22, 1999

◆ Attn. Sam, Cokie, Tim, Bob, Brit et al.

There's a tremendous isolation that goes on in Washington.
You've got to stop watching Sunday morning talk shows.
They create a reality that doesn't exist in the rest of
America. Remarks during visit to give speech in Phoenix, AZ
New York Times, January 3, 1999

◆ And Finally . . .

Choose to defuse.

Public service ad designed to reduce teen violence
New York Times, June 19, 1995

We can kick your city's ass.

Giuliani's choice among five possibilities given him on
David Letterman show for use as New York City's new
tourism slogan, *New York Times,* April 13, 1995

28

And the Future. . . ?

If he is elected to the Senate, Rudy Giuliani refuses to promise to serve a full term in *that* job.

I've seen so many people have to break that commitment that it doesn't make sense to make it if you value your integrity and your honesty.

New York Post, June 17, 1999

You don't know what's going to happen in life. You don't know what opportunities are going to be presented. . . . You shouldn't make commitments like that.

New York Daily News, June 17, 1999

And just what might those "opportunities"—higher than a seat in the U.S. Senate—be?

Hours before her son was sworn in for a second term as Mayor, Helen Giuliani told reporters that she hoped someday to see him "sworn in as President." . . .

. . . The Mayor refused to say whether he shares his 88-year-old mother's aspirations for him to seek a new home at 1600 Pennsylvania Ave.

"My mother is, you know, a mother," Giuliani said. "She's always had very, very high objectives for me."

New York Daily News, January 3, 1998

But with a sweetheart during his teenage years, Rudy Giuliani had not been so reticent.

"He told me he wanted to become the first Italian-Catholic President of the United States," she said. "He

liked to say, 'Rudolph William Louis Giuliani 3d, the first Italian-Catholic President of the United States.'

"We'd joke about it, 'Oh, there's Rudolph William Louis Giuliani 3d, the first Italian-Catholic President of the United States.' He said it enough that it was part of him. He didn't say things lightly."

Recollections of former Giuliani girlfriend
Kathy Livermore, New York Daily News, May 13, 1997

And why not? After all, as the Generalissimo himself said on the day he took power. . .

Nothing is beyond our grasp.

First Inaugural Address, *New York Times,* January 3, 1994